STAGING SHAKESPEAREAN THEATRE

STAGING SHAKESPEAREAN THEATRE

ELAINE ADAMS NOVAK

BETTERWAY BOOKS
CINCINNATI, OHIO

Other fine Betterway Books are available from your local or online bookstore.

04   03   02   01   00   5   4   3   2   1

Library of Congress Cataloging-in-Publication Data

Novak, Elaine Adams.
    Staging Shakespearean theatre / Elaine Adams Novak.
        p.   cm.
    Includes bibliographical references (p.) and index.
    ISBN 1-55870-517-1 (alk. paper)
        1. Shakespeare, William, 1564-1616—Dramatic production. 2. Theater—Production and direction. I. Title.

PR3091.N68   2000
792.9′5—dc21   99-089645
                                                                                                              CIP

Editor: Tara Horton
Production editor: Christine Doyle
Interior designer: Sandy Conopeotis Kent
Cover designer: Amber Traven

On the cover: Top, Adrian Sparks, Tracy Griswold and Edwin Dundon in the Cincinnati Playhouse in the Park's 1982 production of *MacBeth*. Photo by Sandy Underwood; courtesy Cincinnati Playhouse. Bottom, The Cassius Carter Stage at the Old Globe Theatre, Balboa Park, San Diego, California. Courtesy of the Old Globe Theatre.

ABOUT THE AUTHOR

Dr. Elaine Adams Novak is the author of *Styles of Acting* and *Performing in Musicals* and co-author of *Staging Musical Theatre*. She is professor emeritus of theatre at Marshall University and has taught theatre classes and directed plays, musicals and revues. She holds degrees from Marshall College, Columbia University and Ohio State University.

Grateful acknowledgment for their help and support is owed to my family, Edwin Novak, Deborah Novak and John Witek; to friends, Kristine Greenwood, William G. Kearns, Andrew Marcum, Maureen Milicia, James Morris-Smith, Mike Murphy, Judge Dan O'Hanlon and S. Tyler Tackett; and to my editors at Betterway Books, Tara Horton, Terri Wilson and Christine Doyle.

Table of Contents

Preface

The purpose of this book is to offer an easy-to-understand guide for community, college or high school directors and students who want to stage a Shakespearean play.

William Shakespeare's works hold the record for the most films and stage performances in more languages than those of any other dramatist. Through the years many of us have viewed great actors in renowned Shakespearean plays on the professional stage and in films; consequently, some directors of amateur productions may want to try working with the best dramatic writing available, despite the difficulties inherent in these works.

Shakespearean plays are not easy to stage and many directors—both amateur and professional—are afraid to try them. They require more research, analysis and study than modern plays. They need larger casts and contain more scenes than most amateur directors are accustomed to and, of course, they contain poetic, archaic language that can be difficult to understand. They often call for singing, dancing, playing musical instruments, fighting and special effects. Also, they demand from directors imaginative interpretations. This book takes up these and other problems and tries to demystify the process of staging Shakespeare's plays.

Part One of this book deals with the development of playwriting in the Elizabethan-Jacobean era. (*Elizabethan*

concerns the time period of 1558 to 1603 when Queen Elizabeth I reigned England, while *Jacobean* refers to 1603 to 1625 when England was ruled by King James I. Shakespeare lived from 1564 to 1616, during both regimes.) Part One also offers a description of the theatres, the acting and the direction of plays at this time. In addition, it touches on the life and works of Shakespeare and other famous writers of this era.

Part Two discusses preparing a Shakespearean play for production today: selecting a play, researching, analyzing and interpreting your choice, acquiring a staff of workers to assist you and supervising their work.

Part Three describes auditions, casting, rehearsals and performances.

Part Four gives detailed information for preparing and directing *Romeo and Juliet*. The necessary research, analysis and arriving at an interpretation are described. A complete script of *Romeo and Juliet* is included with suggested blocking, lighting, sound, possible cuts and meaning of unusual words. There is also advice on costuming, makeup, scenery, properties, lighting, music and sound.

The appendix, which gives information about major Shakespearean plays, is followed by a list of books for further reading.

✧ Part One ✧

Introduction

Part One discusses the characteristics of the Elizabethan-Jacobean style of playwriting. Next we will look at the theatres, the acting and the direction of plays in this period. This is followed by a review of the life and works of William Shakespeare, other major writers of this time and their most famous plays.

Development of Elizabethan-Jacobean Playwriting

Two great influences, the medieval and the classical, converged in England in the sixteenth century to affect the plays written by Elizabethans. To explain how this came about, let's start in the Dark Ages when there was no theatre to speak of in Europe. There may have been traveling entertainers who roamed the countryside performing their specialties (juggling, singing, dancing, storytelling and so forth) but little is known of their activities.

Medieval Religious Influence

We do know that about A.D. 925 liturgical drama was developing in Europe. At first these religious plays were produced inside cathedrals, monasteries and churches and were acted by the clergy or choir boys in Latin; but by the thirteenth century secular organizations were assisting in the presentation of elaborate outside productions performed by laymen in the local language. These productions grew in size until they were often spectacular

with expensive special effects, stage machinery and flying devices that attracted large crowds.

In the British Isles, amateurs in more than one hundred towns produced religious plays, probably with the help of a few experienced professionals. Some of the presentations were on fixed stages but others were on pageant wagons, which may have had two levels above the wagon wheels. In 1558, however, Queen Elizabeth expressed her disapproval of these religious productions and, thereafter, they diminished in popularity.

The following types of religious presentations were done: **mystery** plays (from the French word *mystère* meaning "trade" for the trade guilds which produced them) were based on the Bible (e.g., *Abraham and Isaac);* **miracle** plays depicted the lives of saints (e.g., *The Conversion of St. Paul);* and **morality** plays, of which the most famous is *Everyman* (c. 1500), demonstrated the struggle between virtues and vices for possession of man's body and soul. These three, along with **folk plays** (e.g., *The Play of Robin and Marion,* which was written about 1283), **farces** (e.g., *The Second Shepherds Play,* written about 1400 which grew out of a religious play) and **secular interludes**, which could be serious or comic (e.g., *Fulgens and Lucrece,* written in 1497 by Henry Medwall), comprise the medieval influence.

From viewing these productions, Elizabethan writers learned to use a loosely organized plot and no unities of time, place or action (the play could cover days, months or years of time, have many short scenes in various locations, which may not be indicated by scenery or props but just mentioned in the dialogue, and use subplots). They could have a mixture of the serious and the comic, moral instruction, singing and music. The actors wore contemporary garments with a few exceptions for characters such as devils and angels. They performed on a platform that had simple set pieces, properties, traps, sound effects, and devices to fly actors to or from the stage.

Classical Influence

Classical influence pertains to the plays of Aeschylus, Sophocles, Euripides and Aristophanes, who wrote in the fifth century B.C. in Greece, and the works of Plautus, Terence and Seneca, whose Roman plays date from the third century B.C. to the first century A.D.

Aeschylus wrote tragedies like *Prometheus Bound* about 468 B.C. and a trilogy entitled the *Oresteia* in 458. Sophocles is noted for such tragedies as *Antigone* (c. 441), *Oedipus Rex* (c. 430), *Electra* (c. 418) and *Oedipus at Colonus* (406). Euripides's tragedies include *Medea* (431), *Hippolytus* (428), *The Trojan Women* (415) and *Electra* (c. 414). Aristophanes's comedies comprise *Knights* (424), *Clouds* (423), *Wasps* (422), *Birds* (414), *Lysistrata* (411) and *Frogs* (405).

Plautus, who wrote his comedies between 205 and 184 B.C., is noted for *The Braggart Warrior, Pseudolus, Amphitryon, The Captives, The Menaechmi* and *The Haunted House*. Terence also created comedies such as *Andria* (166), *Mother-in-Law* (165), *Phormio* (161) and *The Brothers* (160). Seneca, who lived from about 4 B.C. to A.D. 65, produced tragedies like *The Trojan Women, Medea, Oedipus, Phaedra, Thyestes* and *Agamemnon*.

In 1472 the plays of Plautus were printed in Latin and in the next few years those by Terence and Seneca followed. In the early sixteenth century, the Greek writers' plays were published.

In England in the fifteenth and sixteenth centuries, these printed books of plays, especially those by Plautus, Terence and Seneca, inspired a revival of interest in classical learning as British scholars tried to imitate the Roman writers. They copied the Romans' use of a five-act structure; the aside (a brief remark that a character makes to

the audience that other characters onstage pretend not to hear); the soliloquy (a speech made when a character is alone onstage); the "three unities" of (1) **time** (the plot must take place in one day's time period or less), (2) **place** (only one location) and (3) **action** (just one plot—no subplots); and the separation of comedy and tragedy (comedies should have no serious moments and tragedies no funny actions).

From Plautus and Terence, who both wrote comedies, the English learned to use the plot of mistaken identity, disguises, intrigue, sudden disclosures, stock characters (old father, young son, courtesan, scheming servant, quack doctor and braggart warrior), love stories, slapstick and music.

From Seneca, a writer of tragedies, they learned to use the theme of revenge, violence, cruelty, poetry, strong passionate scenes with mad characters, ghosts, confidants, messengers and a chorus. Italian adaptations of Seneca's plays in the Renaissance inspired the English to try blank verse, which has unrhymed lines in iambic pentameter (for a discussion of blank verse, see page 16).

Elizabethan Plays

While some educated Elizabethans followed classical traditions, neoclassicism was never as popular in England as it was on the continent. Most Elizabethan writers were more influenced by the medieval. Their plays exhibit a freedom of imagination and emotions that is not hampered by classical restraint and decorum. Love stories are frequent and the language can be passionate. Often actors had to sing and background music accompanied some scenes. There is much movement involving fighting, fencing and dancing, and the ancient Greeks, who disliked violence onstage, would have been shocked to see the bodies lying on the stage at the end of a typical Elizabethan tragedy.

The Elizabethans also inherited their method of staging from the medieval: a platform stage with little scenery, a few traps in the stage floor, several entrances to the stage, music, sound, special effects and a large cast of male performers who were costumed for the most part in contemporary clothes.

Theatres in the Elizabethan-Jacobean Period

There were outdoor public theatres and indoor private theatres, which are described below. In addition some performances were given at court.

Outdoor Public Theatres

All of London's outdoor public theatres were built outside the city limits. On days of performances, a flag was flown at the top of the theatre so all who saw it would know there was to be a play that afternoon, usually at two or three o'clock. Typically there was an audience of about fifteen hundred to three thousand who paid one penny to stand in the yard around the stage (these people were called the "groundlings") or two or three pennies to sit in the galleries. Some paid more for the privilege of being seated onstage. There were no tickets or programs but food and drinks were sold. While only males acted, women were permitted to be in the audience, which included all types of people, rich and poor.

The theatres were popular and attracted capacity throngs. The spectators surrounded the stage and were quick to let actors know whether they liked or disliked the proceedings by shouting their approval or disapproval. They involved themselves in the play, weeping openly at stirring moments or laughing and applauding when pleased. They came to be entertained and were vocal about their needs.

The outdoor theatres varied in shape and size, but most probably were circular or polygonal. It is thought that the first Globe theatre, which was built in 1599, was polygonal with a diameter of one hundred feet. For seated customers, there were three tiers of galleries that surrounded the yard. The galleries were roofed with thatch but the yard was open to the sun and rain.

The large rectangular stage was about five feet high and projected halfway into the yard. On the first level, the back wall may have had one door on each side and a large curtained opening in the center that could be opened to reveal an inner stage. The stage floor had several traps through which actors could enter or exit and two pillars to support the stage cover. This decorated ceiling was called the "Heavens."

The second level was a balcony used by actors and musicians. It may have had curtains in the back that could be drawn aside to show a second inner stage. This second level was ideal for the balcony scene of *Romeo and Juliet.*

The third level was for musicians but actors may have used it for some scenes, especially when playing gods or spirits who had to be lowered in a mechanical device to the main stage—the *deus ex machina* (god from the machine) of classical theatre. For example, Jupiter in Act V, Scene 4 of *Cymbeline* descends from above to the stage floor "in thunder and lightning sitting upon an eagle."

There was a small orchestra to play background music for some scenes or to accompany songs and dances; there were trumpeters to announce the beginning of the production and to provide flourishes when needed before an entrance or scene; and drummers added realistic sounds to battle scenes. After a play of two to three hours in length, the musicians also accompanied a concert and jig that concluded the entertainment.

There was little scenery onstage, enabling playwrights to change locales quickly. All that was necessary was to indicate the place in the dialogue. If needed, a set piece or prop, such as a throne, table, bed or tree, could be moved onstage to assist the illusion. Hand properties like letters, drinks, flowers and swords were also used.

Lighting was provided by afternoon sunlight coming through the opening in the roof. Night scenes could be suggested three ways: (1) The playwright could simply have a character talk about the darkness of the night; (2) a black cloth could be hung on the "Heavens"; or (3) an actor could carry a candle, torch or lantern—then the audience would know the stage was supposed to be dark. For example, in Act II, Scene 1 of *A Midsummer Night's Dream,* Puck has a line, "I am that merry wanderer of the night," and a little later Oberon says to Titania, "Ill met by moonlight, proud Titania." Both lines help establish that this scene takes place at night. In Act I, Scene 4 of *Romeo and Juliet,* a servant is carrying lanterns to indicate it is a night scene and Romeo has two lines:

> Give me a torch: I am not for this ambling;
> Being but heavy, I will bear the light.

Little attempt was made at historical accuracy in costuming. For the most part, elaborate, beautiful contemporary clothes were worn, with a few exceptions for special characters like animals, fairies, ghosts and witches. The males who played female characters dressed in women's clothing and used appropriate hairstyles and make-up. In Shakespeare's time, when playing *Twelfth Night*, a boy actor would be dressed like a woman to act Viola, who then in the course of the play assumes the disguise of a male, Cesario. The boy actor could probably play Cesario better than Viola.

Special effects included lightning, rain, thunder, rising mists, blazing stars, alarm bells and cannon fire (the theatre had its own cannon).

The two outdoor public theatres with which Shakespeare was associated were The Theatre, built in 1576 and torn down in 1597, and The Globe, which opened in 1599 and burned down in 1613. The Globe's destruction happened during a performance of Shakespeare's *Henry VIII* when a wad fired from the cannon ignited the thatch on the roof. In one hour nothing was left of the building, but luckily no one was hurt. The Globe was rebuilt in 1614 on the old site (with a tiled roof this time) and was in existence until 1644.

Other outdoor theatres included The Curtain, The Rose, The Swan, The Fortune, The Red Bull and The Hope.

Indoor Private Theatres

There were also smaller indoor private theatres in the Elizabethan-Jacobean period which seated about five hundred. Although called "private," anyone who paid the admission price was allowed to enter. The cost was higher than admission to the public theatres but they did provide seats for all customers either on the main floor or in two or three galleries. At one end of the room was a raised stage which probably had three entrances and a balcony. Lighting was by candles.

At first, children's companies played mostly in the private theatres. These companies came from church choir-schools where young boys were trained to sing and act. Audiences enjoyed watching the boys perform and some noted writers like John Lyly and Ben Jonson wrote plays for them. Lyly's *Endimion* was performed by the Children of Paul's before Queen Elizabeth in about 1588. Jonson wrote *Cynthia's Revels* in 1600 and *Poetaster* in 1601 for the Chapel Children at Blackfriars. In 1609 his *Epicoene, or the Silent Woman* was produced by the Children at Whitefriars.

Later, the adult companies sometimes used the indoor theatres in winter months. Starting in 1608 Shakespeare's company, The King's Men, played in an indoor theatre, The Blackfriars, from October to May and in The Globe the rest of the year. When The Globe burned down in 1613, the company moved to The Blackfriars until it was rebuilt.

Court Performances

In addition to the indoor and outdoor theatres, some performances were given at court for Queen Elizabeth. Shakespeare's company was invited several times to provide entertainment for the annual Twelfth Night celebration on January 6, and in 1600 it is thought that the troupe presented Shakespeare's *Twelfth Night* on this occasion.

After James I came to the throne, elaborate productions were devised for invited audiences. Masques, often written by Ben Jonson and designed by Inigo Jones, were favorite court entertainments that mixed songs, dances and spoken scenes.

Acting and Directing in the Elizabethan-Jacobean Period

Information is meager on the acting and directing in this time period but the following is probable.

Acting

The principal acting troupes consisted of about twelve to twenty men, including shareholders, hirelings (actors who were hired for a limited time) and servants (the prompters, stagehands, property men, custodians and money-gatherers). There were also male apprentices who started as young as ten to learn the business. They played pages, children and some women's roles.

In this period, actors had to be versatile because, as

one can see immediately by examining the scripts, in addition to acting they had to sing, dance, fence and play musical instruments. They also had to learn lines rapidly because, with the repertory system, the troupes performed a different show each performance day. They also needed well-projected voices to work in an outdoor theatre to perhaps three thousand people.

Practically nothing is known for sure about the quality and characteristics of the acting in this time. One of the best clues, though, is provided by Shakespeare, who was an actor as well as a playwright. He had this to say about acting when Hamlet is talking to the players in Act III, Scene 2 of *Hamlet:*

> Speak the speech, I pray you, as I pronounced it to you, trippingly on the tongue: but if you mouth it, as many of your players do, I had as lief the town-crier spoke my lines. Nor do not saw the air too much with your hand, thus, but use all gently: for in the very torrent, tempest, and, as I may say, the whirlwind of passion, you must acquire and beget a temperance that may give it smoothness. O, it offends me to the soul to hear a robustious periwig-pated fellow tear a passion to tatters, to very rags, to split the ears of the groundlings, who for the most part are capable of nothing but inexplicable dumb-shows and noise: I would have such a fellow whipped for o'er-doing Termagant; it outherods Herod: pray you, avoid it. . . .
>
> Be not too tame neither, but let your own discretion be your tutor: suit the action to the word, the word to the action; with this special observance, that you o'er-step not the modesty of nature: for any thing so overdone is from the purpose of playing, whose end, both at the first and now, was and is, to hold, as 't were, the mirror up to nature; to show virtue her own feature, scorn her own image, and the very age and body of the time his form and pressure. Now this overdone, or come tardy off, though it make the unskillful laugh, cannot but make the judicious grieve; the censure of the which one must in your allowance o'erweigh a whole theatre of others. O, there be players that I have seen play, and heard others praise, and that highly, not to speak it profanely, that, neither having the accent of Christians nor the gait of Christian, pagan, nor man, have so strutted and bellowed that I have thought some of nature's journeymen had made men and not made them well, they imitated humanity so abominably. . . .
>
> And let those that play your clowns speak no more than is set down for them; for there be of them that will themselves laugh, to set on some quantity of barren spectators to laugh too; though, in the mean time, some necessary question of the play be then to be considered: that's villainous, and shows a most pitiful ambition in the fool that uses it.

Note the points that Hamlet stresses in the above speech. We can assume from them that Shakespeare was concerned about good articulation, appropriate gestures and proper displays of emotions. He urged actors to "suit the action to the word, the word to the action" in order to appear natural. He was against overacting, strutting, bellowing, and comedians who ad-lib and laugh at their own jokes.

Directing

We know little about the acting in this period, but we know even less about the direction of plays. Perhaps the playwright directed his play, if he wished to, or he may have served as an advisor to a senior member of the troupe who did the directing. If the playwright was not available, a senior member may have directed or the actors directed themselves. If Shakespeare talked to actors as Hamlet advised the players, he must have been a good director.

Life and Works of Shakespeare

Shakespeare lived at an exciting time in the history of England. Under Elizabeth I, who came to the throne in 1558, there was great development in many areas. England defeated the Spanish Armada in 1588 and, with the help of the Netherlands, broke Spain's power. Traders set up the East India Company. Explorers, such as Sir Francis

Drake and Sir Walter Raleigh, investigated the West Indies and the coasts of Africa. Francis Bacon became a distinguished philosopher, statesman and writer. Young playwrights, who were known as the University Wits, because most of them had been educated at Cambridge or Oxford, whetted the public's taste for drama. These writers, who paved the way for Shakespeare and Ben Jonson, included John Lyly, George Peele, Thomas Kyd, Robert Greene and Christopher Marlowe.

In 1564 William Shakespeare was born to John and Mary Arden Shakespeare. The third of their eight children, he was christened on April 26 of that year in Stratford-upon-Avon, England. Little is known about his life except that in 1582, at age eighteen, he married Anne Hathaway, age twenty-six, and in the following years three children were born, daughter Susanna and twins Judith and Hamnet (he died at age eleven). About 1587 William left his wife and children in Stratford and went to London where several years later his first plays were produced. It is usually a guess as to when he wrote his plays, but the following are thought to be his earliest works:

The Comedy of Errors
Henry VI (Parts 1, 2 and 3)
Titus Andronicus
The Two Gentlemen of Verona
Richard III

When the plague hit London, as it did in 1592, theatres were closed. Probably a patron, the Earl of Southampton, helped Shakespeare through these years. We do know that Shakespeare dedicated two poems *Venus and Adonis* (1593) and *Rape of Lucrece* (1594) to Southampton. By 1594 Shakespeare was a member of The Lord Chamberlain's Men and owned a share of the company. Around this time, he probably composed the following plays:

The Taming of the Shrew
Love's Labour's Lost
Romeo and Juliet
A Midsummer Night's Dream
King John
Richard II
The Merchant of Venice
Henry IV (Parts 1 and 2)

In 1599 Shakespeare bought a one-tenth interest in The Globe and in the next few years he created the following:

Much Ado About Nothing
Henry V
Julius Caesar
As You Like It
The Merry Wives of Windsor
Twelfth Night
Hamlet
Troilus and Cressida

By the time Queen Elizabeth died in 1603, Shakespeare was considered the leading dramatist and poet of the day. When James I came to the throne, Shakespeare's troupe, The Lord Chamberlain's Men, became The King's Men, and in the following years, he wrote these plays:

All's Well That Ends Well
Measure for Measure
Othello
King Lear
Macbeth
Antony and Cleopatra
Timon of Athens
Coriolanus
Pericles

In 1609 a book of Shakespeare's sonnets was published without his permission, and in his final writing years he composed the following plays:

Cymbeline
The Winter's Tale
The Tempest
Henry VIII (collaborator: John Fletcher)
The Two Noble Kinsmen (collaborator: John Fletcher)

Shakespeare got ideas for his works from many different sources and he penned all types of plays: histories, farces, comedies, pastorals, tragedies and romances or tragicomedies. Shakespeare made fun of all the popular types of plays when he had Polonius in Act II, Scene 2 of *Hamlet* list them as follows: ". . . tragedy, comedy, history, pastoral,

pastoral-comical, historical-pastoral, tragical-historical, tragical-comical-historical-pastoral. . . ."

Shakespeare was also influenced in his writing by the people in his company. He tailored certain parts to fit the talents of different actors, such as Richard Burbage, who played many of Shakespeare's leading roles, including Richard III, Romeo and Hamlet.

Will Kempe, who was a comedian, played parts like Launce in *The Two Gentlemen of Verona*, Peter in *Romeo and Juliet* and Bottom in *A Midsummer Night's Dream*. When Robert Armin succeeded Kempe, Shakespeare wrote for a different type of comic, such as Touchstone in *As You Like It*, Feste in *Twelfth Night* and the Fool in *King Lear*. Because there were no actresses, he had to limit the number of female parts to what the young apprentices could handle.

Shakespeare was a householder, which means he owned part of the theatre, and was a playwright, actor and director. He acted in other writers' plays as well as his own; for example, in 1598 he played a part in Ben Jonson's *Every Man in His Humour* and a little later he was Adam in his own *As You Like It*. It is thought that he made money working in the theatre and retired comfortably to Stratford-upon-Avon.

In 1597 Shakespeare bought New Place, one of the finest homes in Stratford, and in 1602 he purchased 107 acres of the best land in Old Stratford. In 1613, when The Globe burned down, he invested in the building of the new Globe, but he spent the final years of his life in Stratford where he died on April 23, 1616.

In 1623 John Heminges and Henry Condell, who were actors in Shakespeare's company, edited and published thirty-six of Shakespeare's plays, omitting *Pericles* and *The Two Noble Kinsmen*. This is called the First Folio. In 1632, the Second Folio was published, in 1663-4, the Third Folio and in 1685, the Fourth Folio.

Other Elizabethan-Jacobean Playwrights

John Lyly (c. 1554-1606), who became playwright-in-chief to the Children of Paul's, was noted for the delicate, polished prose of his pastoral comedies like *Campaspe*

(1584), *Endimion* (c. 1588), and *Love's Metamorphosis* (c. 1590). Lyly may have been influential when Shakespeare was creating Mercutio's sparkling repartee in *Romeo and Juliet* and such comedies as *The Two Gentlemen of Verona* and *As You Like It*.

George Peele (1556-1596), who was noted for his poetry, wrote *The Arraignment of Paris* which was performed for Queen Elizabeth by the Chapel Children in 1584; but his best known work is *The Old Wives' Tale* (c. 1590), a comedy in which he made fun of the romantic plays of the day.

Thomas Kyd (1558-1594) employed many of Seneca's ideas in *The Spanish Tragedy* (c. 1587): a ghost, messenger, chorus, confidant and soliloquies in a revenge tragedy. The popularity of this play may have led Shakespeare to try another complex revenge tragedy—*Hamlet*.

Robert Greene (1558-1592) wrote romantic and pastoral comedies and is best remembered today for his delightful *Friar Bacon* and *Friar Bungay* (c. 1589).

Christopher Marlowe (1564-1593) had a hit in 1587 and 1588 with plays about the warrior *Tamburlaine the Great* (Parts 1 and 2). About a year later he composed *Doctor Faustus*, which told the story of a scholar who sold his soul to Mephistopheles in exchange for knowledge, power and luxury. Marlowe's *Edward II* (c. 1592) aided the development of the history play and blank verse.

Ben Jonson (1572-1637), probably this period's second best playwright (after Shakespeare), wrote twenty-eight plays. His comedy *Every Man in His Humour* (1598), in which Shakespeare acted a role, was a success but Jonson is best known for creating *Volpone* (1606), *The Alchemist* (1610) and *Bartholomew Fair* (1614). He wrote many masques for the court productions of James I, who made him the first poet laureate of England in 1616. Proud that he had read the classical writers, Jonson commented that Shakespeare "hads't small Latin and less Greek." He reported also: "I remember that the players have often mentioned it as an honor to Shakespeare, that in his writing, whatsoever he penned, he never blotted out a line. . . ." In addition, Jonson wrote that Shakespeare "was not of an age, but for all time."

Thomas Dekker (c. 1572-c. 1632) is credited with

about sixty-five plays, many of them with collaborators. He is best remembered today for a popular romantic comedy, *The Shoemaker's Holiday* (1599).

John Webster (c. 1580-c. 1630) collaborated with Dekker and others but is noted primarily for two Jacobean romantic tragedies, *The White Devil* (1612) and *The Duchess of Malfi* (1614).

Francis Beaumont (c. 1584-1616) and **John Fletcher** (1579-1625) collaborated in 1608 on a romantic tragedy, *The Maid's Tragedy*, and a tragicomedy, *Philaster*, which did much to establish the popularity of these genres in the Jacobean period. Probably Shakespeare was influenced by them when writing *The Tempest* (1611). Beaumont retired several years before he died and thereafter Fletcher alone wrote many plays that are attributed to both of them. As noted earlier, Shakespeare and Fletcher may have collaborated in 1613 on *Henry VIII* and *The Two Noble Kinsmen*.

Preparing to Direct a Shakespearean Play

Part Two is concerned with selecting a Shakespearean play for production, doing the necessary research and analysis, arriving at your interpretation of the work, recruiting a staff of people to help you and supervising their work.

Select a Play

In Part One you will find a complete list of Shakespeare's known plays. If you are charged with directing one of them, your first job is to make a selection. Perhaps you already have a favorite: You have admired *Hamlet* or *Julius Caesar* since you read it in high school or college; you liked a film production of *Romeo and Juliet* or *Othello*; you laughed at a professional production of *As You Like It* or *Twelfth Night*.

Go through the list of Shakespeare's plays and choose the ones you respond to favorably. Then read them carefully, imagining all the while how you would cast each one with the actors available to you, how the play would look on your stage and how your audience would like it. Be sure also that you have sufficient rehearsal time available, because you will probably find that a Shakespearean play will take longer to prepare than a typical two-act modern play. Because of the language difficulty, you had better plan to rehearse several weeks more than you would for a contemporary play.

Narrow the list down to two plays. To make your final choice, ask your theatrical friends and colleagues which one they would prefer to see. If you are in a school situation, you may have to get the approval of a committee or the chairperson of your department or the dean. If you are in a community theatre situation, you may need the consent of a board of directors or, perhaps, the entire membership.

Money is an important consideration, and you may have to prepare a tentative budget for the production that includes probable income and costs. See Figure 2-1 for possible items that may apply to your situation. One item that is found in most modern play budgets, but does not appear in Figure 2-1, is royalty, since Shakespeare's plays are in public domain. The cost of scripts depends on whether you prefer to buy everyone a printed book of the play or to have your cut and edited script typed and duplicated for all who need it.

Just be sure that you end up with a selection you like. You are going to have to spend several months of your life on this production, so be certain you have a play you will enjoy reading, interpreting, teaching and directing.

Research

After you have selected the play, read it several times using different editions, which you can find at your library or bookstore. Look at the following: The Arden Shakespeare, The New Folger Library Edition of Shakespeare's Plays, The New Penguin Shakespeare, The New Variorum Shakespeare and The Newly Revised Signet Classic Shakespeare Series. Samuel French, Inc. publishes acting editions of the best known Shakespearean plays and also vocal music for some of them. Compare them and decide on the one you feel most comfortable using as the script for your production.

Then read what the best literary critics of plays have had to say about the one you've chosen and what theatrical critics have written about well-known productions of

INCOME

Sale of tickets	$
Sale of advertising in programs	$
Sale of refreshments	$
Other income	$
Total	$

EXPENDITURES

Scripts	$
Scenery	$
Properties	$
Lighting	$
Sound	$
Costumes, wigs, shoes, accessories	$
Makeup	$
Music	$
Rental of rehearsal rooms, building spaces and theatre	$
Transportation charges of scenery, props, costumes, equipment	$
Publicity: flyers, postcards, newspaper ads, radio and TV ads, posters, signs, billboards, photographs, personal appearances	$
Postage	$
Telephone	$
Office expenses	$
Tickets	$
Programs	$
Refreshments to be sold	$
Salaries of employees	$
Janitorial services	$
Touring production: transportation, meals, lodging, rental of theatre	$
Insurance	$
Taxes	$
Other expenses	$
Total	$

FIGURE 2-1: **ESTIMATED INCOME AND EXPENDITURES**

your selection. Histories of the theatre describe famous stage plays of the past, while the *New York Theatre Critics' Reviews* criticize New York and regional productions (both can be found in most libraries). Look under the date of the opening performance.

Read about and look at pictures of previous stage productions. If your library has *Theatre World*, you can find photographs and information there about modern productions of Broadway, off-Broadway, touring and resident companies Also, look in theatrical and news magazines, such as *Time, Newsweek, People, Entertainment Weekly*, and *Variety* for information.

See any available live productions, films and videotapes and listen to recordings of the play. These will show you some possibilities for interpretation. But just because a famous actor delivered a line in a certain way, do not feel your performer has to copy it. You probably will get a better result if you work with your actor to get her or him to think and feel like the character does at that moment.

Who are the actors who have played roles in this play? Throughout the centuries most thespians have considered a Shakespearean role as the high point of their careers. Richard Burbage (the first to act many of the leading roles in Shakespeare's tragedies), David Garrick, Edmund Kean (about whom Samuel Coleridge wrote: "To see him act is like reading Shakespeare by flashes of lightning"), Edwin Booth, Henry Irving, Sarah Bernhardt (one of a few women to play Hamlet) and Ellen Terry were great Shakespearean actors of the past. In the twentieth century, John Barrymore, Maurice Evans, John Gielgud, Laurence Olivier, Judith Anderson (another woman to try Hamlet), Orson Welles and Richard Burton played to accolades. Then there are the present actors: Judi Dench, Ian McKellen, Derek Jacobi, Kenneth Branagh, Emma Thompson, Mel Gibson, Ralph Fiennes, Leonardo DiCaprio, Claire Danes, Calista Flockhart and many others.

After some research, you should be able to start making decisions as to what time period and locations you will use. For example, American director Joseph Papp changed *Much Ado About Nothing* from sixteenth-century Sicily to a small American town early in the twentieth century. An Old Vic Theatre production of *The Merchant of Venice*, starring Laurence Olivier with Jona-

than Miller directing, changed the century from the sixteenth to the late nineteenth century. For *A Midsummer Night's Dream*, English director Peter Brook used an all-white set and colorful, loose-fitting costumes, with some actors swinging on trapezes. A 1996 film entitled *Romeo + Juliet*, starring Leonardo DiCaprio and Claire Danes and directed by Baz Luhrmann, changed the place from Italy to modern-day United States where the fighting is with guns instead of swords.

Why do some directors want to do a nontraditional production of a Shakespearean play? Perhaps they

1. like modern costumes better than sixteenth-century;
2. think it will have more appeal for an audience if they use costumes, sets and props that are familiar to them;
3. are tired of doing Shakespeare in the traditional way; or
4. think audiences are bored with seeing traditional productions.

But there is much to be said for leaving the time period and locations as they were in Shakespeare's original script. Consider the verse of the play. If you choose a modern period for your production, is the verse going to seem incongruous? It is the director's decision to make.

Whatever you decide, you should then research the time period and locations and find out as much as you can about the clothes, shoes, hairstyles, makeup, customs, manners, occupations, dances and music of the people in that era and place. For answers, look at histories of the country, costume books, works set in that time period or region and other reference books.

Analyze the Play

In the fourth century B.C., Aristotle wrote about the six parts of the drama: **plot**, **characters**, **thought**, **diction**, **music** and **spectacle**. These are the divisions we shall use to cover analysis. To understand your play thoroughly, the following steps are essential.

Analyze the Plot

What is the plot all about? Was the plot organized by Shakespeare to tell a story, using a cause-to-effect arrangement of incidents, as in *Hamlet?* Was it written to reveal a character, such as Falstaff in *The Merry Wives of Windsor?* Or was it planned to illustrate an idea, such as what happens when an incompetent king is on the throne, as in *Richard II?*

Aristotle wrote that a plot should have a beginning, middle and an end. Can you tell the story of what occurs from the beginning to the end of the play? Are there subplots? Does the plot build to minor climaxes and then to a major climax shortly before the ending?

The plot is the plan or outline of what happens in the play. In the beginning of the work the playwright usually tries to establish the **mood**, **tone** and **style** of the play. Near the beginning of *Hamlet* one of the officers says, "Something is rotten in the state of Denmark," and we know immediately this is a tragedy. The writer **introduces the major characters** and gives **exposition**—the audience is told about the place, time and other information needed to understand the play. There may be an **inciting incident** that starts the main action: A problem may be presented to the protagonist that disturbs the **balance** or **equilibrium**. In *Hamlet* the Ghost of Hamlet's father urges Hamlet to seek revenge for his death by Claudius, who after the murder became king and married Gertrude, Hamlet's mother. Then the **theme** or **major dramatic question** is introduced: Will Hamlet be able to get revenge?

In the long middle section of the plot, there is **conflict** between protagonist (Hamlet) and antagonist (King Claudius). Hamlet is determined to kill Claudius, but finds him at prayer and decides not to do it at that time. **Complications** and **obstacles** occur so that the protagonist cannot accomplish his goal: Mistaking Polonius for the king, Hamlet kills the father of his love Ophelia. Claudius sends Hamlet to England and arranges for his death, but Hamlet escapes and returns to Denmark. And so the **suspense** builds as we wonder if Hamlet will ever succeed. **Discoveries** may happen: Upon returning to Denmark, Hamlet finds Ophelia has killed herself. **Reversals** may occur: Laertes and Hamlet engage in a sup-

posedly friendly fencing match, but Laertes is using a poisoned rapier. Laertes wounds Hamlet, but in the fighting they exchange rapiers and Hamlet stabs Laertes. There may be **surprises**: Queen Gertrude drinks poison Claudius intended for Hamlet. There is a **crisis** when the two forces of conflict meet: Hamlet stabs Claudius with the poisoned rapier. This is followed by the **major climax**, which is the point of the audience's greatest emotional involvement: Hamlet's death.

The third part of the play is the relatively short **ending** (also called the **denouement** or **resolution**): The audience learns that Fortinbras will take over and rule Denmark. The ending relieves the tension and may answer questions raised during the play.

A farce comedy may have a slightly different structure. Let's look at *The Taming of the Shrew*. The beginning has the **introduction of the major characters** and **exposition**: We learn that Baptista has two daughters, Katharina and Bianca, that the latter has many suitors because of her beauty and gentleness, but that Katharina, the older of the two, has a shrewish disposition that drives suitors away. Baptista is determined, however, that Bianca shall not marry until Katharina is married. Gremio and Hortensio, two of Bianca's suitors, vow to try to find a husband for Katharina. Lucentio, who has traveled from Pisa to Padua to study philosophy, is much taken with Bianca and vows to get into her house to see her by pretending to be a schoolmaster. The **tone** is farcical.

In the next scene, there is the **inciting incident** when Petruchio arrives in Padua to visit his friend Hortensio and hopefully to wed a rich woman. Hortensio and Grumio tell him about Katharina and arrange a meeting. Baptista gives his permission for Petruchio to woo Katharina, but when Petruchio and Katharina meet, there is **conflict** as they maneuver for dominance. Abruptly he declares that they shall be married on the next Sunday. The **major dramatic question** is: Will Petruchio be able to tame Katharina?

The wedding day comes but there is no Petruchio. When he does arrive, he is dressed in bizarre clothes, but they are married anyway. After the wedding he insists that she accompany him immediately to his country house. In the next scene, Petruchio enters his home pulling a bedraggled Katharina. In a soliloquy he explains to the audience that ostensibly he is taking good care of her, but he is not letting her sleep or eat in order to tame her. This treatment goes on for several more scenes as **suspense** builds. In the meantime Bianca is married to Lucentio. Finally in the ending the **major climax** is reached when Katharina shows that she, more than Bianca, has become a dutiful, obedient wife.

In studying your play, note the time and day of each scene. Also note the offstage action between scenes. Have hours or days or months gone by? What has happened in these intervals? This is important to know because it will influence what each character is thinking and feeling as the next scene begins. For example, in the third scene of *The Taming of the Shrew*, Petruchio leaves to go to Venice to buy clothes for the Sunday wedding. How long is the interval before the next scene which takes place on Saturday? Probably a day or two. What do you think Petruchio did in Venice? Why did he decide to show up late for his wedding in an outrageous outfit? These are the things that a director should figure out.

Analyze the Characters

First, the director should prepare a list of characters and note in which scenes each one appears. As a help to you in calling actors to rehearsals, indicate on the chart whether each one has lines to say or is silent. If he or she has to do something exceptional, like fight, sing, dance or play a musical instrument, note this also. (See Figure 2-2.)

To visualize each role, study the following:

- What the person says about himself or herself.
- What other characters say about him or her.
- What the individual has done in the past and does during the play.
- How the person changes during the play.

You should know each character so well that you can describe him or her.

Select the important items for each role from the list below and write a description of each character. Examine the following:

- The character's function: Is this person the protagonist (central character) or antagonist (character opposed to the protagonist)? In both cases, more than one person may be involved. Is the character a confidant(e), relative or enemy of one of the principals; comedian; servant; or something else?
- Physical appearance: Age, height, weight, posture, movements, clothing.
- Vocal characteristics: Loudness, rate, pitch, quality, dialect or accent.
- Intellectual and emotional characteristics.
- Personality (e.g., extroverted, funny, somber, kind, evil).
- Occupation, social and economic status.
- Nationality.
- Religion and moral beliefs.
- Character's major goal for entire play.
- Character's objective(s), motivation(s) and action(s) for each scene the person is in.
- Obstacles the person meets in trying to reach the objectives.
- Character's attitude toward everyone else in the play with whom he or she is involved.
- Changes that occur in the individual during the play.
- Special talents needed to act the role, such as swordfighting, singing, dancing or playing a musical instrument.

Let's take one example. Suppose you are directing *Twelfth Night*. It would be wise to write a short description of each character before you cast so you know what you are looking for. This may also be helpful when talking with the actor about the role. For a description of Viola you might write the following:

Viola: The protagonist, the one the audience cares the most about.

Appearance: She must be attractive when dressed as a woman, yet able to look like a young man when in men's clothing. She and her brother Sebastian must be similar enough in height and general appearance to be mistaken for each other as they are supposed to be twins.

Voice: She must be able to talk like a feminine young lady and also a young man.

Intellectual and Emotional Characteristics; Personality: She is a smart, compassionate, earnest young lady.

CHARACTER	I					II					III				IV			V
	1	2	3	4	5	1	2	3	4	5	1	2	3	4	1	2	3	1
Duke Orsino	✓			✓					✓									✓
Curio	✓		E	E					✓									E
First Musician	PS							P	P									P
Second Musician	PS							P	P									P
First Lord/Officer	E		E	E					E					✓				✓
Second Lord/Officer	E		E	E					E					✓				E
Valentine	✓			✓	E				E									E
Viola		✓		✓	✓		✓		✓		✓			✓				✓
Captain		✓																
First Sailor		E																
Second Sailor		E																
Sir Toby Belch			✓		✓			✓		✓	✓	✓		✓	✓	✓		✓
Maria			✓		✓			✓		✓	✓	✓		✓		✓		E
Sir Andrew Aguecheek			✓					✓		✓	✓	✓		✓	✓			✓
Feste, a clown					✓			✓S	✓S		✓			✓	✓	✓S		✓S
Olivia					✓						✓			✓	✓		✓	✓
Malvolio					✓		✓	✓						✓		✓		✓
First Lady					E											E		E
Second Lady					E											E		E
Fabian					E					✓		✓		✓	E			✓
Sebastian						✓							✓		✓		✓	✓
Antonio						✓							✓	✓				✓
Priest																	E	✓

✓ =Speaks   E=Extra (Does not speak, sing, dance, fight or play an instrument)   S=Sings   F=Fights
D=Dances   P=Plays

FIGURE 2-2: **CAST CHART FOR** *TWELFTH NIGHT*—**WHO IS IN EACH SCENE AND WHAT THEY DO**

Occupation: After being shipwrecked, she persuades the captain of the ship to help her disguise herself as a young man named Cesario and to get a job serving Duke Orsino.

Major Goal: After meeting and working for Orsino, Viola develops aspirations to be his wife, and this is her major goal that guides her actions in all of her following scenes.

Obstacles: After Orsino sends Viola (disguised as Cesario) to woo Lady Olivia for him, Olivia becomes an obstacle to Viola's obtaining her major goal since Olivia falls in love with her.

Attitudes Toward Others: Viola tries to be a good employee and woo Olivia for Orsino. She is genuinely upset when Olivia persists in wanting her. To the other characters she encounters, Viola feels intellectually superior.

Changes in Viola During Play: In the beginning she is a pitiful shipwrecked young lady who does not know whether her brother Sebastian is dead or alive. In the last scene of the play, Viola is happy to find her brother and be able to reveal to everyone that she is a woman. She is happier still when Orsino asks her to marry him and when Olivia, who is now married to Sebastian, calls her Sister.

Another point to consider when analyzing characters is character relationships: Who is related to whom? Which characters love or, at least, are friendly to each other? Which characters hate one another?

Let's switch to another play. This time a tragedy, *Romeo and Juliet*. There are two families who hate each other: the Capulets and the Montagues. This situation affects everything that happens in the play. When Romeo (a Montague) and Juliet (a Capulet) fall in love, grave problems develop that are only resolved by their deaths. Like other Shakespearean tragedies, there are multiple deaths: Mercutio (friend of Romeo) is slain by Tybalt (nephew of Lady Capulet) and in vengeance Romeo kills Tybalt. Later, Romeo slays Paris (another suitor of Juliet), then kills himself. When Juliet sees Romeo is dead, she commits suicide. Only then do the Capulets and Montagues decide they must reconcile.

Analyze the Thought

Under this heading we should study the theme, messages to the audience and other major ideas expressed in the play. In reading the play you have selected, be on the lookout for Shakespeare's major ideas, such as the following:

Hamlet has a theme of revenge. It is in the tradition of Seneca, the Latin playwright who wrote revenge tragedies and used ghosts in his plays. As explained earlier, Hamlet is seeking revenge because the Ghost of his father told him he was murdered by Claudius.

As You Like It shows a contrast between the sophisticated selfishness of the court and the faithfulness and simplicity found in the country. In this pastoral comedy Shakespeare is satirizing some of the absurdities of pastoral dramas and romantic comedies.

Richard II raises the question: What can be done about an incompetent king? In this study of power politics, the answer is that Richard deposes himself.

Antony and Cleopatra demonstrates the tragedy that comes from an illicit love affair. Other ideas have to do with showing the practical, efficient, disciplined life of the Romans versus the luxurious, enjoyable, beautiful life of the Egyptians.

Analyze the Diction

Diction means the playwright's choice of words. Plot, characters and thought are revealed to the audience through the words. Unfortunately, the words used in the Elizabethan-Jacobean period may not have the same definitions that we give them today. The director, therefore, should work on the play from an edition that has good footnotes which will explain what the words and phrases meant to Shakespeare. You may also have to consult a dictionary, encyclopedia, atlas or other reference book. Examine every line carefully. Be sure you understand what Shakespeare had in mind before you proceed to the next line.

Is there an underlying meaning, which is called the **subtext**? Is a character saying one thing but thinking something different? Look at *Hamlet*. At the end of Act I, Hamlet, who is going through an upsetting scene with the Ghost of his father, says to Horatio and Marcellus:

> But come;
> Here, as before, never, so help you mercy,
> How strange or odd soe'er I bear myself,
> As I perchance hereafter shall think meet
> To put an antic disposition on, . . .

In the following scenes when Hamlet is assuming an "antic disposition" that he speaks of above, you must consider the subtext that he is putting on this act.

Look in a dictionary for the **pronunciations** of words. Will you be able to help when an actor asks, "How do you pronounce this word?" As an example, inspect the opening

---

Some of Shakespeare's words have changed in meaning since he used them; other words have become obsolete. Note what the following words meant to Shakespeare:

a:	in, on	**heavy:**	sad
ability:	means, wealth	**holp:**	helped
addition:	title, name	**modern:**	common
carry:	manage	**moe:**	more
close:	secretive	**mows:**	faces
conceit:	conception, idea	**pregnant:**	resourceful
confusion:	overthrow, ruin	**teen:**	sorrow
fume:	mist	**trow:**	believe

speech of Titania in Act II, Scene 2 of *A Midsummer Night's Dream*. Underlined are some words that an actor may need help with even though all are in a modern dictionary:

> Come, now a <u>roundel</u> and a fairy song;
> Then, for the third part of a minute, hence;
> Some to kill <u>cankers</u> in the musk-rose buds,
> Some war with <u>rere</u>-mice for their <u>leathern</u>
>   wings, . . .

A little later in the same scene Lysander has the line:

> Two bosoms <u>interchainèd</u> with an oath; . . .

When you see an accent mark on a final syllable, as in the line above, you should sound that syllable; therefore, *interchainèd* should be pronounced with four syllables.

Jokes need study because it may not be apparent at first what's funny about a line. For example, in the first four lines of Act II, Scene 4 of *Romeo and Juliet*, Mercutio is having fun with the Nurse and in the following speech and song he makes puns on the word *hare*, which means *rabbit* or *harlot*, and *hoar*, which is defined as *moldy* and pronounced like *whore*.

> No hare, sir; unless a hare, sir, in a lenten pie, that
> is something stale and hoar ere it be spent. (*Sings*)
>   An old hare hoar,
>   And an old hare hoar,
> Is very good meat in Lent:
>   But a hare that is hoar
>   Is too much for a score,
> When it hoars ere it be spent.

Consider **figures of speech** such as the **simile** (comparison of two unlike things that is usually introduced by *like* or *as*), the **metaphor** (comparison that is made when a word or phrase is used in place of another), the **personification** (attributing human qualities to an object or abstraction) and the **allusion** or **reference**. You will find examples of most of these in the excerpt below from Act II, Scene 2 of *Antony and Cleopatra*. **Sensory images** (words that stimulate the senses of sight, hearing, taste,

touch or smell) are found in abundance in the following speech in which Enobarbus describes Cleopatra:

> The barge she sat in, like a burnish'd throne,
> Burn'd on the water: the poop was beaten gold;
> Purple the sails, and so perfumèd that
> The winds were love-sick with them; the oars were
>   silver,
> Which to the tune of flutes kept stroke, and made
> The water which they beat to follow faster,
> As amorous of their strokes. For her own person,
> It beggar'd all description: she did lie
> In her pavilion—cloth-of-gold of tissue—
> O'er-picturing that Venus where we see
> The fancy outwork nature: on each side her
> Stood pretty dimpled boys, like smiling Cupids,
> With divers-colour'd fans, whose wind did seem
> To glow the delicate cheeks which they did cool,
> And what they undid did.

To help your actors interpret sensory images, be sure they understand them and can visualize them. They must get a vivid picture in their minds before they can speak the words meaningfully.

Like many playwrights of this time period, including Thomas Kyd and Christopher Marlowe, Shakespeare wrote most of his plays in **blank verse**—only about 28 percent of the lines in his plays are in **prose**. Some low comedians talk in prose, and when Hamlet and King Lear act insane, they speak prose. Most of the time, however, we are dealing with blank verse, as in Enobarbus's speech above.

Let's define blank verse: It is a type of unrhymed poetry with no stanzas; it has five metrical feet to a line, called *pentameter*, and the rhythm is iambic. An *iamb* is a metrical foot which consists of one unstressed syllable followed by a stressed syllable. For an example, look at the fifth line of Enobarbus's speech. The line is marked with ˘ for unaccented syllables and ´ for accented syllables. A straight line is at the end of each foot:

> Whĭch tó | thĕ túne | ŏf flútes | kĕpt stróke, | ănd máde |

At times, Shakespeare wrote two or three lines to make five metrical feet, as in *Othello*:

OTHELLO: Mĭstréss! |
DESDEMONA: M̆y lórd? |
OTHELLO: What wóuld | yŏu wíth | hĕr, sír? |

At the end of some scenes Shakespeare used a **rhyming couplet**, which is two lines that rhyme. For an example see the end of Act I, Scene 1 of the *Romeo and Juliet* script in Part Four of this book:

ROMEO: Farewell: thou canst not teach me to forget.
BENVOLIO: I'll pay that doctrine, or else die in debt.

Shakespeare also used rhyming couplets in longer passages and, in addition, he put in some **sonnets**, which have fourteen lines in iambic pentameter and a definite rhyme scheme. For an example, look at the Prologue to *Romeo and Juliet* on page 75 in Part Four.

In reading blank verse in rehearsal, try to help the actors note the rhythm and rhyme scheme, if any. In rehearsal, actors should be aware of the verse but, after they memorize the text, they should think only of the meaning of the lines. In performance, actors must forget about the verse.

Not every line Shakespeare wrote scans perfectly for various reasons: Perhaps that is the way Shakespeare wanted it, some words may have been lost, or the word may have been pronounced differently in the Elizabethan period. Other words may have been changed or eliminated or added through the years by editors.

Analyze the Music and Sound

Aristotle wrote about the importance of music because it was a prominent part of ancient Greek productions in the fifth and fourth centuries B.C.. Today we include all sound in this category—the performers' speaking and singing voices, live and recorded music and sound effects—everything the audience hears from the stage.

In Shakespeare's day, music was also important. There were about six instrumentalists, playing lutes, viols, pipes, sackbuts and citterns, to make background music for some scenes and to accompany songs and dances. Hautboys are called for in some plays—these are oboes. In addition, there were trumpeters and drummers to provide fanfares and drum rolls. The words to songs are in the plays, but, unfortunately, none of the music that was used in the original productions of Shakespeare's plays has been preserved. It is thought, though, that Shakespeare wrote many of the lyrics to fit popular tunes of the day. Shakespeare, like many Elizabethan gentlemen, evidently had a good knowledge of musical instruments and music.

For your production, the time period and country you have selected will influence the music to be used. For example, if you have decided on setting your production of *Much Ado About Nothing* in the United States in the 1890s, you might select waltz music of that period.

Survey your script to see where you need music: At the beginning or ending, for scene changes, for songs, dances or as background music for certain scenes? You should know what common stage directions mean; for example, "flourish" or "tucket" means a fanfare of trumpets or cornets, "sennet" is a signal call on a trumpet or cornet for an entrance or exit on the stage, and "alarum" or "alarum with excursions" calls for exciting warlike sounds as soldiers move across the stage.

After you know where you want music, investigate what type of music would be the best to use. If you are not knowledgeable in this area, go to a good music library and seek the help of a music librarian. This person should be able to assist you with recordings or sheet music. Some famous composers have written music for Shakespearean plays, such as Felix Mendelssohn who wrote an overture to *A Midsummer Night's Dream* in 1826 when he was seventeen years old. Seventeen years later, he composed thirteen additional numbers for this play, including the "Wedding March" that many brides choose for their ceremonies. In Suggested Reading at the end of this book, you will find some listings under "Music in Shakespeare's Plays" that may be of help.

If the budget can afford it, however, consider asking a local musical composer to write an original score for your play and have a small group of musicians play it at each performance.

Whether you use recordings or live musicians in an orchestra pit, backstage, onstage or elsewhere is up to the director. If you use live musicians, you will probably need a conductor. For the songs, you may require the coaching of a musical director and for the dances, a choreographer.

In addition to recorded music, the sound designer handles the amplification of performers' voices. If you are playing in a small indoor theatre, amplification should not be needed, but if you are performing outdoors, it probably will be. This designer also does recorded sound effects, like church bells ringing or birds chirping. Recordings of almost any sound effect can be bought from theatrical supply houses, but if a sound effect is not available, a good sound designer should be able to create it.

Analyze the Spectacle

This category includes everything the audience sees on the stage—all the visual elements: the performers and their movements (blocking, dancing, swordfighting), the scenery, properties, costumes, makeup, hairstyles, lighting and special effects.

First look at the type of stage on which you will perform: Is it an indoor proscenium arch stage, arena stage or thrust stage? Is it an outdoor stage? What is the shape of it and what kind of facilities does it have? A **proscenium arch stage** has an arch that separates the audience from the acting area and helps to focus the spectators' attention on the performers by hiding the lighting equipment, stage machinery and technical workers who are backstage. The audience sits in rows of seats facing the proscenium stage, which is the most common type of

stage in the United States (see Figure 2-3). An **arena stage** or **theatre-in-the-round** has a stage in the middle of a space with the audience sitting on all four sides around the performers (see Figure 2-4). With a **thrust stage** the audience is seated on three sides; on the fourth side may be a stagehouse or wall through which actors, scenery and props may enter and leave the stage (see Figure 2-5). This is the type of stage Shakespeare probably had for most of his productions.

Think about the scenery and props that you would like to have for your production. The best advice is probably to keep it simple, as it was in Shakespeare's day, because you must be able to change scenes quickly.

Consider the costumes: They may be authentic for the time and place of the play; they may be Elizabethan or Jacobean; they may be of no particular time period or locale; they may be of another era that is compatible with the play; or they may be contemporary clothes.

Give thought to the makeup, hairstyles, lighting and special effects (such as lightning, thunder, rain, snow, fog and smoke). What problems do you foresee here?

Dancing and swordfighting or fencing are also part of the spectacle. If you are not an expert in these areas, you should try to find people who are and let them stage the fights and dances. Know what you want, though. For fights, how long the fight should last; who wins; who is wounded or killed; and where on the stage the fighting begins, where it moves to and where it ends. For dances, where on the stage each dance takes place, who will dance, what music will be used and how long each will last.

Normally the director does not have to design any of the above, but you have to know what you want so you can talk to designers about your ideas.

Preparing a Rundown (or Outline)

As you analyze the script, prepare a rundown or outline giving for each scene the place, time, characters in the scene and anything else that you want to record, such as set requirements, props, music, songs, dances and fighting. For an example, see Figure 2-6, which gives this information for the first three scenes of the comedy *Twelfth Night*, or Figure 4-1, which is a rundown of the entire play of *Romeo and Juliet*. It will help you visualize

TIP

How do you know in advance what the playing time of your show will be? The best way is to time it with a stopwatch as you read the play aloud—or get a couple of actors to do it for you—with the variations in tempo you would like for each scene. Be sure to include the time that songs, dances, fights, scene changes and intermission(s) will take. This should give you a rough estimate of the playing time.

FIGURE 2-3: **EXAMPLE OF A PROSCENIUM ARCH STAGE**
Macbeth as produced by Marshall University Theatre, Huntington, West Virginia.
Direction by Eugene J. Anthony and scene design by Mike Murphy.
Photograph by Brett Hall

the production and will assist you in getting ready for conferences with the designers, with casting and planning a rehearsal schedule.

Cutting and Editing the Text

After you have completed your analysis, you should consider cutting and editing the text. Perhaps you want to produce a complete *Hamlet*, but if you do, you will probably have more than a four-hour presentation. Modern American audiences are accustomed to plays lasting about two hours or less and may get restless at a much longer production. So again it is the director's decision: Can you cut the play? Do you want to cut it?

Are there individual lines you would like to cut for one

reason or another? Perhaps you do not understand a line or you may think a line or passage adds nothing to the scene. All of Shakespeare's plays are in public domain, so you have the right to make any changes you wish in the script; however, if you stray too far from the original, you may find that the Shakespeare lovers in your audience—and there will be many—will dislike your production.

Intermission(s)

You should also decide where you want to take an intermission or two. Do not feel you have to take one at the end of an act. Keep in mind Shakespeare did not put his scenes into a five-act structure—this was done by later editors. So take your intermission(s) where you

FIGURE 2-4: **EXAMPLE OF AN ARENA STAGE**
The 225-seat Cassius Carter Centre Stage, located in the Old Globe's three-theatre complex in Balboa Park, San Diego, California. *Photo courtesy of the Old Globe Theatre*

want them. For one intermission, look for a good place to stop about half way through the play or just a little longer. Try to end the first part on a minor climax or where something vital is happening, so the audience will want to come back for the second part to see how it is resolved. For two intermissions, look at places that are about one-third and two-thirds of the way through the script.

Interpret the Play

After the above research, analysis and editing, your next step is interpretation. Here the director should think about how this play should look and sound. By looking at old pictures of productions, you can get an idea of how the play was produced in the past, and you will see most Shakespearean plays have been done in a variety of

styles. Here is a description of a few of them:

Elizabethan: Since the new reconstruction of The Globe theatre opened in London in 1997, interest has grown in producing Shakespearean plays as they were done originally: in the daytime with an open roof, a projecting stage with the audience standing or sitting around it and no microphones or spotlights. If you do not want to go this far away from styles used in our present theatre, look at the following possibilities.

Formalism: This is a neutral type of stage, similar to Shakespeare's original. One or two pieces of furniture may be onstage to establish a location, but this type relies on steps, ramps, different levels, drapes and screens to provide an interesting background that is no specific place until localized by the dialogue.

Selective realism: This style is more selective than realism. Only a few of the necessary details needed to

FIGURE 2-5: **EXAMPLE OF A THRUST STAGE**
The thrust stage at the new Globe Theatre, Shakespeare's Globe, London, England.
Photograph by Richard Kalina

portray a location are onstage with a greater emphasis on theatricality.

Theatricalism: No attempt is made to hide the fact that the audience is in a theatre watching a play. Lights are visible; actors may change costumes in view of the audience; stagehands may come onstage to change scenery and props.

Symbolism: This style makes use of symbols onstage to suggest the meaning of the play.

Expressionism: As the leading character becomes disturbed, the scenery, properties, lighting, costumes and sound become distorted to show how the person views the world.

Impressionism: There is an emphasis on heightening the mood in a nonrealistic but atmospheric way.

Constructivism: Steps, ramps, ladders and platforms are used to suggest the skeletal construction of a building, house, church and the like.

Multimedia: Slide, film or television projections on multiple screens combine with live performers, stereophonic sound and unusual lighting for another theatrical style.

Some may wonder why **realism** is not listed above since it is a popular style today for modern one-set plays. Realism attempts to give the illusion of an actual place and to do so the designer often uses elaborate scenery, furniture and props. With Shakespeare's short scenes in various locations, it would be too difficult to change realistic sets quickly. This is why Shakespeare's plays are usually done in another style.

It is the director's choice. Decide for yourself the style and interpretation. This is your concept for this play and you should communicate it to everyone who works on the production.

Twelfth Night

I-1: Duke Orsino's palace in Illyria
Time: Morning of first day
Speaking: Duke Orsino, Curio, Valentine
Singing and playing: First Musician (plays lute), Second Musician (plays pipe)
Extras: First and Second Lords/Officers
Furniture and props: Bench for Duke Orsino, lute for First Musician, pipe for Second Musician, swords
        for Curio, Valentine, First and Second Lords/Officers.

I-2: The seacoast near Olivia's house
Time: Later on the first day
Speaking: Viola, Captain
Extras: First and Second Sailors
Props: Gold chain worn by Viola, chest

I-3: Olivia's house
Time: Evening of the first day
Speaking: Sir Toby Belch, Maria, Sir Andrew Aguecheek
Furniture and props: Table and two chairs, riding crop for Sir Toby, fancy handkerchief with lace on edge,
        swords for Sir Toby and Sir Andrew, two cups or tankards for wine, bottle of canary wine

---

FIGURE 2-6: **RUNDOWN (OR OUTLINE) OF ACT 1, SCENES 1, 2 AND 3 OF** *TWELFTH NIGHT*

Acquire a Staff of People to Assist You

The director cannot do all the work alone. You need a business manager; publicity manager; stage manager; designers of scenery, lighting, sound and costumes; property master; technical director; and, perhaps, a musical director/conductor, choreographer and fight director.

> **TIP**
>
> If you have a small organization, consider giving one person two or three of the following jobs. The scene designer may also like to be the lighting designer; the business manager may also supervise the sound. Actors can also handle some positions, such as publicity manager or program manager, in addition to appearing onstage.

You will also need managers of programs, tickets, refreshments and house. (See Figure 2-7.) The work involved in these jobs is described below.

Business Manager

The most important work for this manager is to raise the money to finance the production, prepare a budget and pay all the bills. Other jobs include the following:

- Acquiring rooms or a theatre for auditions, rehearsals, technical work and performances.
- Signing contracts for rentals or purchase of supplies and equipment and hiring of employees.
- Setting ticket prices and policies, usually with the advice of the director and others.
- Supervising the sale of tickets and refreshments.
- Keeping accurate records for each performance of the number of tickets sold at each price and audi-

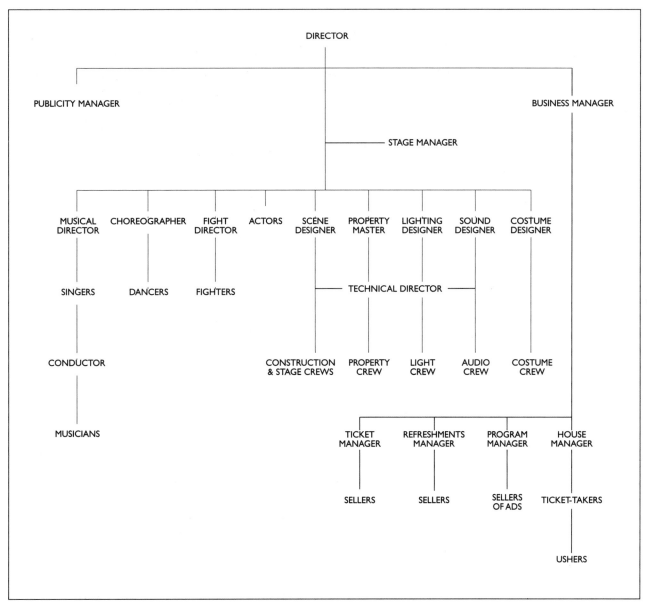

FIGURE 2-7: **SUGGESTED ORGANIZATION FOR A SHAKESPEAREAN PLAY PRODUCTION**

ence attendance.
- Closing the production, which involves making sure all rented and borrowed items are returned in good condition and those bought or built are properly stored, sold or thrown out.

Publicity Manager

This manager supervises all publicity and promotion for the play, which may include the following:
- Preparing and distributing posters, flyers and postcards.

- Writing newspaper, radio and TV ads and releases.
- Arranging for signs and billboards.
- Booking personal appearances of performers.
- Being the liaison person with the media, trying to get all publicity possible.

Stage Manager

The stage manager's principal work is to assist the director in every way possible at auditions, rehearsals and performances. During run-throughs, technical and dress rehearsals and performances, the stage manager is in charge backstage. Because this person has so many responsibilities, an assistant may be necessary. The work includes the following:

- Preparing an up-to-date list of addresses and phone numbers of everyone working on the production.
- At rehearsals and performances, posting sign-in sheets for actors and crews and telephoning those who are absent or late.
- In rehearsals, chalking or taping the floor to indicate where scenery will be and putting chairs where furniture will be located.
- Prompting and keeping the promptscript up-to-date by recording blocking, stage business, line changes, cuts or additions to the script; technical cues for scene and property shifts, lights, sound, music and curtains; floor plans of sets; plots for lights, sound, props and costumes.
- Assigning dressing rooms.
- Rehearsing understudies.
- Keeping in a safe place valuable items (like watches, money, jewelry) that performers do not want to leave in a dressing room while they are onstage.
- Checking on all technical elements before dress rehearsals and performances.
- Notifying performers and crews of the time by calling "Half hour, please," "Fifteen minutes, please," "Five minutes, please," and "Places, please," before the first act begins. At intermission(s), the stage manager calls "Five minutes, please" and "Places, please."
- Keeping order and quiet backstage and enforcing any regulations about smoking, eating or drinking.
- Notifying the house manager when the house may be opened to the audience. This is usually thirty minutes before curtain.
- Starting the first act and following acts after the house manager informs the stage manager the audience is seated.
- Making an announcement on a backstage microphone when an understudy is to play a role. This is usually done as the houselights are dimming before Act I begins. If there is enough time to prepare it, a piece of paper announcing the cast change

should be inserted in all programs.

- Calling performers to the stage for their entrances. (This is not necessary if the theatre is equipped with a stage-monitoring system allowing performers to follow the progress of the show in their dressing rooms.)
- Prompting and giving technical cues.
- Telling actors when they may or may not go onstage.
- Stopping the show if an emergency occurs and explaining to the audience what happened.
- Deciding at curtain call when to close the curtains for the last time and bring up the houselights.
- Keeping an accurate record of the playing time of acts and the length of intermission(s).

Scene Designer

The scene designer provides a visual environment appropriate for each scene of the play and supplies the specifications for the construction and painting of the scenery. For a Shakespearean play, a major consideration is that sets be constructed so they can be changed quickly.

A good design can help the audience understand the following:

- Place and time period (Italy, town, fifteenth century).
- Style and genre of play (selective realistic or expressionistic, comedy or tragedy).
- Mood and atmosphere (happy, sad, ominous).
- The type of people who live in the environment depicted onstage.

This designer provides the director with a **ground** (also called **floor**) **plan** which is a line drawing of the set as seen from above (see Figure 2-8). A **rendering** (perspective drawing of the set onstage) and a **model** (three-dimensional representation of the set) may also be done.

The scene designer dresses the scene with set or trim properties, such as furniture, draperies or flowers, and supervises special effects, like fog or smoke. Assistants include the technical director, master carpenter, construction crew, property master and crew and the stage crew (stagehands and riggers).

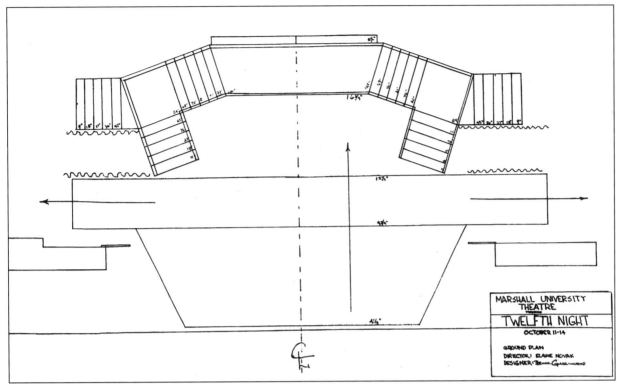

FIGURE 2-8: **GROUND PLAN BY BRUCE GREENWOOD FOR MARSHALL UNIVERSITY THEATRE'S PRODUCTION OF** *TWELFTH NIGHT*

Property Master

While the scene designer is responsible for selecting or designing set or trim properties, the property master and crew acquire or construct and take care of these items. As for hand props, such as money, flowers, drinks, the director or stage manager should make a list and oversee the acquisition or preparation of them by the property crew. Props that are part of a costume, like a handkerchief, handbag or cane, are selected by the costume designer.

Lighting Designer

The lighting designer makes visible what the audience needs to see and adds color, light and shade to the sets. This entails acquiring and placing lighting equipment and making a light plot, which indicates the type, size and location of all lighting instruments, the area that each will light, the colors of filters and the circuitry. This designer also prepares an instrument schedule, which gives information about each lighting instrument, and supervises the focusing of the instruments and the operation of the control board.

The lighting can help the audience understand the following:

- Genre of play (farce, romance).
- Mood and atmosphere (happy, sad).
- Time of day and year (day, night, summer, winter).
- Weather conditions (sunny, stormy).
- The important part of the stage or the people, props or scenery that should be emphasized.
- Some special effects, like lightning.
- Indicating the end of a scene through a fade-out or blackout and the beginning of the next scene through a cross-fade, fade-in or bump-up.

The lighting designer is assisted by a master electrician and the light crew.

Sound Designer

The sound designer is concerned with making audible what the audience needs to hear, which includes amplifying voices and musical instruments, playing recorded sound effects and music and supervising operation of the control board.

Sound may help the audience to understand the following:

- Place of a scene (street, wooded areas).
- Time of day (clock striking the hour).
- Mood and atmosphere (pastoral sounds).
- Weather (thunder).
- Offstage occurrences (battle sounds).

The audio crew assists the sound designer.

Costume Designer

This designer, who is responsible for providing appropriate costumes for the cast, may want to design them and have them made locally. Other options are to rent, buy or borrow them. In any case, the costume designer takes accurate measurements of the performers as early as possible.

Costumes can help the audience understand the following:

- Age of the character.
- Socioeconomic status (wealthy, poor).
- Occupation (farmer, soldier).
- Character relationships (members of a family may wear the same colors).
- Genre of play (tragedy, comedy).
- Mood and atmosphere (funny, dramatic).
- Time period and place (44 B.C. Rome, 1398 London).
- Time of day (day clothes, evening dress).
- Occasion (wedding, funeral).

This designer is responsible for costume accessories that are worn (wigs, hats, swords) or carried in the hands (fans, handbags, canes). Other duties include supervising the fitting of costumes, alterations, repairs, laundering, and dress parade (held several days before dress rehearsals where the actors put on their costumes for the costume designer and director to approve). This designer may also oversee performers' hairstyles, mustaches, beards and makeup.

The wardrobe supervisor and costume crew assist the costume designer.

Technical Director

This director is in charge of coordinating the technical elements, which include the following:

- Purchasing needed equipment and supplies.
- Constructing and painting scenery (as designed by the scene designer).
- Building, buying, renting or borrowing properties.
- Shifting, repairing and striking sets and properties.
- Supervising the work of all technical crews.

Musical Director/Conductor, Choreographer and Fight Director

Whether you employ these people depends on your budget, your play, your own capabilities and your cast's competence. If you think you can handle these jobs, there is no reason to look elsewhere; however, if you cannot coach the singers, conduct the musicians, choreograph the dancers and design the fights, you may need some help unless your cast can do it.

If you are using recorded music or no music at all, you obviously will not need a conductor. If you have only a few musicians, one of them may assume the leadership. If you have expert singers, they may not need the assistance of a musical director. If you have excellent dancers, they may be able to handle their own choreography. If you have experienced swordsmen, they may be able to arrange their own fight. The director decides.

Program Manager

This person sells ads for the program and oversees the writing of the program. At its simplest, the program may consist of the front and back of one sheet of paper. Or it may be folded to make a four-page program. If you sell a lot of program ads, it can go to many pages especially if you want to include photographs and biographies of the director, musical director/conductor, choreographer, fight director, designers and cast. If an elaborate program is desired, the program manager will have to start early to prepare it—probably about the time that rehearsals start.

At a minimum the program should contain the following information:

- Name of the producing organization, title of the play, name of author and dates, times and places of performances (see Figure 2-9).
- Name of director, musical director/conductor, choreographer and fight director.

- Designers of scenery, lighting, sound, costumes, makeup, hairstyles, and technical director.
- Cast of characters and musicians.
- Places and times of scenes.
- Production staff: Stage manager, rehearsal pianist, master carpenter, master electrician, audio technician, master carpenter, property master, wardrobe supervisor and managers of business, publicity, programs, tickets, refreshments and house.
- Crews: List everyone who worked on the play.
- Acknowledgments: List everyone who supplied materials or services.
- House rules: An example would be the following: "Please do not smoke, eat, drink or use a camera, recording device, personal telephone or beeper in this theatre."
- Sponsors and patrons.
- Coming events.

Ticket Manager

This manager works under the business manager and is responsible for the following:

- Ordering or making the tickets.
- Training the ticket-sellers
- Taking reservations and selling tickets at the box office and by mail and telephone.
- Keeping records for each performance of the number of tickets sold at each price and audience attendance.
- Banking the receipts.

Refreshments Manager

This person is responsible for selling refreshments before the performance, at intermissions and after the performance. Responsibilities include the following:

- Purchasing supplies.
- Obtaining city or state permits (if needed).
- Maintaining high standards of cleanliness.
- Training sellers.
- Turning over receipts to the ticket manager.
- Keeping records of sales.

House Manager

This manager is in charge of the house, which is the audience's area. This person should be prepared to handle all emergencies that may happen to spectators: illness, heart attack, fire, robbery, malfunction of the heating or cooling system and so forth.

The house manager is in charge of the ticket-takers and ushers and should instruct them in the following:

- Seating plan.
- Location of rest rooms, telephones and water fountains.
- Escorting members of the audience to their seats and giving one program to each with a smile.
- Assisting the disabled.

The house manager's supervisory duties also include the following:

- Checking on the temperature and cleanliness of the house.
- At 30 minutes before starting time, the stage manager should notify the house manager that all is ready backstage and the house may be opened to the audience.
- Stopping audience members with food or drinks from entering the house.
- Reminding spectators with cameras, tape recorders, personal phones and beepers that they may not be used in the theatre.
- At starting time, the house and stage managers should confer about beginning the performance. If spectators are waiting to be seated, the managers may decide to wait five minutes.
- When the audience is seated, the house manager so notifies the stage manager and closes the doors to the house. If there are latecomers, they may be kept in the lobby until there is a break in the onstage action, such as the end of a scene or act; then they may be ushered to vacant seats near the door. (During an intermission, they can be taken to their correct seats.)
- At intermission, when the houselights come up, the house manager or ushers should open the doors to the house and remain available to answer questions about the location of rest rooms, telephones, and

Marshall University Theatre

presents

A wittie and pleasant Comedie called

THE TAMING OF THE SHREW

As it was acted by His Majesties servants at The Blacke Friers and The Globe

Written by Will. Shakespeare

(As found on the title-page to the 1631 Quarto edition)

8:15 p.m. - November 6, 7, 8, 9, 1968

Old Main Auditorium

FIGURE 2-9: **FRONT COVER OF PROGRAM FOR MARSHALL UNIVERSITY THEATRE'S PRODUCTION OF** *THE TAMING OF THE SHREW*
Program courtesy of Marshall University Theatre

so forth. Several minutes before the end of the intermission, the house manager should warn the audience with flashing lights, a bell or announcement that the next act is about to begin. When the audience is seated, the house manager informs the stage manager of this and then closes the doors to the house. If there is another intermission, this is repeated. At the end of the performance, the house

manager opens the doors so the audience can depart.

- Handling lost-and-found items.
- Seeing that fire and smoking regulations are obeyed.
- Keeping order in the house which may involve insisting that noisy spectators or crying children be quiet or leave.

The Taming of the Shrew

Time: Late sixteenth century
Place: Italy

MEN

PETRUCHIO:
1. Traveling costume with cloak, sword, whip, and hat with feathers
2. Grotesque wedding costume in bright colors, ragged trunks and tights, old boots, torn cloak, broken sword and bizarre hat trimmed with ribbons and feathers
3. Elegant costume with short cape and hat

BAPTISTA:
1. Elaborate costume suitable for older gentleman

LUCENTIO:
1. Rich traveling costume for young nobleman
2. Doctor's black gown and hat to wear when disguised as schoolmaster
3. Elegant wedding costume with short cape and hat

FIGURE 2-10: **DIRECTOR'S AND COSTUME DESIGNER'S LIST OF COSTUMES FOR** *THE TAMING OF THE SHREW*, **continued on page 30**

Supervise the Technical, Business and Publicity Work

Experienced people need little supervision but if you have beginners, the director, assisted by the stage manager, will have to oversee their work.

Before auditions you should meet with the designers of scenery, lighting, sound and costumes, the property master, technical director and stage manager. At this conference you must be sure everyone agrees as to the play's time period, locations, interpretation, genre, theme, mood and atmosphere. All technical elements must work together to contribute to the audience's understanding of plot, characters and theme.

Colors to be used in the scenery, properties, lighting and costumes should be discussed and, if the director favors certain colors, this is the time to communicate it to the designers.

At this conference the director should accomplish the following:

- The director and scene designer should agree on the ground plans for the sets (see Figure 2-8 or Figure 4-4).
- The director and the costume designer should agree on the costume list (see Figure 2-10 or Figure 4-6).
- The director should give a preliminary prop list to the property master. (The director can take this from the rundown sheet, an example of which is Figure 2-6 or Figure 4-1.)
- Handling of special effects (such as the storm in Act I, Scene 1 of *The Tempest*) should be discussed with the entire group.

After the designers have had time to finalize their plans, they should submit them to the director for approval. The latter may then accept them or ask for revisions.

About halfway through rehearsals, the director should provide the final prop list (see Figure 3-4 or 4-5), a cue sheet for lights (see Figure 3-5 or 4-7) and another cue sheet for sound (see Figure 3-6 or 4-3). The director should also confer with the costume designer to see if there are any problems with hairstyles, wigs and makeup for the cast.

As for the business and publicity work, the business manager and publicity manager should take charge of these; but if they are unable to do so, the director or stage manager must step in and take over.

Now it is on to auditions, casting, rehearsals and performances—what Part Three is all about.

The Taming of the Shrew (cont.)

HORTENSIO:
1. Plain but good costume with short cape and hat
2. Doctor's black gown and hat to wear when disguised as schoolmaster
3. Rich wedding costume

GREMIO:
1. Elaborate costume for this elderly man with armhole cloak and tall hat with plumes

TRANIO:
1. Servant's costume with tunic and cap
2. Rich costume with scarlet cloak

VINCENTIO:
1. Rich costume suitable for older nobleman

GRUMIO:
1. Servant's costume with cap
2. Grotesque outfit with ragged, colorful clothes, old boots, broken sword, bizarre hat with feathers

BIONDELLO:
1. Servant's costume with cap

CURTIS:
1. Servant's costume with cap

FOUR SERVANTS:
1. For each, a servant's costume with cap

TAILOR:
1. Fancy costume with cap

HABERDASHER:
1. Similar to tailor's costume, but not as fancy

PEDANT:
1. Plain, dark costume with cloak for elderly man
2. Better costume

WOMEN

KATHARINA:
1. Riding dress with hat and whip
2. Elaborate wedding gown and veil, cloak and hat
3. Torn, soiled version of wedding gown
4. Elegant gown

BIANCA:
1. Elegant dress and cap
2. Elegant gown

WIDOW:
1. One modest dress, cloak and cap

FIGURE 2-10: **continued**

✦ Part Three ✦

From Auditions Through Performances

Part Three is concerned with auditioning actors for your Shakespearean production plus other performers you might need: singers, dancers, swordsmen and musicians. After that, we shall take up casting the play, rehearsals (orientation, reading, blocking, developing, polishing, technical and dress) and performances.

Auditions

About two weeks before auditions, the director or publicity manager should write an announcement about auditions that will motivate prospective performers to come to tryouts. This notice may be sent to school or local newspapers and radio and television stations or used as posters or handouts in classes. It should state the title and author of the play; the name of the producing organization; dates, times and places of tryouts; and dates of performances. Also, you may want to publicize descriptions of the characters. If any of these must sing, dance, fight or play a musical instrument, this should be mentioned. Ask singers to come with their own music and be prepared to sing one minute of a song of their choice. Dancers should wear or bring dancing clothes and shoes to auditions. Musicians should furnish their own instruments (see Figure 3-1).

Because of the difficulties in reading Shakespeare's lines without advance preparation, it might be wise to prepare copies of the excerpts from the play that you plan to have actors read at auditions. You can make these available to anyone who wants to study them before tryouts.

Audition Information Form

The director should prepare an information form for candidates to complete at the time of auditions. Before you do this, you will need to plan a tentative rehearsal schedule, since you will want to indicate on the form the days of the week and the hours that you intend to rehearse (see Figure 3-2).

The audition information form may include the following:

- Name to be used on the program and in publicity.
- Address (with zip code).
- Telephones (with area code).
- Social security number or student number.
- Class or grade (if in a school situation).
- Hometown (if needed for publicity).
- Height (without shoes).
- Weight.
- Age.
- Color of hair.
- Training and experience in acting.
- (If singing, dancing, swordfighting or playing a musical instrument is important to your production, ask about their training and experience in these.)
- Commitments that will interfere with rehearsals. (State when rehearsals will be held so that they can

AUDITIONS FOR
Romeo and Juliet
BY WILLIAM SHAKESPEARE

Monday, Feb. 22, from 2 to 4 P.M. and from 6:30 to 9 P.M. in the Theatre
Callback will be on Tuesday, Feb. 23, from 6:30 to 9 P.M. in the Theatre
Rehearsals will begin on Wednesday, Feb. 24. Performances will be on April 21-24.

NEEDED: 25 MEN, 7 WOMEN

ROMEO:	Attractive, romantic, young, impulsive, rash. During the play, he grows to manhood. Swordfighter.
JULIET:	Beautiful, romantic, delicate, refined, charming. Fourteen years old. She grows from child to woman during the five days of this play.
MERCUTIO:	Witty, talkative, courageous, poetic, often flippant and cynical. Kinsman to Prince, friend to Romeo. Swordfighter.
NURSE:	Eccentric, garrulous, coarse, bawdy woman of middle age or older.
FRIAR LAURENCE:	Genial, kind, sympathetic, intelligent man of middle age or older.
PRINCE ESCALUS:	Strong, dignified, stern leader.
CAPULET:	Wealthy, hot-tempered, talkative, master of his house, middle-aged.
LADY CAPULET:	Dignified lady of about twenty-eight. Sophisticated, kind mother of Juliet.
MONTAGUE:	Well-to-do middle-aged man.
LADY MONTAGUE:	Mother of Romeo. Has three lines.
BENVOLIO:	Nephew to Montague, friend to Romeo. Spirited, fiery. Swordfighter.
TYBALT:	Nephew to Lady Capulet. Hot-tempered, fiery, tall. Swordfighter.
PARIS:	Young, handsome kinsman to Prince. Loves Juliet. Swordfighter.
SAMPSON:	Comic servant to Capulet; little man. Swordfighter.
GREGORY:	Servant to Capulet; taller than Sampson. Swordfighter.
BALTHASAR:	Servant to Romeo. Swordfighter.
ABRAHAM:	Servant to Montague. Swordfighter.
PETER:	Attendant to Nurse.
CHORUS:	Dignified, authoritative; must have good speaking voice. May double.
APOTHECARY:	Thin, poor.
FRIAR JOHN:	Franciscan monk.
THREE WATCHMEN:	Strong, authoritative. Only the first has lines to say.
ROSALINE and TWO LADIES:	No lines but will dance and appear in several scenes.
OLD CAPULET:	Capulet's cousin. Has two lines.
TWO GENTLEMEN:	No lines but will dance and appear in several scenes.
TWO SOLDIERS:	Strong, tall. No lines.

FOR MORE DETAILS, SEE DR. E.A. NOVAK IN THE THEATRE DEPARTMENT
THIS IS A MARSHALL UNIVERSITY THEATRE PRODUCTION

FIGURE 3-1: **ANNOUNCEMENT OF AUDITIONS FOR *ROMEO AND JULIET***

Name as you want it on program (please print):

Address (with zip code):

Height (without shoes):

Weight:

Telephones (with area code):

Age:

Color of hair:

Social Security Number:

Class:

Hometown (needed for publicity):

Training in acting:

Experience in acting:

Rehearsals will normally be from 6:30 till 9:30 P.M. on Monday through Friday but there may be some rehearsals in the afternoons or on weekends. Put an X in the squares below to indicate the times that you CANNOT rehearse:

	Mon.	Tue.	Wed.	Thu.	Fri.	Sat.	Sun.
1:30-2:30 P.M.							
2:30-3:30 P.M.							
3:30-4:30 P.M.							
6:30-7:30 P.M.							
7:30-8:30 P.M.							
8:30-9:30 P.M.							

Commitments that will interfere with rehearsals:

Men only: Do you sing well?   How long and where have you studied singing?

Men only: Can you play the guitar, mandolin, lute, or flute well?
                    Do you read music?

I will accept any role in this production (please circle one): Yes No

If not cast, I would like to work on the jobs circled: Props   Building sets   Sound   Stage crew
Lighting   Costumes   Makeup   Selling refreshments   Ushering

FIGURE 3-2: **AUDITION INFORMATION FORM FOR** *TWELFTH NIGHT*

indicate which ones they cannot attend.)

- I will accept any role in this production (please circle one): Yes   No
- If not cast, I would like to work on the jobs circled: Props   Building sets   Sound   Stage crew Lighting   Costumes   Makeup   Selling Refreshments   Ushering

Open or Private Auditions

There are two kinds of auditions that you might use: open or private. In open auditions, all candidates who wish to try out gather in a large room or theatre to audition and watch the others do so. The director may make a brief opening speech, which can include the following:

- Introduce members of the production team who are present.
- Mention the performance dates (so no one will try out who has a conflict with performances).
- If a role has already been cast (as with a guest performer), tell them it is not available.
- Briefly review the plot of the play, descriptions of the principal characters and your concept for the production.
- Inform them where and when a callback list (and, later, a cast list) will be posted or give them a telephone number they can call to find out if they are on the lists.
- Tell them the procedure for reading auditions. If you are testing for singing, dancing, swordfighting or playing a musical instrument, let them know how it will be done.
- Give them a chance to ask questions.

Begin the audition by selecting one to three people to read a three-to-four-minute excerpt from the play. For example, if you are directing *Romeo and Juliet*, you might have prospective leads read part of the balcony scene (Act II, Scene 2). To try out for the roles of Mercutio or Benvolio, they might read from Act II, Scene 1, while Act I, Scene 3 is good to use for those who might play Lady Capulet, the Nurse or Juliet. To audition just one person, select a soliloquy or long speech, such as Mercutio's description of Queen Mab in Act I, Scene 4.

The director should go to tryouts with about twelve scripts for actors to read from and a list of page numbers for the fifteen or more excerpts that will be used to audition all of the major characters. After getting one to three people to stand in front of the others, give them scripts, assign them parts, and tell them the page number and the line where they are to start reading. After about three minutes, stop them with a "Thank you." Then ask other people to read the same scene or a different one. Proceed until everyone has had an opportunity to try out, changing the scenes frequently. Then ask the candidates to read other roles than they did the first time.

In private or closed auditions, the aspirants are given an appointment for a specific time. They are then ushered into a room where the only people present are the director, stage manager and others in the producing organization. Each candidate may audition alone by reading a soliloquy or long speech or by reading a short scene with the stage manager or with one or two of the other hopefuls. Auditions for singing, swordfighting and playing a musical instrument can be handled in the private audition, but auditioning for dancing may be difficult. Probably dancers will have to audition at another time and place with the choreographer.

There are advantages and disadvantages to both types of auditions. The open audition allows the director to see all of the candidates together in one place. How they look and work together is evident as various combinations of people read different scenes. Disadvantages are that some actors get nervous auditioning in front of an audience and others may get upset if they are not allowed to read as often as other people.

Private auditions can be held in a small room or office. Actors usually feel more comfortable in this type of tryout and may, therefore, make a better impression. Private auditions give the director the opportunity to talk with each candidate about items on the audition form and perhaps get to know them a little better than at an open tryout. Also if the actors have an appointment, they should not have to wait long to try out. The disadvantages are that the director hears them read only once and does not have the chance to see and hear them read with many other people. Also, if there are a large number of candidates, it will take a lot of time because you will have to allot at least seven minutes or more to each person. If you expect many to try out, you should select open auditions.

Now let's look at the audition procedure if you have singing, dancing, swordfighting or playing musical instruments in your production.

SINGING

In *Twelfth Night,* Feste, the clown, sings four solos but, in addition, he has to be a good comedian. (The part was originally acted by Robert Armin, who succeeded Will Kempe as the leading comedian in Shakespeare's company and became noted for his singing.) The musical director or director will have to arrange for a tuned piano and accompanist so prospects can bring their own music and sing one minute of a song of their choice. The musical director may advise on casting but the director must make the selection.

In other plays, actors may sing but perhaps not as well as Feste. For example, the director should ask those auditioning for Desdemona in *Othello* to sing, but in Act IV, Scene 3, Desdemona is sad and worried and is singing softly, almost to herself, although Emilia is present. You should cast Desdemona for her acting ability and beauty, not her singing, but, of course, she has to be able to sing in tune.

DANCING

In *A Midsummer Night's Dream* dancers may include Puck, First Fairy, Peaseblossom, Cobweb, Moth, Mustardseed, Oberon's Elves and others. At auditions the choreographer may teach prospective dancers a short combination of steps. Then the dancers can show the choreographer and director what they can do. The choreographer may advise on casting everyone except Puck. A major role like Puck must be cast for acting ability and appearance, not his dancing skill, so the director must make this decision.

SWORDFIGHTING

In *Romeo and Juliet* the following engage in swordfighting: Romeo, Mercutio, Benvolio, Tybalt, Paris, Sampson, Gregory, Balthasar and Abraham. It is not necessary to bring swords to auditions. The director or fight director can just talk to aspirants about their training and experience in fencing and swordfighting. If no one has this skill, your best bet is to cast athletic men who can learn how to do it quickly. For this you may need the advice of your fight director.

PLAYING MUSICAL INSTRUMENTS

A rehearsal pianist (if needed) and nonspeaking musicians (in such plays as *Twelfth Night* and *Othello*) may be selected by the musical director. This can be done at regular auditions or, if you expect a large number of musicians to try out, at a special audition just for them. A piano should be provided for pianists, but other musicians should bring their own instruments. Ask them to play about one minute of any selection. If the musicians have lines to say, they must read for the director who should cast them with the advice of the musical director.

Callback

If you have a large number of candidates, the director should plan to hold at least two open auditions and then a callback. After the second open audition, the director should prepare a list of those who may read, sing or dance again at a callback. Eliminate the people you cannot use in this production and call back the possible ones.

This is an opportunity for the director to see and hear actors read different roles with various people to determine who can handle the parts vocally and physically, who responds to whom and who fits your image of the characters. It also gives you the chance to view the singers and dancers once more.

Casting the Play

Casting is the place where a director makes or breaks the show. It is probably the most important part of directing a production, so take your time, consider what you know about each candidate and try to come up with the best cast possible. Think about each person's education, training and experience in previous productions and the way the aspirant performs on and off stage. Ask yourself: Of all the people who auditioned, who is the best actor for

TIP

You may be able to cast one actor in two or three roles. For example, the part of Chorus in *Romeo and Juliet* speaks only in the prologues to Acts I and II (and the latter is often cut as it is in the script of *Romeo and Juliet* featured in Part Four.) You need a good performer for the part of Chorus, but you hate to put one of your best actors in a role that has only fourteen lines. In this case you might try having this actor double—that is, play two roles. Perhaps he could be Chorus and Friar Laurence.

No director likes to have an actor who is only in one scene near the beginning of the play and then has nothing else to do in the show except wait for curtain call. Doubling may be the answer or putting the actor to work doing a technical job, such as serving as a dresser to other actors.

this role? Who will please the audience the most? Who will work well with the others in the cast? Who will work hard with me to produce a great play? Start with the principal roles, then work down to the midsize and smaller parts and finally the extras or walk-ons (the ones who have no lines). And take your time—don't rush! If necessary, you can call performers back for additional auditions.

Announcing the Cast

If you are certain that the cast you have put together is the one you really want, you can head up the announcement with "Cast List." If, however, you think there may be some changes needed, title it "Tentative Cast List." This will warn performers that you may want to make some alterations in the first week or two of rehearsals. And don't be afraid to make changes. If an actor is not working up to your expectations or is habitually late or absent, dismiss the person. Don't think about hurt feelings—you must do what is best for the play.

Underneath the title, list the characters (in the order of speaking or appearance in the play, or in the order found in the script under Cast of Characters or Dramatis Personae) with the names of the actors cast in the roles. Other information you should include: where scripts can

be obtained and the date, time and place of the first rehearsal with the names of performers who are needed at that time. Remind them to bring their script and a pencil, and end with thanking all who auditioned (see Figure 3-3).

Understudies

Unless the play will run for a long time or you are concerned that an actor cast in the show will be unable to make all performances, understudies probably are not necessary. If you want to be on the safe side and select understudies, however, put the stage manager in charge of their rehearsals. They should also be invited to watch regular rehearsals.

Rehearsals

In this section we shall take up planning a rehearsal schedule that will give you adequate time to prepare your play. Then we will look at various problems you may encounter in orientation, reading, blocking, developing, polishing, technical and dress rehearsals.

As for the technical work, the scene and costume designers and property master need to go to work immediately. As noted in Part Two, by this time the director and scene designer should have agreed on ground plans for the sets, the director and costume designer should be in accord on the costumes and the director should have given a preliminary prop list to the property master. A final prop list and cues for lights and sound may wait till the play is blocked. (See Director's Supervisory Duties on page 47.)

Planning a Rehearsal Schedule

The total number of rehearsals will vary depending on the difficulty of the play and the skills of the actors. If you plan to rehearse five times a week for about three hours each, your tentative rehearsal schedule may look something like the one on page 38. Since not every Shakespearean play requires singing, dancing, swordfighting or live music, you will not find time allotted to these rehearsals. If you have one or more of these in your production, you will have to work these rehearsals into the schedule.

Cast List for Twelfth Night

(in order of appearance)

Orsino, Duke of Illyria ....(Names of those cast in this column)

Curio, gentleman attending the Duke ....

First Musician ....

Second Musician ....

First Lord/Officer, in service of the Duke ....

Second Lord/Officer, in service of the Duke ....

Valentine, gentleman attending the Duke ....

Viola, sister of Sebastian ....

Captain ....

First Sailor ....

Second Sailor ....

Sir Toby Belch, uncle to Olivia ....

Maria, gentlewoman attending Olivia ....

Sir Andrew Aguecheek ....

Feste, a clown ....

Olivia, a countess ....

Malvolio, steward to Olivia ....

First Lady in waiting to Olivia ....

Second Lady in waiting to Olivia ....

Fabian, servant to Olivia ....

Sebastian, brother to Viola ....

Antonio, a sea captain ....

Priest ....

CAST: Please initial by your name to indicate that you accept this role.
You may get a script in the theatre office.

FIRST REHEARSAL: Wednesday, Sept. 4, 6:30 P.M., in Theatre. Everyone in the cast is needed. Bring your script and a pencil.

MY THANKS TO ALL WHO AUDITIONED—YOU WERE GREAT!

(Name of Director)

FIGURE 3-3: **ANNOUNCEMENT OF CAST**

1st Week:

Mon.   Two open auditions in the afternoon and evening.

Tue.   Callback.

Wed.   *Orientation:* Complete cast needed; measure for costumes.

Thu.   *Reading rehearsals:* Reading of play; discussion of meanings and pronunciations of words with those playing speaking roles.

Fri.   Same.

2nd Week:

Mon.   Continue work on the meanings of words and scenes with those playing speaking roles; try improvising some difficult sections.

Tue.   Reading and discussion of the first half of the play with those playing speaking roles; focus on line interpretations, variety and articulation.

Wed.   Reading and discussion of the last half of the play with those playing speaking roles; focus on line interpretations, variety and articulation.

Thu.   *Blocking Rehearsals:* Block Act I with those playing speaking roles.

Fri.   Continue work on Act I by adding those playing nonspeaking parts; focus on plot and movement.

3rd Week:

Mon.   Block Act II with those playing speaking roles.

Tue.   Continue work on Act II by adding those playing nonspeaking parts; focus on plot and movement.

Wed.   Block Act III with those playing speaking roles.

Thu.   Continue work on Act III by adding those playing nonspeaking parts; focus on plot and movement.

Fri.   Block Act IV with those playing speaking roles.

4th Week:

Mon.   Continue work on Act IV by adding those playing nonspeaking parts; focus on plot and movement.

Tue.   Block Act V with those playing speaking roles.

Wed.   Continue work on Act V by adding those playing nonspeaking parts; focus on plot and movement.

Thu.   *Developing Rehearsals:* Review first half of play with everyone in these scenes; focus on characterizations and voice.

Fri.   Review last half of play with everyone in these scenes; focus on characterizations and voice.

5th Week:

Mon.   Act I with everyone; everything must be memorized—no scripts onstage from here on; focus on accurate memorization, listening to other actors and stage business (detailed activities devised to assist actors with characterizations, such as handling a cane).

Tue.   Act II with everyone; focus on memorization, listening and stage business.

Wed.   Act III with everyone; focus on memorization, listening and stage business.

Thu.   Act IV with everyone; focus on memorization, listening and stage business.

Fri.   Act V with everyone; focus on memorization, listening and stage business.

6th Week:

Mon.   *Polishing Rehearsals:* Run-through of first half of the play with props; focus on tempos, building to climaxes, concentration, energy and ensemble playing.

Tue.   Run-through of last half of the play with props; focus on tempos, building to climaxes, concentration, energy and ensemble playing.

Wed.   Run-through of entire play with props.

Thu.   Run-through of entire play with props.

Fri.   *Technical Rehearsals:* Dress parade before a run-through of the entire play with props. (The dress parade involves actors wearing their costumes for the costume designer and director to approve. This is usually done onstage under stage lights. It is also a time when the director and costume designer can talk to each performer about hairstyles, wigs and makeup. Alterations needed to costumes are noted and then the actors change into rehearsal clothes for a run-through of the play.)

7th Week:

Mon. Rehearsal for scenery, properties, lighting and sound designers and crews with director, stage manager and technical director—*no actors or musicians are needed.*

Tue. Run-through with actors, scenery, properties, lighting, sound and music.

Wed. Same.

Thu. *Dress rehearsals:* Actors in costumes and makeup, all technical elements and music; block curtain call.

Fri. Same.

8th Week:

Mon. Same; production photographs taken during and/or after rehearsal.

Tue. Same.

Wed. *Performances begin.*

If you play more than one week, you should schedule a refresher rehearsal each week for the day prior to performances.

TIP

Everyone connected with the play must be aware of the rehearsal schedule, but it is difficult to plan a seven-week schedule and stick to it. It is best to post only one or two weeks at a time so the schedule can be revised to take care of any problems that arise.

Orientation

The first rehearsal is a good time to get everyone acquainted. The director can introduce the stage manager and other members of the producing organization to the cast. The director may also ask the cast members to introduce themselves. Then the director can tell the cast about the plans for the play: the time period and locations of scenes; style and interpretation; genre, mood and atmosphere; and ideas for the sets and costumes. If the scene and costume designers have some designs ready to share with the cast, they will be interested to see them. It is also a good time to talk about hair, especially if you want some of the men to grow longer hair, beards or mustaches.

Next, the director should discuss the plot and theme or major ideas to be stressed in the production. All actors should be encouraged to read the play carefully to determine who are the characters and what are their relationships, objectives and motivations and what obstacles they encounter in trying to achieve their goals (see Analyze the Characters on pages 13-15).

Remind the cast of the company's rules, such as:

1. Be on time for rehearsals. Encourage them to arrive ten to fifteen minutes early to warm up their voices and bodies, study their lines or just relax and focus on the role and the play.

2. Rehearsals will end at—(give them the approximate time).

3. Be quiet and attentive during rehearsals.

4. Write in your scripts with pencil and bring both to every rehearsal.

5. Notify the stage manager if you must miss a rehearsal. (Give them the phone number to call.)

6. Ask the stage manager's permission if you must leave a rehearsal before it is finished.

7. Do not smoke, eat or chew gum during rehearsals. (Bottled water is permissible.)

8. Keep the rehearsal, makeup and dressing rooms clean.

9. Wear shoes similar to what you will use in performance.

10. If you will wear a long skirt or robe in the play, bring a similar garment to rehearse in.

Then, take time to answer any questions they may have about the play, rules of the organization or anything else that is a concern. The director should try to inspire confidence—your cast must think that you know what you are doing. The director should also try to develop a good relationship with the cast by encouraging them to relax and enjoy the experience. In order to make them feel comfortable, the director should endeavor to provide a nonthreatening space in which to work.

A play production involves the collaboration of a great number of people. The director heads this group—the team—but he or she needs to instill in the team the desire for success. Like the coach of a football team, the director must inspire and encourage, build confidence, listen to problems, stimulate imaginations and be a friend to all. Make it fun to come to rehearsal, not a chore. Have a good time and your team will too.

This orientation session may also be a good time for publicity. While the entire cast is together, the publicity manager may want to arrange for pictures to be taken to accompany an announcement of the cast.

Last, you should have everyone measured for costumes. The costume designer and crew must go to work immediately and they need accurate measurements.

TIP

Have a plan for every rehearsal you hold. Don't waste the actors' time by making them wait for you to decide what you want to do next. If they feel you are working hard and efficiently, they will likely reciprocate. If they think you don't care about the play, they won't care either. Keep the rehearsal moving toward your goal for that day.

Show them you are concerned about everyone. Be enthusiastic! Praise them when they do well. Help them when they don't.

Reading Rehearsals

Because Shakespeare's language presents difficulties to modern actors, it is best to start rehearsals with working on the words. This is so important that five rehearsals have been scheduled for reading and discussion, with the actors who have speaking roles, the director and the stage manager sitting in a circle or around a large table. Until the actors understand the plot, characters, thought and diction, the director should not start blocking.

You should provide the cast with scripts that have good footnotes since these will eliminate a good number of questions about meanings of words and lines. This is the time, too, to give the cast any changes in the script: cuts, additions, substitutions of words or alterations of scene order.

One question that will come up is: Should we use the Standard English dialect? For actors in the United States, the answer is No. The Standard American dialect will do just fine. After all, most of Shakespeare's plays are set in such places as Ephesus, Athens, Thebes, Venice, Verona, Messina, France, Illyria, Vienna, Rome, Padua, Denmark, Bohemia, and other non-English locations, so there is no logical reason to use a Standard English dialect when acting them. But you may ask: What should we use when we act English history plays, such as *Henry VIII*, or a comedy set in England, *The Merry Wives of Windsor*? The answer is you can use the Standard American dialect here too because it is thought to be as close or even closer to the original Elizabethan speech of Shakespeare than today's Standard English dialect.

BLANK VERSE AND RHYMING COUPLETS

The actors should be conscious of Shakespeare's **blank verse** and the **rhyming couplets** that he often used to end a scene. As stated earlier, most of the lines that Shakespeare wrote for his plays are in blank verse, which is unrhymed iambic pentameter, but in *A Midsummer Night's Dream* he often employed rhyming couplets, in which every two lines rhyme, such as this speech from Act II, Scene 1, when Oberon speaks to Puck:

> I know a bank where the wild thyme blows,
> Where oxlips and the nodding violet grows,
> Quite over-canopied with luscious woodbine,
> With sweet musk-roses and with eglantine:
> There sleeps Titania sometime of the night,
> Lull'd in these flowers with dances and delight;
> And there the snake throws her enamell'd skin,
> Weed wide enough to wrap a fairy in:
> And with the juice of this I'll streak her eyes,
> And make her full of hateful fantasies.
> Take thou some of it, and seek through this grove:
> A sweet Athenian lady is in love
> With a disdainful youth: anoint his eyes;
> But do it when the next thing he espies
> May be the lady: thou shalt know the man
> By the Athenian garments he hath on.
> Effect it with some care that he may prove

More fond on her than she upon her love:
And look thou meet me ere the first cock crow.

Then Puck ends the scene with a rhyming line:

Fear not, my lord, your servant shall do so.

Actors should study the verse in rehearsal, but in performance they must forget about the meter and rhyme scheme. Their concentration should be on listening to the speeches of the other characters and thinking the thoughts and feeling the emotions of the character.

FIGURATIVE LANGUAGE

Analyze the figurative language: the **allusions** (references), **similes** (comparisons that are usually introduced by *like* or *as*), **metaphors** (comparisons made when a word or phrase is used in place of another), **personifications** (attributing human qualities to an object or abstraction) and other figures of speech (see pages 15-17). In Act II, Scene 2 of *Romeo and Juliet*, Romeo uses a metaphor and personification in the following excerpt:

But soft! What light through yonder window
    breaks?
It is the east, and Juliet is the sun.
Arise, fair sun, and kill the envious moon,
Who is already sick and pale with grief,
That thou her maid art far more fair than she: . . .

Later, he uses a simile and an allusion when he is comparing Juliet to a winged messenger of heaven (an angel):

O, speak again, bright angel! for thou art
As glorious to this night, being o'er my head,
As is a wingèd messenger of heaven
Unto the white-upturnèd wondering eyes
Of mortals that fall back to gaze on him
When he bestrides the lazy-pacing clouds
And sails upon the bosom of the air.

For actors to interpret figurative language well, they first must understand it and then visualize it. Once they can see the image in their minds, they should be able to interpret it meaningfully.

ARCHAIC WORDS

When actors have **archaic words** to say, they should speak them distinctly and hope the context of the sentence plus appropriate gestures will communicate meaning to the listeners. Look at a soliloquy by Viola in Act II, Scene 2 of *Twelfth Night*:

How will this fadge? My master loves her dearly,
And I, poor monster, fond as much on him,
And she, mistaken, seems to dote on me.

Fadge means "succeed" or "fit together" and, if the actress will emphasize the word or make a small gesture while saying it, it should carry meaning to the audience.

ARTICULATION AND BREATH CONTROL

In order to speak the lines of Shakespeare well, actors need good **articulation** with adequate **breath control**. Articulation involves moving your lips, tongue, jaws and teeth and hard and soft palates to speak distinctly enough to be understood easily. Breath control concerns inhaling and exhaling to provide an adequate supply of breath to support your words so they carry to the back row of the audience. To improve these, have the actors work on Lady Macbeth's difficult soliloquy from Act I, Scene 5 of *Macbeth*:

Glamis thou art, and Cawdor; and shalt be
What thou art promised: yet do I fear thy nature;
It is too full o' the milk of human kindness
To catch the nearest way: thou wouldst be great;
Art not without ambition, but without
The illness should attend it: what thou wouldst
    highly,
That wouldst thou holily; wouldst not play false,
And yet wouldst wrongly win: thou 'ldst have,
    great Glamis,
That which cries "Thus thou must do, if thou
    have it;

And that which rather thou dost fear to do
Than wishest should be undone."

ASIDES AND SOLILOQUIES

Two devices encountered in Shakespeare's plays are the **aside** and the **soliloquy**. An *aside* is a brief remark a character makes to the audience that other people onstage pretend not to hear. Editors usually mark these comments with [*Aside*] so directors and actors will know how to handle them. The person making the aside may turn toward the audience or move closer to the audience to say the remark. Other people onstage should pretend not to hear it. One example occurs in Act II, Scene 2 of *Romeo and Juliet* when Romeo says:

[*Aside*] Shall I hear more, or shall I speak at this?

A *soliloquy* is a speech given when a character is alone onstage. The question that needs answering is this: Is the character talking to the audience or speaking aloud his thoughts? Director and actor should discuss this. Most of the time you will find that the speaker should share it with the audience. Here for directors and actors to study is the most famous soliloquy ever written: From Act III, Scene 1 of *Hamlet*, the title character is speaking:

To be, or not to be: that is the question:
Whether 'tis nobler in the mind to suffer
The slings and arrows of outrageous fortune
Or to take arms against a sea of troubles,
And by opposing end them? To die—to sleep—
No more; and by a sleep to say we end
The heartache, and the thousand natural shocks
That flesh is heir to. 'Tis a consummation
Devoutly to be wish'd. To die—to sleep.
To sleep—perchance to dream: ay, there's the rub!
For in that sleep of death what dreams may come
When we have shuffled off this mortal coil
Must give us pause. There's the respect
That makes calamity of so long life.
For who would bear the whips and scorns of time,
Th' oppressor's wrong, the proud man's contumely,
The pangs of despised love, the law's delay,

The insolence of office, and the spurns
That patient merit of th' unworthy takes,
When he himself might his quietus make
With a bare bodkin? Who would fardels bear,
To grunt and sweat under a weary life,
But that the dread of something after death,
The undiscovered country, from whose bourn
No traveller returns, puzzles the will
And makes us rather bear those ills we have
Than fly to others that we know not of?
Thus conscience does make cowards of us all;
And thus the native hue of resolution
Is sicklied o'er with the pale cast of thought,
And enterprises of great pitch and moment
With this regard their currents turn awry
And lose the name of action.

PHRASING

Another important consideration is **phrasing**. Encourage actors to pause only at logical places. Do not let them pause at the end of every line just because it is the end of the line: have them continue until the end of the thought. Punctuation may be a guide in most cases to pausing but not always. Look at the above soliloquy. You probably will not want Hamlet to pause at the end of the second line because the thought continues to line 3; however, even though there is no punctuation mark at the end of line 3, you may want him to take a slight pause there before going to line 4. You and your actor must analyze the lines and make your own decisions.

When speaking blank verse, the poetry should be clear and distinct, but it should not sound "hammy" or "sing-song." The best advice you can give your actors is to concentrate on being the character and expressing the thoughts and feelings in the lines, and the poetry and rhythm of the lines should come through automatically.

When you encounter a scene that is difficult to understand, one exercise that may help is to have the actors improvise the scene. Let them put it in their own words. Another exercise you might want to try is to have actors improvise what the characters were doing in the intervals between scenes. This may help them start the next scene

TIP

It is not a good idea for the director to interpret lines for an actor and ask for an imitation of your reading. You will get better results if the actor figures it out for himself. Encourage the actor to experiment with different choices for the lines, then settle on the one you and the actor think is best.

with the right objectives, motivations, attitudes, thoughts and feelings.

Five reading rehearsals should be sufficient for most casts; however, if you have experienced Shakespearean actors, they may not need this many. The director should decide when the cast is ready to progress to blocking rehearsals.

Blocking Rehearsals on a Proscenium Arch Stage

On the rehearsal schedule, ten rehearsals are devoted to blocking (planning the major movements of characters). You may not need this many or you may need more. Change the rehearsal schedule to suit you and your cast.

Your blocking will depend on the type of stage you are using. First, is an explanation of blocking on a proscenium arch stage, and later, information will be given about blocking on arena and thrust stages (see Figures 2-3, 2-4 and 2-5).

The proscenium arch stage has an arch which conceals the *fly loft* or *flies*. This is the place above the stage where curtains, drops, scenery and lighting equipment may hang and be lowered to the stage through a *rigging system*. The stage floor may have *traps* through which scenery, props and actors may enter or exit. The floor may also have a *revolve*, which is a circular turning platform, and *tracks* for moving wagons, scenery or properties.

The scene designer should provide the director with a ground (or floor) plan for the sets. (See Figure 2-8 for a ground plan for *Twelfth Night* or Figure 4-4 for a ground plan for *Romeo and Juliet*.) Now you can begin to think about blocking. Always go to a blocking rehearsal with a rough plan for the major movements written in your script.

These will probably be changed in rehearsal but it is a starting place. And do listen to the ideas of your actors: They may have some excellent suggestions.

The stage manager should ready the rehearsal room by chalking or taping the floor where scenery will be and placing rehearsal chairs where furniture will be located. This person should also check up on tardy or missing actors and read the parts of those who are absent. He or she holds the promptscript and records in pencil all blocking and changes in the script that are decided upon in rehearsals.

At the first blocking rehearsal, inform the cast about the placement of scenery, properties, furniture, steps, levels, entrances and exits. Block the scenes in order so actors can better understand why certain things happen in the plot; and do talk about the plot, taking the time to explain events and answer questions. Before each scene, describe the characters' objectives, motivations, actions and attitudes toward others. Be sure to discuss character relationships: who is friendly, loves, hates or is indifferent to whom. The director should also talk to actors about their costumes, shoes, makeup and hairstyles in each scene and, as mentioned earlier, encourage them to come to rehearsals with shoes that are similar to what they will wear in performances because shoes affect how a character walks and stands. Women and men who will be costumed in a long dress or robe should bring to rehearsals ankle-length clothing to get accustomed to wearing it.

At the first blocking rehearsal for each act, block the act with speaking roles only. Then at the second rehearsal of the act add the nonspeaking parts. This procedure should be followed also for the last four acts. The reason for not calling extras to the first rehearsal of each act is that blocking the speakers may take a long time and the nonspeakers will have nothing much to do but stand around and wait.

Be certain actors record their blocking in their scripts in PENCIL so it can be changed if necessary. They can use the abbreviations and symbols described on page 44.

STAGE AREAS, ABBREVIATIONS AND SYMBOLS
The names and abbreviations of the fifteen areas of a large proscenium arch stage appear on the chart on page 44.

BACK WALL OF STAGE

Up Right-UR	Up Right Center-URC	Up Center-UC	Up Left Center-ULC	Up Left-UL
Right-R	Right Center-RC	Center-C	Left Center-LC	Left-L
Down Right-DR	Down Right Center-DRC	Down Center-DC	Down Left Center-DLC	Down Left-DL

(AUDIENCE)

When a performer is standing in center stage facing the audience, the right areas are to the actor's right and the left areas are to the left. Upstage is in back of the actor and downstage is in front.

When you are writing in the director's script or the stage manager is writing in the promptscript, use abbreviations and symbols to save time; for example, you can refer to characters by the first letter or two of their names and indicate a *cross* (an actor's move to another location) by ✕. For instance, if you want Ophelia to move down center to Hamlet, you can indicate it briefly in your script as O ✕ DC to H. Use an upward arrow ↑ to indicate that a character rises and a downward arrow ↓ when the character sits. A ∨ can indicate which direction a character is facing, such as ∨, ∧, < or > . In places where you think there should be a pause, write l. For a longer pause, write ‖. If you don't like these symbols, make up your own. Every director does.

BODY POSITIONS

In giving directions to performers about body positions use the following terms:

Full front: The actor faces the audience.

One-quarter left: The actor is in a position halfway between full front and left profile.

Profile left: The actor faces left with profile to the audience.

Three-quarter left: The actor is in a position halfway between left profile and full back.

Full back: The actor's back is to the audience.

Three-quarter right: The actor is in a position halfway between full back and right profile.

Profile right: The actor faces right with profile to the audience.

One-quarter right: The actor is in a position halfway between right profile and full front.

MORE TERMS

Other terms that directors may use in blocking are:

Cross in back (or cross above): Move on the upstage side of another person or property.

Cross in front (or cross below): Move on the downstage side of another person or property.

Dress stage (or counter): Move slightly or change position to balance the stage after another performer has made a cross. (If two standing actors are sharing a scene in opposite one-quarter positions and the director tells one to cross the other, the moving actor will normally walk in front of the stationary person to the place specified. The latter may then have to counter to visually balance the stage.)

Take stage: Take a dominant position onstage.

Give stage: Take a less dominant position.

Make an open turn: Turn toward the audience.

Make a closed turn: Turn away from the audience.

Open up: Turn more toward the audience.

Cover: Stand in front of an actor or property so that the audience cannot see the person or the object.

Focus: Look at a specific person or people or object(s).

STAGE PICTURES

The audience must be able to see, hear and understand the characters and the plot, and it is the director's job to make each stage picture communicate to the audience the intellectual and emotional qualities of the moment. The proscenium arch is a large frame for the stage picture, so the director's job is to create meaningful pictures for the audience.

The director must control the audience's attention by getting them to look at the important character and ignore the others. For example:

- A person who is facing the audience in a full-front position is more attention-getting than those in other body positions.
- The highest or tallest actor onstage will also receive attention.
- A performer who is in a downstage or center area is more likely to get the audience's interest than those in other areas.
- An actor wearing a brightly colored or light-colored costume will get attention.
- Spotlighting will emphasize a person.
- If everybody onstage is looking at one actor, that person will draw the audience's attention.
- A performer who is moving and gesturing will capture the spectators' interest.
- An actor who is speaking will receive attention.
- A person who is alone and isolated from a group of people draws attention.
- An actor who is doing something different from everyone else onstage will draw the audience's interest.

BALANCE

Most of the time the stage should appear balanced, but an asymmetrical balance is usually better than a symmetrical. The latter often seems too artificial, so most directors opt for asymmetrical balance in which both sides of the stage will be different but the audience will feel that there is a visual balance. Scenery and properties do, of course, contribute to the stage picture.

There may be places in the script, however, when the director wants the stage to seem unbalanced in order to provoke tension in the audience, but most of the time the director will opt for a balanced stage to make the spectators feel comfortable.

MOVEMENT

Movements help to show character and character relationships, contribute to the plot and add excitement. Keep the following in mind, though, when moving actors:

- There must be a reason—a motive, a purpose—for every move onstage.
- Usually a speaker moves on his or her lines and does not move when another character is talking.
- A speaking character will normally cross in front of other actors rather than in back of them so the speaker may be heard and seen.
- Unless there is some reason in the script, actors should avoid sidestepping, backing up onstage and standing in straight lines or a semicircle with other characters.
- When blocking three or more actors, the director will sometimes use triangular arrangements with the emphatic person at the apex.

SPECIAL PROBLEMS

Street scenes are frequent in Shakespeare's plays such as *Romeo and Juliet* and *Richard III*. They call for walk-ons and small parts like servants, soldiers, attendants, citizens and others. Explain to all of these actors the situation, mood, thoughts and emotions of the scene. Give each a characterization (age, nationality, function in play, posture, movements, intellectual characteristics, objective, motivation, attitude) and tell them when and where to enter, move, focus and exit.

Swordfighting must be carefully choreographed and rehearsed frequently. The most important consideration is that no one gets hurt. Macbeth and Young Siward fight with swords in Act V, Scene 7 of *Macbeth* and Young Siward is killed; then in Scene 8 in "another part of the field" Macbeth and Macduff fight. They exit fighting and Macbeth is killed offstage. If the director does not feel competent to handle fight scenes, a fight director should be employed.

Stabbing with daggers is called for in some plays such as Act III, Scene 1 of *Julius Caesar*. The easiest way to conceal a stabbing is to have the victim downstage of the stabber(s) so that the receiver's body hides the movement. Unfortunately, actors have been injured—even killed—by using real knives onstage. For safety, sharp daggers or knives should not be employed. Use only rubber or collapsible knives.

Falling occurs in fight scenes and elsewhere. After Iago stabs Emilia in Act V, Scene 2 of *Othello*, Gratiano says, "The woman falls." The safest way to fall is along one side of the body. While staying as relaxed as possible, the actor should fall to the side of a leg, hip, torso and shoulder, then carefully lay the side of the head on the floor. Hands should be close to the body so the actor is not tempted to use them to break the fall; feet should not bounce. Tell the actor that the fall does not have to be fast. If furniture or a property is nearby, perhaps it can be used to slow the descent. Stage the fall so the person lands with his or her back to the audience in an upstage area, a dark area or behind furniture. The body should be concealed as much as possible from the spectators. If the victim must be seen, be sure the head is closer to the audience than the feet (as feet can look funny).

Bowing was done by gentlemen from medieval times to the late nineteenth century. Through the years bows have changed but one that was done in the Elizabethan period is as follows: Stand with feet apart, weight on both feet, with one foot slightly forward. While taking off your hat, bend both knees; while putting your hat back on, straighten the knees. When James I came to the throne in 1603, bows became a little more elaborate: Step back on either foot and bend the back knee while removing the hat and placing it over the chest. As you straighten the knee, the hat may be returned to the head. For bows in other time periods, consult books on manners and customs in period plays, which are listed in Suggested Reading (page 181).

Curtsying has not changed much through the years so an Elizabethan curtsy is like a nineteenth-century one: The woman places the ball of one foot in back of the other and keeps her weight on both feet as she bends her knees. She may incline her head toward the person to whom she is curtsying. Maids in period plays make what is called a "bob" curtsy upon entering or leaving rooms: that is, the maid quickly bends her knees slightly as she nods her head.

Getting laughs (where you want the audience to laugh) can present problems. Shakespeare wrote different kinds of comedies: farce (such as *The Taming of the Shrew*), romantic comedy (*As You Like It*), light lyrical comedy (*A Midsummer Night's Dream*) and dark comedy

(*Measure for Measure*). There are also comedy scenes in tragedies, like the Porter's scene in Act II, Scene 3 of *Macbeth*. And there are funny scenes in the history plays, like Falstaff and his pals provide in *Henry IV*, Parts 1 and 2. What will get laughs? Humorous situations in the plot, funny characters, witty lines, surprises, puns and mispronunciations of words—these are some possibilities. Also, consider blocking comic movements and business or having actors use unusual speaking voices, bizarre props, or funny costuming, facial expressions, makeup or hairstyles. Be sure to warn your actors about talking through laughs. If the audience responds with big laughter to something onstage, actors should freeze unless humorous movements or facial expressions are feeding the laugh. When the laughter begins to die out and the next speaker thinks the following line can be heard, the actor should speak the words loudly and clearly.

Blocking Rehearsals on Arena and Thrust Stages

Arena staging also goes by the name of theatre-in-the-round, circle or circus staging. The audience sits on four sides of the acting space which may be a circle, an oval, a rectangle or an irregular-shaped area. Usually there are four aisles leading to the playing area that can also be used for performing as well as moving properties and scenic pieces in and out (see Figure 2-4).

In thrust staging, the audience sits on three sides of the playing space (see Figure 2-5). In back of the fourth side may be a wall or stagehouse through which performers, scenery and props may enter or leave the stage.

The main advantage these two have over a proscenium stage is that actors and audience are closer together and the latter may, therefore, get more involved in the play. Also there is less need for elaborate scenery so production expenses are smaller.

The disadvantages are, because spectators may be only a foot or two from the stage, the actors have to be more realistic with their makeup and costumes. They also have to concentrate more so as not to be distracted by the audience. From the spectators' point of view, they may miss the scenic effects a proscenium stage can provide.

STAGE PICTURES

Everything that was written above about getting attention on a proscenium arch stage also pertains to arena and thrust with the exception of body positions and stage areas. The following are especially useful to arena/thrust stages: *height of the actor, brightly colored costume, spotlighting, focus, moving, speaking, isolation from others* and *contrast in action.* The need for balance on a stage is also valid.

The director can block a play by telling actors to go to various properties or furniture or other actors. Also you may think of the stage as a compass with areas labeled North, South, East and West or as a clock with twelve areas and a thirteenth one in the center.

Blocking on arena or thrust stages usually involves moving actors more often than on a proscenium stage so they do not have their backs to a part of the audience for a long time. The director should try to see to it that all sections of the audience see the faces of the actors as much as possible. In blocking two actors, if the director can allow at least four feet between them, they will be more visible than if they are close together. A position called *twisting the pairs* is often used: Rather than facing each other directly, the two actors make opposite one-quarter turns, which make the two visible to more parts of the audience.

Acting in the aisles is often done, especially when an actor is entering or exiting.

Lighting is important because scenes begin and end with light changes. Scene changes must be done in the dark (or almost dark) unless the theatre has an elevator stage to raise or lower a set to another level for changing.

In arena staging, furniture, properties and set pieces should be low and movable. The same is true of the thrust stage except that in the back there can be tall scenery and furniture, windows, doors and stairs.

Other Rehearsals

While the director is busy with blocking, other rehearsals must be held: The choreographer should begin rehearsing the dancers; the musical director should work with musicians and singers; the fight director should develop and teach the fencing matches and/or swordfights. These should continue until they are ready for performances.

Director's Supervisory Duties

After blocking is completed, the director should be able to make a final prop list and give it to the property master (see Figure 3-4 or Figure 4-5). If necessary, however, it can be changed later on.

I-1: *Palace of Theseus*
  2 throne chairs on raised platform
  2 candelabra on either side of chair
  1 sword for Theseus

I-2: *Quince's house*
  1 rustic bench
  1 bucket for Quince
  5 scrolls for Quince
  1 larger scroll on floor

FIGURE 3-4: **DIRECTOR'S PROPERTY LIST FOR THE FIRST ACT OF *A MIDSUMMER NIGHT'S DREAM***

The director should also be able to write a lighting cue sheet (see Figure 3-5 or Figure 4-7) for the lighting designer and a sound cue sheet (see Figure 3-6 or Figure 4-3) for the sound designer. These also can be altered later if the need arises.

Developing Rehearsals

Blocking will be on the director's mind until dress rehearsals but other concerns must also be given consideration. Helping actors obtain a good characterization is foremost, but they must also be working on voice, memorization, listening to other actors and stage business.

CHARACTERIZATIONS

The next seven rehearsals should be devoted to seeing the actors grow in their roles. The objective is to create well-rounded characters. An actor can prepare a role by working emotionally, technically or using a combination of the two. You may find that some actors have a preference for one of these and the director should

I-1:   Room in Duke's palace. Actors begin entering through the audience and go to DRC steps to reach stage. They need to be lighted on their way through audience. When you light actors, take down houselights. Bring up stage lights. This is a daytime indoor scene. At the end of scene, as actors are exiting, black out.

I-2:   Seacoast. Again we have actors entering through the audience and go to DRC steps to reach stage. At end of music bridge, light them on their way to stage. Bring up stage lights. Daytime outdoor scene. At end of scene, as actors are exiting, black out.

I-3:   Dining area in Olivia's house. Evening indoor scene. At end of music bridge, bring up stage lights. At end of scene, as actors are exiting, black out.

I-4:   Duke's palace. Daytime indoor scene. At end of music bridge, bring up stage lights. At end of scene, as Viola and attendants are exiting, black out.

I-5:   Living room of Olivia's house. Daytime indoor scene. At end of music bridge, bring up stage lights. At end of scene, as Olivia is exiting, black out.

FIGURE 3-5: **DIRECTOR'S INSTRUCTIONS FOR LIGHTING THE FIRST ACT OF** *TWELFTH NIGHT*

OVERTURE: Begin on cue from stage manager.

END OF I-1:   Lucentio has the last line: "If you ask me why, sufficeth, my reasons are both good and weighty." Business follows this line. Blackout will come as Biondello almost gets offstage. Begin music bridge.

END OF I-2:   As actors start to exit right, black out. Begin music bridge.

END OF I-3:   At end of scene, Tranio is alone center. His last line is: "A child shall get a sire, if I fail not of my cunning." Black out. Begin music bridge.

END OF I-4:   At end of scene, Hortensio is alone center. His last line is: "Hortensio will be quit with thee by changing." Black out. Begin music bridge.

END OF I-5:   No music at end of scene.

FIGURE 3-6: **DIRECTOR'S INSTRUCTIONS FOR SOUND IN THE FIRST ACT OF** *THE TAMING OF THE SHREW*

talk to the actor in terms that she or he will understand.

1. Emotional actors: Called emotional, intuitive or Method actors, these performers prefer to work from the inside to the outside. This means that they prepare internally, thinking the thoughts and feeling the emotions of the character, hoping that the external manifestations are then valid.

2. Technical actors: These performers prefer to work from the outside to the inside. They analyze carefully the outer manifestations of the thoughts and emotions rather than trying to experience them internally. They adopt an appropriate posture, movements, gestures, facial expressions, voice and dialect in an effort to have a believable characterization.

3. Internal-external actors: These performers prepare to act a role by working on both the internal and the external aspects of the character.

To help actors with their characterizations, encourage them to analyze the role by determining the following about their character:

Objectives: What is the character's major goal for the entire play? What does the character want in each scene?

Motivations: What moves the character to take action?

Actions: What does the character do to achieve his or her objective?

Obstacles: What obstacles keep the character from achieving the objectives?

Attitudes: What attitudes does the character show toward others in the play?

Thoughts: What is the character thinking in each scene?

Feelings: What is the character feeling in each scene?

An actor can get ideas for a role by examining the following:

- What your character says about himself or herself in the play.
- What other characters says about your character, if they are speaking the truth.
- What your character has done prior to the beginning of the play.
- What your character does during the play.
- How the character changes during the play.

An actor can also get ideas for characterizations by doing the following:

- Observing people who are similar to the character in age, occupation, temperament or some other significant way.
- Examining personal memories of similar experiences that are close to the character's.
- Researching the life of a historical character, such as Cleopatra or Julius Caesar.
- Using Konstantin Stanislavsky's "magic if." The famous Russian director, actor and teacher wrote that an actor should ask, "What would I do IF I were this person in this situation?" Then the actor should let his imagination go to create a character. (See Stanislavsky's books listed in Suggested Reading page 180.)

If certain scenes are difficult for the actors, try the following exercises:

- Have the actors speak out loud what the characters are thinking before each line of the dialogue. Stanislavsky called this "vocalizing the inner mono-

TIP

A director can often help an actor by listening to him or her. Sometimes actors have better instincts about how a character would behave in a situation than the director. Listen to them!

logue." It is a good way to find out if the actors truly understand the scene.

- Have the actors improvise what they were doing for about five minutes before the difficult scene begins.
- Encourage them to take risks by trying different interpretations of the scene. Some will be terrible or not appropriate, but one might be excellent.

VOICE

Be sure the actors are projecting and articulating the words well. If you are rehearsing in a theatre, move to a back row to determine this. If someone has difficulty with projection, ask the speaker to imagine that he is aiming his voice to those seated in the back. If someone has trouble with articulation, ask the actor to form the words more precisely. Repeat the scene until it can be heard and understood.

The actor should also have enough variety in delivery to be interesting to the spectators. The speakers must vary the pitch, rate, loudness and quality of their voices to capture and hold the audience's attention. If an actor is lacking in variety, you might tape the delivery of several speeches and play it back so the person can hear the fault. Or it is possible that the actor has not thought sufficiently about his vocal characterization. The actor's voice should reflect the character's age, intellect and emotional state. Think about how the *quality* of the character's voice may be different from the actor's voice: Should it be more throaty, thin, nasal, harsh, strident or gentle? Should the *pitch* be higher or lower? Should the *rate* of speaking be faster or slower? Should the character speak *louder* or *softer* than the actor?

MEMORIZATION

Be sure the actors have memorized their lines accurately. No one should get in the habit of paraphrasing lines. When this occurs, the stage manager should be instructed to stop the actor immediately and inform the person of the correct line.

When an actor has difficulty with a line, it may be that the individual does not understand the character's objective, motivation and action for the scene and you may have to review these as well as what the character is thinking and feeling at this moment.

If the actor continues to have difficulty memorizing lines, suggest the following:

1. Record all the lines in your scenes and listen to the playback, speaking your lines with the recording.
2. Work with someone who will read the other parts and prompt you when necessary.
3. Walk around the room doing the blocking as you repeat the lines.

LISTENING

Check up on whether actors are really listening to other people onstage or just standing there waiting to hear their cue? They should be listening, thinking about what they heard and responding as though they just had the idea that causes them to say their line.

STAGE BUSINESS

After actors get the scripts out of their hands, you can begin to think about **stage business**. This is the term for the usually small activities actors do to help with their characterizations, not major movements as in blocking. For the Elizabethan era it includes a woman's fanning herself or a man's looking at his pocket watch and such everyday activities as drinking, eating, reading or sewing.

Polishing Rehearsals

During polishing rehearsals, the director continues work on blocking but must also pay attention to the tempos of scenes, building to climaxes and the actors' concentration, energy and ensemble playing.

TEMPOS AND CLIMAXES

The director must be concerned with a proper pace and flow throughout the play. Some scenes will have an overall fast rate, some will be medium and a few slow, but in all scenes there will be many variations of speed. If you feel a scene is going too fast ask the actors to slow down the pace; if too slow, ask that cues be picked up promptly or overlapped (this means an actor starts talking before the previous actor has finished) and that pauses be shortened or eliminated. Also later, in technical and dress rehearsals, there should be *no waiting* for scene or costume changes! If there is, rehearse the change until it can be done quickly.

A *climax* is a place in the play that creates great interest and tension in the audience. Building to a climax usually involves increasing the play's intensity, tempo, volume and movement. There are minor climaxes during the play but the major climax comes shortly before the denouement. For example, in Act II, Scene 6 of *Romeo and Juliet* there is a minor climax when they marry. In Act III, Scene 1 there are two minor climaxes: one when Tybalt kills Mercutio and the second when Romeo kills Tybalt. Another minor climax occurs when Romeo kills Paris in Act V, Scene 3, but the major climax occurs when Juliet awakes, finds that Romeo is dead and stabs herself. Be sure there is a proper build in excitement for these climactic moments.

CONCENTRATION

During run-throughs, actors must concentrate on staying in character. They should not be distracted by anything. They should be listening to the other actors, thinking about the scene and feeling the emotions. If anything unexpected occurs, such as a prop not being in the correct place or an actor being late, actors should practice ad-libbing in character until they can get back to the script.

ENERGY

It takes a lot of energy to perform well onstage. Encourage actors to get enough rest and take care of their health. Before each run-through, dress rehearsal and performance, do exercises of about five to ten minutes in length to warm up their voices and bodies and get the energy level up. Try the following exercises:

1. Stand with feet about twelve inches apart. As you inhale, raise your arms to the sides and then over your head. Silently blow the air out of your mouth as you bring your arms down. Repeat.

2. As you inhale and raise your arms again, reach above your head as high as you can. Go up on your toes and stretch for a count of four. Exhale as you bring your arms back to your sides. Repeat.

3. With arms above your head, lunge forward on your right leg, gently stretching for four counts. Repeat on the left leg.

4. Facing front, stretch your right arm over your head as you bend to the left, then bend to the right with left arm over your head. Repeat.

5. Vigorously shake your hands for five seconds, then relax them by moving the hands in circles from the wrists. Shake your arms, then relax them by swinging them in big circles. Shake the torso, then relax by bending at the waist to the left, forward and to the right.

6. Move your head slowly to look left, then slowly look right. Move your head to the center and look down, then look up. Repeat.

7. Tense all the muscles of your face and hold for four counts; then relax by moving the jaw around, sticking out the tongue and moving it around and moving the lips from pucker to broad smile.

8. Yawn before singing "mee," "may," "mah," "moh," "moo." Raise the pitch one tone to sing "nee," "nay," "nah," "noh," "noo." Raise the pitch another tone to sing "tee," "tay," "tah," "toh," "too."

9. Sing "mee" up the scale for one octave using one syllable for each tone. Sing "may" down the scale. Repeat with "mah" and "moh."

10. Take a line from the play you are presenting and ask them to repeat it three ways: (1) Softly, as in a private conversation. (2) Medium loudly, as though projecting on a stage. (3) Loudly, as if talking outdoors to thousands of people. Remind them to keep the throat and neck muscles relaxed. Do the same with another line.

ENSEMBLE PLAYING

By this time in rehearsals, the actors should be an ensemble. In other words, they are working together for the good of the play. It is called **group creativity** or **ensemble playing**. The director should encourage this in every way possible.

Technical Rehearsals

The **dress parade** is held before a run-through so the director and costume designer can look at actors wearing their costumes under stage lights and make any changes they wish before dress rehearsals. It also gives them the opportunity to talk with the performers about hairstyles, wigs and makeup. Notes are taken on needed alterations and then the actors change to rehearsal clothes for a run-through.

The next technical rehearsal the director holds is for technicians only—no actors or musicians are needed. It is a rehearsal for designers, technical director, stage manager and crews to work out problems with the scene and property shifts, light and sound cues, special effects and other technical concerns.

Then at the next two rehearsals actors work with scenery, properties, lighting, sound and special effects in run-throughs of the play. Now everyone should be ready for dress rehearsals.

The cast may need some special instructions for these final rehearsals and performances. If you think they do, you may want to select some of the items from the following list to instruct your cast either orally or in writing:

- If you cannot be present for a dress rehearsal or performance, notify the director or stage manager immediately. [Give them the phone numbers to call.]

- Check in one hour before the starting time of dress rehearsals or performances. Do not leave the theatre without notifying the stage manager.

- At one hour before performances, there will be announcements and a group warm-up that will last no longer than fifteen minutes. Please be present.

- Don't leave watches, money, jewelry and other valuables in unlocked dressing rooms. Give them to the stage manager to keep during the rehearsal or performance.

- Remember that the stage manager is in charge backstage and needs your cooperation.
- Costumes and wigs will be provided, but you must supply your own stage makeup and undergarments. You are also expected to do your makeup and hair according to the director's or costume designer's instructions. [If you have beginners, it would be wise to appoint a couple of experienced people to supervise makeup, wigs and hairstyles.]
- Take care of your costumes and hang them up after taking them off. If you have costume problems, talk to the wardrobe supervisor.
- Check on your props *before* you need them onstage and return them to the prop table when you are finished with them.
- Be quiet in the wings and other areas near the stage while the play is on.
- When onstage, if a prop or part of a costume should accidentally fall to the floor, pick it up if you are nearby because the audience will watch it until someone takes it away.
- If you forget your lines, ad-lib until you can return to the script. Don't wait to be prompted.
- At curtain call, there will be *no* presentations of flowers or curtain speeches. After the last curtain call, clear the stage quickly.
- [If actors are expected to assist with striking the set, tell them when to report.]

Dress Rehearsals

During the last four rehearsals, actors wear costumes, makeup, hairstyles and wigs and the show is performed with all technical elements like a performance. Director and designers should sit in the house and take notes on anything they dislike about the play; then try to get it corrected before the next rehearsal or performance.

As mentioned above, stage makeup and a hairstyle are usually the actor's responsibility. For hygienic reasons, each actor should own and use only his or her cosmetics. What should be acquired? Some actors may not need any makeup, but most will need, at a minimum, a foundation, eyebrow pencil, powder and puff, cleansing cream and tissues. If, however, you are directing a play with some difficult character makeups, such as *The Tempest*, you may want to bring in a cosmetician and hairstylist to help with the makeup and hair for Caliban, Ariel and some other characters.

During the first dress rehearsal the director should check the appearance of each actor to be certain he or she is the character that you envisioned. If you find that a costume or makeup change is delaying the play, you must arrange for dressers to assist the change so the actor can get onstage at the right time.

The end of the first dress rehearsal is an appropriate time to block and rehearse the **curtain call**. Usually actors wear their last costume for this. The procedure is to bring the cast onstage to bow in order from the least to the most important character. If any women are wearing long dresses, they may prefer to curtsy. Men should put their heels together and bow from the waist. Their hands may stay at their sides or be brought together above the knees. After the stars bow, the entire company may join hands for another bow. After this, the front curtain may descend or the stage lights black out. All onstage should hold their positions because if there is great applause the stage manager may call for another bow. It is the stage manager's decision as to how many curtain calls are taken. At the end, the front curtain falls or the stage lights black out and houselights are brought up so that the audience can see to depart.

Performances

At an hour and forty-five minutes before the play performance is scheduled to begin, the stage manager or technical director should open the theatre. Doors should be unlocked, lights turned on and sign-in sheets posted for technicians and cast.

At an hour and thirty minutes before starting time, technicians should check in to make sure all technical elements are ready for the performance. This may involve examining all lighting and sound equipment, mopping the stage floor, checking all scenery and props and setting the stage for the first scene. In the dressing rooms, the wardrobe supervisor and costume crew should be getting the costumes ready. In the front of the house, the house manager and ticket sellers should make certain everything is in order. The house manager should be sure enough programs are available, the heating or cooling system is operating and the house is clean.

At one hour to curtain, actors should sign in and go to the designated place for the director's announcements and brief warm-up, which should last no longer than fifteen minutes. After this, the actors go to their dressing rooms where they have about forty-five minutes to get into costume and makeup. If an actor should have a complicated makeup, he or she should arrive earlier. The director may stay backstage with the actors checking on makeup, hair and costumes, answering questions and calming the nervous, but by curtain time the director should be in the audience to see how the people respond. He or she should take notes on things to fix before the next performance.

At forty-five minutes to starting time, sellers of refreshments, ticket-takers and ushers should be ready to receive the audience. The house manager should instruct new ushers about the seating plan, location of rest rooms, telephones, water fountains and how to give each customer a program with a smile.

At thirty minutes to curtain, all technical elements should be ready for the performance. The stage manager can now inform the house manager that the house may be opened to the public. Backstage, the stage manager delivers warning calls of "Half hour, please," "Fifteen minutes, please" and "Five minutes, please." The proper response from actors and technicians is "Thank you."

At five minutes to curtain, the stage manager should be certain that stage crews and musicians are in place.

At two minutes to curtain, the stage manager calls "Places, please" and everybody in the first scene should go immediately to the stage.

At starting time, the stage manager should confer with the house manager about whether the play can begin on time. If a large number of audience members is waiting to be ushered to seats, the house manager may ask that the curtain be delayed five minutes. At that time, the house and stage manager should talk again and, as quickly as possible, the stage manager should call for houselights to fade out and for the performance to begin. Now the house manager should close the doors to the house and keep latecomers outside in the lobby until there is a break in the onstage action, such as the end of a scene. Then the latecomers can be taken to empty seats near the door. (Later, at intermission they can be ushered to their correct seats.)

During performances, the stage manager prompts, gives cues for the technical work, maintains order backstage and records the running time of acts and intermissions. He or she will also have to call actors to the stage if there is no stage-monitoring system in the dressing rooms and greenroom (a room backstage where performers can rest when not needed onstage). For this purpose, the stage manager will need one or two assistants.

At the first intermission (which is usually ten or fifteen minutes in length), the stage manager should bring the houselights up and the house manager should open the doors of the house. Backstage at intermission, the stage manager calls "Five minutes, please" and three minutes later, "Places, please." At this time a warning bell or flashing lights or an announcement on a public address system should notify the audience the play is about to resume. After checking to be sure everything is ready, the stage manager calls for the houselights to fade out as the house manager closes the doors. If there is a second intermission, the above is repeated.

At the end of the performance, after curtain calls, the stage manager asks for the houselights to come up and the house manager opens the doors so the audience may depart.

Before leaving the theatre, actors should hang up their costumes and clean up the dressing and makeup rooms. The crews should clean the stage area, store away props and scenery and lock up equipment. Ushers should clean the house.

After everyone has left the theatre, the stage manager or technical director may lock up the theatre.

Now let's consider preparing and directing a specific Shakespearean play, one that is a favorite of many, *Romeo and Juliet*. This is the subject of Part Four.

✧ Part Four ✧

Preparing and Directing
Romeo and Juliet

Part Four involves the preparation and direction of *Romeo and Juliet* for performance: the needed research, analysis and interpretation of the play and a complete script with suggested cuts, blocking, sound and light cues and notes on definitions of unusual words and other aspects of the script. (For help with auditions, casting, rehearsals and performances, please refer to Part Three.)

Research

Scholars have traced the story line used in *Romeo and Juliet* back to a Greek medieval romance of the fifth century. Later authors wrote similar tragic stories of young lovers, but Shakespeare's source was probably an English poem of 1562 by Arthur Brooke entitled *The Tragicall Historye of Romeus and Juliet.* Brooke wrote in his preface that he had seen "the same argument lately set forth on stage," so it is possible Shakespeare also saw a stage version for which the script is lost.

It is thought that Shakespeare's *Romeo and Juliet* was first performed in London in 1595 or 1596 with Richard Burbage playing the role of Romeo and Will Kempe the part of Peter. The first quarto of this play was printed in 1597. (The word *quarto* describes the size of a book. If each sheet of paper was folded twice, making eight pages printed on the front and back, the bound book containing these sheets was called a quarto. If each sheet was folded once, making four pages, it was termed a folio.) The 1597 quarto of *Romeo and Juliet* is a bad pirated version, so a second quarto, presumably supervised by actors in Shakespeare's company or by Shakespeare himself, was published in 1599. This was the basis for later quartos as well as the First Folio (see page 7).

In many respects Shakespeare's *Romeo and Juliet* is like other Elizabethan tragedies in that it shows the influence of the Roman playwright Seneca: the use of a chorus, the passionate scenes, the foreboding of evil, the sense that fate is motivating the tragedy, the bloodshed and the horrors of the graveyard.

Although Shakespeare wrote this play in the late sixteenth century, it is often done with costumes and sets of the fifteenth century, which may suggest that the story is from an earlier period. The places are the Italian towns of Verona and, for one scene (Act V, Scene 1), Mantua. The action begins on a Sunday morning and ends with the dawn of Friday.

Analysis and Interpretation

To analyze this play, examine the plot, characters, thought, diction, music and sound and spectacle; then think about the best way you can interpret your ideas for the stage (see also Part Two). In addition, we shall consider cutting and editing the text, taking an intermission and blocking the curtain call.

Plot

The plot tells the story of two "star-cross'd" lovers, Romeo and Juliet, who meet at a party in her home in Verona. She is a member of the Capulet family—he is a Montague. No Montagues were invited to the Capulet home because of a long-standing feud between the two families, but Romeo was persuaded to put on a mask and crash the festivities in order to see a girl he was infatuated with, Rosaline. Once Romeo sees Juliet, however, he forgets about other girls.

In the famous balcony scene, Romeo overhears Juliet confess her love for him. Overjoyed, he reveals his presence and the young lovers decide to be married. The next afternoon they are wed by Friar Laurence.

After the wedding, Romeo tries to stop a fight between his friend, Mercutio, and Tybalt, a Capulet, with the result that Mercutio is slain by Tybalt. Enraged, Romeo kills Tybalt, his wife's cousin. Prince Escalus banishes Romeo but the Nurse arranges for Romeo to spend the wedding night with Juliet in her bedroom. At dawn, he departs for Mantua. Meanwhile Juliet's father, knowing nothing of Juliet's marriage to Romeo, makes plans for her to marry Paris, a kinsman of Prince Escalus. Juliet refuses.

In desperation, Juliet consults Friar Laurence who advises her to agree to the marriage with Paris. His plan is for her to drink a potion that will give her the appearance of being dead for forty-two hours, then the Friar will notify Romeo to return to rescue her. She takes the drug and is presumed dead the next morning. Her grieving family and Paris place her in the Capulet burial vault.

But before the Friar's news about the fake death can reach Romeo in Mantua, Romeo is told Juliet is dead. Immediately Romeo buys poison and goes to Juliet's tomb to perish with her. There he meets Paris, who decides that Romeo should not live because he killed Juliet's relative, Tybalt. They fight and Romeo slays Paris. Then Romeo enters the tomb, sees Juliet, drinks the poison and dies.

When Juliet wakes up, she discovers Romeo's body and learns from Friar Laurence what happened. She then kills herself with Romeo's dagger. Affected by the many deaths in their families, the Capulets and Montagues decide to reconcile.

The genre of this famous play is a tragedy in which Shakespeare used a cause-to-effect arrangement of the events. (In other words, an incident causes an effect, which in turn causes another incident to occur and so on throughout the play.) The plot builds to a major climax when Juliet discovers that Romeo is dead and then kills herself.

Preparation to direct *Romeo and Juliet* should involve writing a rundown or outline of the play (see Figure 4-1).

Characters

In your study of the characters, it helps to know who is in each scene and who speaks, fights, sings, dances or plays a musical instrument (see Figure 4-2). This is especially useful in planning a rehearsal schedule or preparing an announcement of auditions. (See the announcement of auditions for *Romeo and Juliet* in Part Three, Figure 3-1.)

Two of the greatest parts ever written for young people are Juliet and Romeo. They are attractive, romantic leads who fall in love at first sight. She is very young—almost fourteen—but she grows in maturity and depth in the course of the few days of the play. Romeo, who is rash and impulsive, is just a little older than she and one of the unluckiest characters ever created. If he had waited just a few minutes longer to drink the poison, Juliet would have awakened to find him present and there would have been a happy ending. (Actually, in the Restoration period, one version did allow Romeo and Juliet to live.) But Shakespeare was writing a tragedy and in a tragedy the protagonists usually die.

Two of the most interesting and funniest characters in the play are Romeo's friend Mercutio and Juliet's Nurse. Mercutio, whose name comes from the Italian word for the Roman god Mercury (the gods' messenger), is a well-born gentleman, a kinsman to Prince Escalus. A satirical commentator, he is lively, happy, exciting, witty and fanciful, much like his namesake. His famous "Queen Mab" speech of Act I, Scene 4 is about dreams

> Which are the children of an idle brain,
> Begot of nothing but vain fantasy. . . .

Both Mercutio and the Nurse can be bawdy. The Nurse, who raised Juliet, appears to have a real affection

Romeo and Juliet

Prologue: A public place in Verona
Speaking: Chorus (one person)
Extras: Mercutio, First and Second Vendors, First and Second Gentlemen, First and Second Ladies
    Capulets: Old Capulet, Sampson, Gregory, Tybalt, Rosaline, Peter
    Montagues: Romeo, Abraham, Balthasar, Benvolio
Props: Swords for Sampson, Gregory, Tybalt, Romeo, Abraham, Balthasar, Benvolio, Mercutio
    Fountain
    One tray of fruit and one tray of scarves for two vendors
    Coins for two gentlemen and Rosaline
    Dice for Mercutio

I-1: Same set with fountain
Time: 9 A.M., Sunday
Speaking: Sampson, Gregory, Abraham, Benvolio, Tybalt, First, Second and Third Watchmen, Citizens,
    Capulet, Lady Capulet, Montague, Lady Montague, Prince Escalus, Romeo
Swordfighting: Sampson and Abraham, Gregory and Balthasar, Tybalt and Benvolio
Extras: Old Capulet, Peter, First and Second Vendors, First and Second Gentlemen, First and Second Ladies,
    First and Second Soldiers.
Props: Swords for fighters above plus Romeo and Montague
    Weapons for watchmen and soldiers

I-2: Same set with fountain
Time: Later, Sunday
Speaking: Capulet, Paris, Sampson, Benvolio, Romeo
Extras: First Vendor, First Gentleman
Props: List of guests for Capulet
    Tray of fruit for vendor
    Coins for First Gentleman and Paris

I-3: Room in Capulet's house
Time: Later, Sunday
Speaking: Lady Capulet, Nurse, Juliet, Sampson
Furniture and Props: Settee, small table, chair
    List of guests for Lady Capulet

I-4: Street in Verona (same as I-2 with or without fountain)
Time: Sunday night

FIGURE 4-1: **RUNDOWN (OR OUTLINE) FOR CUT VERSION OF *ROMEO AND JULIET***

Speaking: Romeo, Benvolio, Mercutio
Extras: Abraham, Balthasar, First and Second Gentlemen
Playing: Abraham plays tabor
Props: Two lighted lanterns for Balthasar
     Two lighted torches for First and Second Gentleman
     Tabor (drum), stick and Mercutio's mask for Abraham
     Masks for Romeo, Benvolio, First and Second Gentlemen

I-5: Room in Capulet's house with settee, chair, small table (same as I-3)
Time: Later, Sunday night
Speaking: Capulet, Old Capulet, Romeo, Balthasar, Tybalt, Juliet, Nurse, Lady Capulet
Dancing: Paris and Juliet, Benvolio and First Lady, Mercutio and Second Lady, Tybalt and Rosaline, First
     Gentleman and Lady Capulet
Extras: Sampson, Gregory, Peter, Abraham, Second Gentleman
Props: Three small trays of food and drinks to be offered to guests by Sampson, Gregory, Peter
     Tybalt's rapier for Sampson
     Five masks from I-4 are worn in this scene

II-1: Capulet's orchard and Juliet's balcony
Time: Later, Sunday night
Speaking: Romeo, Benvolio, Mercutio
Props: Garden bench
     Masks carried by Benvolio and Mercutio

II-2: Same set with garden bench (same as II-1)
Time: Immediately after II-1
Speaking: Romeo, Juliet, Nurse

II-3: Outside Friar Laurence's cell
Time: 4 A.M., Monday
Speaking: Friar Laurence, Romeo
Props: Large standing cross (about four feet high)
     Wicker basket of herbs and flowers for Friar Laurence

II-4: Street in Verona with fountain (same as I-2)
Time: Noon, Monday
Speaking: Mercutio, Benvolio, Romeo, Nurse, Peter
Singing: Mercutio

FIGURE 4-1: **continued**

Props: Pink flower for Mercutio to wear behind his ear
   Two shopping (string) bags and fan for Peter
   Coins in pouch for Romeo

II-5: Capulet's orchard with garden bench (same as II-2)
Time: Shortly after noon, Monday
Speaking: Juliet, Nurse
Extra: Peter
Props: One shopping (string) bag and fan for Peter
   One shopping (string) bag for Nurse

II-6: Outside Friar Laurence's cell with large cross (same as II-3)
Time: 1 P.M. on Monday
Speaking: Friar Laurence, Romeo, Juliet

III-1: Street. in Verona with fountain (same as II-4)
Time: 2 P.M. on Monday
Speaking: Benvolio, Mercutio, Tybalt, Romeo, First Watchman, Prince Escalus, Lady Capulet, Montague, Sampson
Swordfighting: Tybalt and Mercutio, Tybalt and Romeo
Extras: Abraham, Balthasar, First and Second Gentlemen, Gregory, Second and Third Watchmen, First and Second Soldiers, Nurse, Peter, First and Second Ladies, Rosaline, Old Capulet, Capulet, Lady Montague, Friar John, Apothecary, Citizens
Props: Swords for Tybalt, Mercutio, Romeo
   Handkerchief for Mercutio
   Shopping (string) bags for Peter and Gregory
   Weapons for three watchmen and two soldiers

III-2: Capulet's orchard with garden bench (same as II-5)
Time: Sunset, Monday
Speaking: Juliet, Nurse
Extra: Peter
Props: Rope ladder for Nurse
   Ring for Juliet
   Flask for Peter

III-3: Friar Laurence's cell
Time: Night, Monday
Speaking: Friar Laurence, Romeo, Nurse

FIGURE 4-1: **continued**

Furniture and Props: Desk, chair, candle in holder, matches, books, writing materials
    Dagger for Romeo
    Ring for Nurse

III-4: Room in Capulet's house with settee, chair, small table (same as I-5)
Time: Late night, Monday
Speaking: Capulet, Paris, Lady Capulet
Extra: Sampson
Props: Lighted candle for Sampson

III-5: Juliet's bedchamber
Time: Dawn, Tuesday
Speaking: Romeo, Juliet, Nurse, Lady Capulet, Capulet
Furniture: Bed with pillows and covers

IV-1: Friar Laurence's cell (same as III-3)
Time: Late afternoon, Tuesday
Speaking: Friar Laurence, Paris, Juliet
Furniture and Props: Desk, chair, candle in holder, matches, books, writing materials
    Dagger for Juliet
    Glass vial on desk

IV-2: Hall in Capulet's house
Time: Evening, Tuesday
Speaking: Capulet, Lady Capulet, Nurse, Juliet
Extra: Sampson, Gregory
Props: List of guests for Capulet

IV-3: Juliet's bedchamber (same as III-5)
Time: Night, Tuesday
Speaking: Juliet, Lady Capulet
Extra: Nurse
Props: Dagger and vial under pillows on bed
    One of Juliet's dresses for the Nurse

IV-4: Hall in Capulet's house (same as IV-2)
Time: 3 A.M., Wednesday
Speaking: Capulet
Extra: Nurse

FIGURE 4-1: **continued**

IV-5: Juliet's bedchamber (same as IV-3)
Time: Morning, Wednesday
Speaking: Nurse, Lady Capulet, Capulet, Friar Laurence, Paris
Extra: Juliet

V-1: In front of an apothecary shop on a street in Mantua
Time: Day, Thursday
Speaking: Romeo, Balthasar, Apothecary
Props: Money pouch for Romeo
     Vial offstage (in apothecary shop)

V-2: Outside Friar Laurence's cell with large cross (same as II-6)
Time: Evening, Thursday
Speaking: Friar John, Friar Laurence
Props: Basket of flowers for Friar Laurence
     Letter for Friar John

V-3: Churchyard and the Capulet tomb
Time: Before dawn, Friday
Speaking: Paris, Page, Romeo, Balthasar, Friar Laurence, Juliet, First Watchman, Prince Escalus
Swordfighting: Paris and Romeo
Extras: Capulet, Lady Capulet, Nurse, Montague, Second and Third Watchmen, First and Second Soldiers, Sampson, Abraham, Benvolio, Old Capulet, Peter, First and Second Gentlemen, Citizens
Props: Bier with pillows
     Wall bracket to hold torch
     Five torches (lighted) for Page, Balthasar, Peter, Sampson, Abraham
     Damp cloth for extinguishing flame for Page
     Flowers for Page
     Four lanterns (lighted) for Friar Laurence and three watchmen
     Crowbar and spade for Friar Laurence
     Swords for Paris and Romeo
     Dagger in scabbard for Romeo (worn at waist)
     Letter for Romeo
     Vial for Romeo
     Money pouch for Romeo
     Weapons for three watchmen and two soldiers

FIGURE 4-1: **continued**

CHARACTER	I						II						III					IV					V		
	P	1	2	3	4	5	1	2	3	4	5	6	1	2	3	4	5	1	2	3	4	5	1	2	3
Chorus/Fr. Laurence	✓								✓			✓			✓			✓				✓		✓	✓
Vendor/Apothecary	E	E	E										E										✓		
Vendor/Friar John	E	E											E										✓		
First Gentleman	E	E	E		E	D							E												E
Second Gentleman	E	E			E	E							E												E
Old Capulet	E	E				✓							E												E
Sampson	E	✓F	✓	✓		E							✓	E				E							E
Gregory/Page	E	✓F				E							E					E							✓
Tybalt	E	✓F				✓D							✓F												
Rosaline	E					D							E												
Peter	E	E				E			✓	E			E	E											E
Romeo	E	✓	✓		✓	✓	✓	✓	✓	✓		✓	✓F		✓		✓						✓		✓F
Abraham	E	✓F		EP	E								E												E
Balthasar	E	F		E	✓								E										✓		✓
Benvolio	E	✓F	✓		✓	D	✓		✓				✓												E
Mercutio	E				✓	D	✓			✓S			✓F												
First Lady	E	E				D							E												
Second Lady	E	E				D							E												
First Citizen		✓											E												E
Second Citizen		✓											E												E
Third Citizen		✓											E												E
First Watchman		✓											✓												✓
Second Watchman		✓											E												E
Third Watchman		✓											E												E
Capulet		✓	✓			✓							E			✓	✓		✓		✓	✓			E
Lady Capulet		✓		✓		✓D							✓			✓	✓		✓	✓	✓				E
Montague		✓											✓												E
Lady Montague		✓											E												
Prince Escalus		✓											✓												✓
First Soldier		E											E												E
Second Soldier		E											E												E
Paris			✓			D										✓		✓				✓			✓F
Nurse			✓			✓	✓		✓	✓			E	✓	✓		✓	✓	E	E	✓				E
Juliet			✓			✓D	✓			✓	✓			✓			✓	✓	✓	✓		E			✓

✓ =Speaks   E=Extra (Does not speak, sing, dance, fight or play an instrument)   S=Sings   D=Dances   F=Fights   P=Plays

FIGURE 4-2: **CAST CHART FOR CUT VERSION OF *ROMEO AND JULIET*—WHO IS IN EACH SCENE AND WHAT THEY DO**

for her, yet in Act III, Scene 5 she and Juliet have a serious disagreement about what Juliet should do. She is an eccentric middle-aged woman of experience who adds humor to this tragedy.

Other important characters in this large cast include the following: Friar Laurence, a mature monk who is the voice of reason and tries to do his best to help his young friends; Tybalt, a strong-willed, hot-tempered fighter who is quick to draw his sword; Paris, a young, good-looking count who believes he is in love with Juliet although she has given him no encouragement; Prince Escalus, a relative of Paris and Mercutio and a strong leader who tries to rule Verona in a fair and just way; Lady Capulet, Juliet's mother who is only about twenty-eight but thinks she knows what is best for her daughter; and Lady Capulet's much older husband, Capulet, who is wealthy, talkative and strong-willed.

Thought

The underlying theme of *Romeo and Juliet* is that a feud between families can only bring tragedy. The Prince in Act V, Scene 3 summarizes the situation when he exclaims:

> Where be these enemies? Capulet! Montague!
> See, what a scourge is laid upon your hate,
> That heaven finds means to kill your joys with love.
> And I for winking at your discords too
> Have lost a brace of kinsmen: all are punish'd.

Called a tragedy of fate, the Chorus in the prologue says:

> A pair of star-cross'd lovers take their life. . . .

Star-cross'd means that the lovers were thwarted by unfavorable positions of the stars and thus were doomed by fate to tragedy.

Diction

One of the most lyrical of all of Shakespeare's plays, *Romeo and Juliet* includes types of poetry popular in the sixteenth century; for example, there are three **sonnets** (the *sonnet*, as defined in Part Two, is a poem of fourteen lines in iambic pentameter that rhyme according to a

prescribed scheme). These sonnets are found in the prologues to Act I and Act II and the meeting of Romeo and Juliet in Act I, Scene 5. Other types of poetry are a **serena** in Act III, Scene 2, which is a lyric in which Juliet details her feelings as she waits for her lover; an **alba** in Act III, Scene 5, which shows the lamentations of lovers over the coming of the dawn; and an **elegy** in Act V, Scene 3, in which Paris expresses sorrow for Juliet's death as he puts flowers on her tomb.

In addition, the writing of Mercutio's "Queen Mab" speech of Act I, Scene 4, which is described above, is greatly admired as is Juliet's potion speech of Act IV, Scene 3. Another scene—Act II, Scene 3—should be noted because it is entirely in **rhyming couplets**, in which every two lines rhyme (see Blank Verse and Rhyming Couplets on page 40).

Be certain your actors understand the intellectual and emotional content of the lines and that they are thinking the right thoughts and feeling the emotions of the moment when they say the words.

Music and Sound

In Part Two of this book, it was noted that *music and sound* involve everything the audience hears from the stage: the performers' speaking and singing voices and live and recorded music and sound effects.

To begin the play, about one minute of music is needed for the pantomime in the prologue. If you take an intermission at the end of Act II, Scene 6, you will need about twenty seconds of music to end the scene. Then after intermission you may want to have about thirty to sixty seconds of music to start Act III. You might find something suitable by examining fifteenth-century court music.

In Act I, Scene 5 Capulet calls for musicians to play so guests at his party may dance. If you are using recorded music or if you have live musicians whom you do not want to bring onstage, Capulet may call to the musicians as though they are in an adjoining room. They play two times: A possible social dance that might be used for the first is the pavane because there is music available for this slow dance which is in 2/4 time. (See the section entitled Dancing on page 65.) The same music could also be used for the second time as Romeo and Juliet meet and talk.

Note that this music must be soft and slow and good background music for an important scene.

In Act II, Scene 4, Mercutio sings a six-line song that starts "An old hare hoar. . . ." Mercutio does not have to sing well—just loud as he taunts the Nurse. If you are looking for music to use for this song, consider putting the words to an old English children's tune, such as "Here We Go Round the Mulberry Bush."

In Act IV, Scene 4 music—perhaps a fanfare—is heard offstage as Paris and musicians approach the Capulet house. In Act IV, Scene 5, three musicians speak with Peter. As mentioned earlier in Part One of this book, there were musicians present at public performances in the Elizabethan period, so it would be easy to have them come onstage to play or to act. If live musicians are not feasible for your production, recorded music can be used in Scene 4 and the dialogue with Peter in Scene 5 can be cut.

As for sound effects, the following are needed: church clock striking the hour; rain and thunder sounds; birds chirping; alarm bells and drums; and the tolling of church bells. After blocking the play, the director should provide the sound designer with a cue sheet (see Figure 4-3).

Spectacle

As stated in Part Two, *spectacle* covers everything the audience sees on the stage: the scenery, costumes, makeup, hairstyles, properties, lighting, special effects and the performers and their movements (blocking, dancing, swordfighting). Note: there is nothing in this version of *Romeo and Juliet* that can be called a special effect.

SCENERY

The places to be depicted are in the Italian towns of Verona and Mantua. The time is July, as stated in Act I, Scene 3. The fifteenth century is a popular choice for *Romeo and Juliet* but you may prefer another time period.

A style to consider is formalism, which is defined in Part Two as a "neutral type of stage, similar to Shakespeare's original." It may have platforms of different heights, steps, ramps, and, of course, *Romeo and Juliet* must have a balcony. For each scene, one to a few props may be put onstage to establish a location, such as a fountain may be added for the scenes in the public place

in Verona or a garden bench for Capulet's orchard.

There are twenty-five scenes in the play: Six take place in a public place or street in Verona; one on a street in Mantua; five within the Capulet house; four in Capulet's orchard; five outside or in Friar Laurence's cell; three in Juliet's bedchamber; and one at her tomb in the churchyard. With so many different scenes, the scene designer is challenged to provide simple settings that can be changed quickly.

Before auditions, the scene designer and director should agree on the ground plans for the sets, such as Figure 4-4 for *Romeo and Juliet*. The scene designer may also want to do models and renderings of the sets.

A note about Act III, Scene 4, which takes place in a room in Capulet's house: This is a short scene that can be played without furniture, if that will speed up the scene changes.

Another note about Act III, Scene 5: Editors of Shakespeare's play have usually indicated that it is located in Capulet's orchard with Juliet's balcony onstage; however, most directors today cannot resist putting Romeo and Juliet in her bed for an interior scene. There are a few lines for Juliet to say as Romeo is supposed to be climbing down from the balcony but these lines work all right with her speaking to him in the bedroom.

The most difficult set to design is Act V, Scene 3 which is located in the churchyard and the Capulet tomb. The script suggests that part of the stage should be a churchyard and the rest of the stage the Capulet tomb. There is a door to the tomb which takes a crowbar and other implements to open. In the cut version of this script, the door and tools have been eliminated. Juliet is simply lying on a bier with pillows in very dim light at one side of the stage. If you do not like this simplification, you can restore the cut lines.

PROPERTIES

Before auditions, the director should give the property master a preliminary prop list. Then several weeks later, the director or stage manager should prepare a final prop list, such as Figure 4-5 for *Romeo and Juliet*.

Note: Torches are called for in Act I, Scene 4 and Act

Prologue:	Begin one minute of music on stage manager's cue.
I-1:	After blackout on Prologue, church clock strikes nine times.
I-5:	After Capulet says, "Foot it, girls" and dancers are ready to begin, play 1:40 of dance music. After Tybalt exits and Romeo moves to Juliet, begin softly 1:20 of music.
II-3:	After blackout on II-2, church clock strikes four times.
II-6:	After Friar's last line, begin 20 seconds of music.
	Intermission: Ten minutes.
III-1:	On stage manager's cue, begin one minute of music.
III-3:	On blackout for III-2, begin rain and thunder sounds. (This is a mild summer rain, not a violent storm.) Fade rain out shortly after dialogue begins.
III-5:	On blackout for III-4, begin faint bird sounds (it is supposed to be a lark). Fade out after dialogue begins.
V-3:	After Juliet stabs herself, alarm bells and drums make a loud noice while various groups enter. (Lines are cut; this is in pantomime.) After Prince examines bodies on bier, cut this sound. After Prince's last line, use church bells tolling (as mournfully as possible) until lights have blacked out.

FIGURE 4-3: **SOUND FOR CUT VERSION OF** *ROMEO AND JULIET*

V, Scene 3. If you do not want this fire hazard onstage, substitute lanterns.

COSTUMES

Before auditions, the director and costume designer should agree on a costume list, such as Figure 4-6. For young men, fifteenth-century costumes feature short tunics which end at about the top of the legs and are accompanied by belts, tights, capes, hats and slippers. Older men use longer tunics with armhole cloaks, tights, hats and slippers. Wide, padded shoulders were fashionable for both young and old men. The servants wear plain tunics, belts, tights, hats and slippers. The two friars are in Franciscan monks' robes with sandals. The apothecary's outfit should be shabby to show how poor he is. The watchmen and soldiers need official-looking uniforms.

Women's dresses and gowns are to the floor and are worn with some sort of hair covering. The waistlines tend to be high and the headdresses elaborate. For street scenes, women need cloaks, some of which have hoods.

The colors of costumes can be indicative of the wearer's personality; for example, white and pastel colors are often selected for innocent young girls like Juliet.

Colors may also help the audience to know who is related to whom. For instance, the Capulets may be costumed in certain colors (such as orange, yellow and brown) and the Montagues in other colors (like blue, black and gray). In addition, colors may give the audience information about the plot, such as Lady Capulet's dressing in black after Tybalt's death to point up the emotions felt in the Capulet family.

MAKEUP AND HAIRSTYLES

In the fifteenth century, wealthy adult women might use some makeup for pale complexions with cheek and lip rouge, but you probably will not want much makeup on young girls like Juliet. Women's hair was long, sometimes with braids, but caps, hats and various hair coverings concealed the hair much of the time.

Men should not appear to have on makeup: any

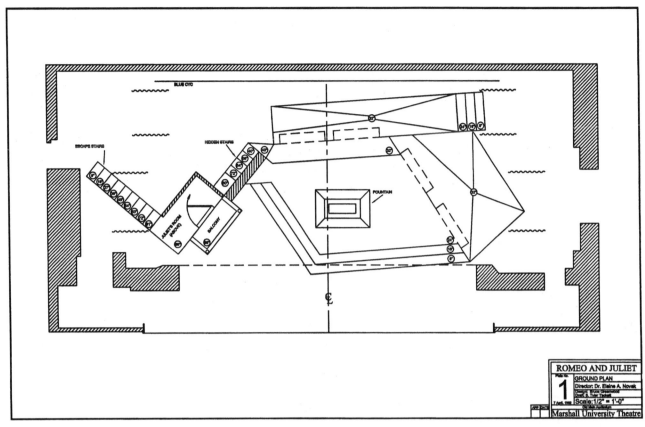

FIGURE 4-4: **GROUND PLAN BY BRUCE GREENWOOD (DRAFTED BY S. TYLER TACKETT) FOR MARSHALL UNIVERSITY THEATRE'S PRODUCTION OF** *ROMEO AND JULIET*

stage makeup must be very subtle. The hair may be shoulder-length or a little shorter, often with bangs across the forehead. Older men may have beards and mustaches.

If the director foresees any problems with costumes, hairstyles, wigs or makeup, a discussion with the costume designer is in order.

LIGHTING

Several weeks into rehearsal the director should prepare a lighting cue sheet, such as Figure 4-7 for *Romeo and Juliet.* This should be discussed with the lighting designer who may have discovered certain problems with the lighting that the director had not noticed.

DANCING

As mentioned above, the pavane is a social dance that might be used in Act I, Scene 5. The couples who may dance are Juliet and Paris, Benvolio and First Lady, Mer-

cutio and Second Lady, Tybalt and Rosaline and (if a fifth couple is needed) Lady Capulet and First Gentleman. A slow dance in 2/4 time, it begins and ends with the gentlemen bowing and the ladies curtsying to eight slow counts each time. (See Part Three for how to do an appropriate bow and curtsy.)

The pavane dancers all face in the same direction as they move up and down the room. (If you do not have this much space onstage, the couples can move in a circle.) The couples hold hands in a low position with the gentleman on the left. Starting with the left foot, they step forward on the toe, then drop the heel as they bring the right foot close to the left; then repeat on the right foot. This is followed by three steps on the toes of left, right, left, lower the left heel as the right foot closes. The sequence is then repeated starting on the right foot. To get variety, you can do it backwards. Facing in the same direction, step back on the toe of the left foot, lower the left heel as you draw

Prologue: *A public place in Verona*

Fountain, which has space to sit

Steps up to stage from auditorium

One tray of fruit, one tray of scarves (supported with straps around the neck) for two vendors

Coins for two gentlemen and Rosaline

Dice for Mercutio

Swords for Sampson, Gregory, Tybalt, Romeo, Abraham, Balthasar, Benvolio, Mercutio

I-1: *A public place in Verona* (same set with fountain)

Weapons for three watchmen and two soldiers

Swords listed for men above plus one for Montague

I-2: *A street in Verona* (same set with fountain)

List of guests for Capulet

Tray of fruit for First Vendor

Coins for First Gentleman and Paris

I-3: *Room in Capulet's house*

Settee

Small table

Chair

List of guests for Lady Capulet

I-4: *A street in Verona* (same as I-2 with or without fountain)

Two lanterns (lighted) for Balthasar

Two torches (lighted) for First and Second Gentlemen

Tabor (drum) and stick and Mercutio's mask (with "beetle brows") for Abraham

Masks for Romeo, Benvolio, First and Second Gentlemen

I-5: *Room in Capulet's house* (same as I-3)

Settee, table, chair

Three small trays of food and drinks to be offered to the guests by Sampson, Gregory and Peter

Tybalt's rapier for Sampson

Five masks from I-4 are worn into this scene

II-1: *Capulet's orchard and Juliet's balcony*

Garden bench

Masks carried by Benvolio and Mercutio

II-2: *Capulet's orchard and Juliet's balcony* (same as II-1)

Garden bench

II-3: *Outside Friar Laurence's cell*

Large standing cross about four feet high

Wicker basket of herbs and flowers for Friar Laurence

II-4: *A street in Verona with fountain* (same as I-2)

Two shopping (string) bags and fan for Peter

Pink flower for Mercutio to wear behind his ear

Coins in puch for Romeo

FIGURE 4-5: **PROPERTY LIST FOR CUT VERSION OF** ***ROMEO AND JULIET***

II-5:   *Capulet's orchard*
Garden bench
One shopping (string) bag for Nurse
One shopping (string) bag and fan for Peter

II-6:   *Outside Friar Laurence's cell with large cross*

III-1:   *A street in Verona with fountain (same as I-4)*
Swords for Tybalt, Mercutio, Romeo
Handkerchief for Mercutio
Shopping (string) bags for Peter and Gregory
Weapons for three watchmen and two soldiers

III-2:   *Capulet's orchard (same as II-5)*
Garden bench
Rope ladder for Nurse
Ring for Juliet
Flask for Peter

III-3:   *Friar Laurence's cell*
Desk
Chair
Candle in holder with matches
Books
Writing materials
Dagger for Romeo
Ring for Nurse

III-4   *Room in Capulet's house (same as I-5)*
Settee
Chair
Small table
Lighted candle for Sampson

III-5:   *Juliet's bedchamber*
Bed with pillows and covers

IV-1:   *Friar Laurence's cell (same as III-3)*
Desk
Chair
Candle in holder with matches
Books
Writing materials
Dagger for Juliet
Glass vial on desk

IV-2:   *Hall in Capulet's house*
List of guests for Capulet

FIGURE 4-5: **continued**

IV-3: *Juliet's bedchamber* (same as III-5)

Dagger and vial under pillows on bed

One of Juliet's dresses for Nurse

IV-4: *Hall in Capulet's house* (same as IV-2)

IV-5: *Juliet's bedchamber* (same as IV-3)

V-1: *In front of an apotechary shop on a street in Mantua*

Pouch with money for Romeo

Vial offstage (in apothecary shop)

V-2: *Outside Friar Laurence's cell with large cross* (same as II-6)

Basket of flowers for Friar Laurence

Letter for Friar John

V-3: *Churchyard and Capulet tomb*

Bier with pillows (bier must be large enough for two people)

Wall bracket to hold torch

Dagger in scabbard (worn at waist), letter, money pouch and vial for Romeo

Five torches (lighted) for Page, Peter, Balthasar, Sampson, Abraham

Damp cloth for extinguishing flame for Page

Flowers for Page

Four lanterns (lighted) for Friar Laurence and three watchmen

Crowbar and spade for Friar Laurence

Swords for Paris and Romeo

Weapons for three watchmen and two soldiers

FIGURE 4-5: **continued**

the right foot back to it. Then step back on the toe of the right foot, lower the right heel as you draw the left foot back. Then take three steps on the toes left, right, left, lower the left heel as you draw the right foot to it. Repeat going backwards starting on the right foot.

A little later in the scene Romeo and Juliet meet. Music is playing softly but there is no dancing.

SWORDFIGHTING

Swordfights in Act I, Scene 1 start off with four servants fighting: Sampson with Abraham and Gregory with Balthasar. Benvolio rushes in to try to break it up. Tybalt sees Benvolio with his sword out and immediately challenges him, so we have three couples fighting onstage.

This attracts a crowd, the watchmen, Prince Escalus and soldiers who manage to stop the fight.

In Act III, Scene 1, Tybalt is insulting Romeo who will not fight with him because Tybalt is his wife's relative. Mercutio, who does not understand Romeo's apparent timidity, takes on Tybalt in what should be an expert fight between two experienced swordsmen. Romeo then tries to stop the fight. He stands between the fighters with his arms out. Tybalt thrusts under Romeo's arm and stabs Mercutio. Tybalt runs away, Mercutio goes offstage to die and Romeo becomes infuriated. When Tybalt returns, he and Romeo engage in a brief vigorous fight in which Tybalt is killed.

The last fight is in Act V, Scene 3 in the churchyard

Romeo and Juliet

MEN

MONTAGUES:

Romeo (son to Montague):
1. Rich-looking tunic, belt, hat, tights, slippers, mask
2. Add cape to (1)
3. Different street costume
4. (Tomb scene) Black tunic, cape, belt, money pouch, dagger in scabbard (worn at waist)

Benvolio: (nephew to Montague):
1. Rich-looking tunic, belt, hat, tights, slippers, mask
2. Add cape to (1)

Montague (father of Romeo):
1. Elegant tunic, belt, armhole cloak, hat, tights, slippers

Balthasar (servant of Romeo):
1. Plain tunic, belt, cap, tights, slippers
2. Cape and boots for V-1

Abraham (servant of Montague):
1. Plain tunic, belt, cap, tights, slippers

CAPULETS:

Tybalt (nephew to Lady Capulet):
1. Rich tunic, belt, hat, tights, slippers, mask
2. Add cape to (1)

Capulet (father of Juliet):
1. Elegant tunic, armhole cloak, hat, tights, slippers
2. Another elegant costume in black for use after Tybalt's death

Gregory (servant of Capulet):
1. Plain tunic, belt, pouch, cap, tights, slippers

Sampson (servant of Capulet):
1. Plain tunic, belt, pouch, cap, tights, slippers

Peter (attendant to Nurse):
1. Plain tunic, belt, pouch, cap, tights, slippers

Old Capulet (cousin):
1. Elegant costume, tights, slippers

OTHER MEN:

Mercutio (kinsman of Prince; friend of Romeo):
1. Elegant tunic, hat, tights, belt, slippers, mask
2. Another elegant street costume, hat, cape

Escalus, Prince of Verona:
1. Elaborate tunic, cloak, hat, tights, slippers

FIGURE 4-6: **FIFTEENTH-CENTURY COSTUMES FOR CUT VERSION OF *ROMEO AND JULIET***

Paris (young nobleman, kinsman to the Prince):	1.	Elegant tunic, belt, hat, tights, slippers
	2.	Another elegant street costume, hat, cape
Chorus:	1.	Plain, black, full-length robe, sandals
Friar Laurence:	1.	Brown Franciscan monk's robe with hood, scapular, skullcap, rosary, sandals
Friar John:	1.	Brown Franciscan monk's robe, scapular, skullcap, rosary, sandals
Apothecary (a poor man):	1.	Dark, shabby full-length robe, belt, pouch, cap, slippers, apron
First Gentleman (a masker, dancer at the ball, citizen of Verona):	1.	Rich costume for young man, hat, tights, slippers, cape, mask
Second Gentleman (a masker, dancer at the ball, citizen of Verona):	1.	Rich costume for young man, hat, tights, slippers, cape, mask
First Watchman (leader of three watchmen):	1.	Official-looking uniform, hat, boots
Second Watchman:	1.	Official-looking uniform, hat, boots
Third Watchman:	1.	Official-looking uniform, hat, boots
First Soldier (guard to Prince Escalus):	1.	Uniform, hat, boots
Second Soldier (guard to Prince Escalus):	1.	Uniform, hat, boots
First Vendor:	1.	Shabby tunic, cap, tights, slippers
Second Vendor:	1.	Shabby tunic, cap, tights, slippers
Page to Paris:	1.	Tunic, cap, tights, slippers, cape
First Citizen:	1.	Tunic, cap, tights, slippers
Second Citizen:	1.	Tunic, cap, tights, slippers

FIGURE 4-6: **continued**

Third citizen:	1.	Tunic, cap, tights, slippers

WOMEN

Juliet (daughter to Capulet):	1.	Elegant ball gown, cap
	2.	Nightgown and robe
	3.	Elegant dark-colored dress, cap
	4.	Rich, light-colored gown, cap
	5.	Hooded cloak for visits to Friar Laurence that will completely cover nightgown worn underneath

Nurse (to Juliet):	1.	Dark, heavy-looking dress, apron, headdress and wimple, money pouch

Lady Capulet (mother of Juliet):	1.	Elegant costume, headdress, for home and the ball
	2.	Another elegant dress in black for use after Tybalt's death
	3.	Cape to be worn in street scenes

Lady Montague (mother of Romeo):	1.	Elegant costume and headdress for wear in street scenes

Rosaline:	1.	Ball gown, cap
	2.	Cape for wear in street scenes

First Lady:	1.	Ball gown, cap
	2.	Cape for wear in street scenes

Second Lady:	1.	Ball gown, cap
	2.	Cape for wear in street scenes

FIGURE 4-6: **continued**

when Paris decides to challenge Romeo because he killed Juliet's cousin, Tybalt. Romeo does not want to fight but is provoked; he kills Paris after a short swordfight.

Cutting and Editing the Text

If the complete text is played, it will probably take about three hours and fifteen minutes or more, depending on the tempo of the acting of scenes and the length of swordfights, dancing, scene changes and intermission(s). If you take the cuts suggested in the following script, it will be about one hour less.

About the cuts: You may not agree with any of them. All of Shakespeare's lines have been included in the following script so you can restore what has been cut. Or perhaps you want to cut other lines. It is the director's choice.

Intermission

Because this is a long play, it is suggested that you have only one intermission of ten minutes, but the director should make this decision. For one intermission, the two best places are after Act II, Scene 6 or after Act III, Scene 1. Both scenes have interesting events that should assure an audience wanting to return after the intermission to see what happens next.

Prologue: When one minute of music begins, start fading out houselights to blackout by fifteen seconds. Immediately bring up full stage lighting.

Daytime exterior. Street in Verona. Full stage is used.

Spot Chorus as he enters (other actors freeze at this time). Immediately take out stage lights leaving Chorus in spotlight until end of speech, then black out.

I-1: Clock will strike nine times. On the sixth bell, bring up stage lights.

It is 9 A.M. on a hot summer day on a street in Verona, Italy. We use the full stage.

As Benvolio and Romeo exit at end of scene, fade stage lights out quickly.

I-2: After a three-second blackout, bring up stage lights quickly.

Daytime exterior. Street in Verona. We use the full stage.

As Benvolio and Romeo exit at end of scene, fade stage lights out quickly.

I-3: As soon as furniture and actors are onstage, bring up lights in furniture area.

Daytime interior. Room in Capulet's house. We use only the area around the furniture.

As actors exit, fade stage lights out quickly.

I-4: As soon as furniture is removed, bring up stage lights.

Night exterior. Street in Verona. We use the full stage.

As actors exit, fade stage lights out quickly.

I-5: As soon as furniture is set and actors are onstage, bring up stage lights.

Night interior. Room in Capulet's house. We use the full stage.

After last line, fade stage lights out quickly.

II-1: After furniture is removed, bring up stage lights.

Night exterior. Capulet's orchard. We use the full stage.

II-2: There is no break between Scene 1 and 2. Do *not* fade out at the end of Scene 1.

Same lighting as used in Scene 1. When Juliet's balcony doors are open, light shines from her bedroom. When the two are both near the balcony, bring down stage lights in other areas.

As Romeo exits, fade stage lights out quickly.

II-3: After clock strikes four times and large cross is in place, bring up stage lights.

It is daybreak exterior. Outside Friar Laurence's cell.

As actors exit, fade stage lights out quickly.

II-4: When fountain is in place, bring up stage lights.

It is noon on a hot summer day. Exterior. Street in Verona. We use full stage.

After last line, fade stage lights out quickly.

II-5: When garden bench is in place, bring up stage lights.

Afternoon exterior. Capulet's orchard. We use full stage.

After last line, fade stage lights out quickly.

II-6: When cross is in place, bring up stage lights.

Afternoon exterior. Outside Friar Laurence's cell.

When twenty seconds of music starts, begin fading out stage lights and bring up spot on three actors at cross. At end of music, black out.

FIGURE 4-7: **LIGHTING FOR CUT VERSION OF *ROMEO AND JULIET***

Intermission: After actors have left stage, bring up house lights for ten minutes.

III-1:   When one minute of music starts, start fading out house lights at thirty seconds; at forty-five seconds there should be a blackout, then immediately bring up stage lights.

Afternoon exterior. Street in Verona. We use full stage.

As Prince Escalus and others exit, fade stage lights out.

III-2:   When garden bench is in place, bring up stage lights.

Exterior sunset. Capulet's orchard. We use full stage.

After last line, fade stage lights out quickly.

III-3:   As soon as furniture is in place, scene begins with entrance of Friar through door.

It is a rainy night and this should be visible when door is open. When Friar lights candle on desk, bring up dim lighting.

Night interior. Friar Laurence's cell. We use only the area around the door and furniture.

When Romeo exits through door and Friar blows out candle, black out stage lights.

III-4:   As soon as furniture is set, bring up dim stage lights.

Late night interior. Capulet's room. We use only the area around the furniture.

As actors exit, fade out stage lights quickly.

III-5:   As soon as actors are in bed, bring up stage lights.

Dawn interior. Juliet's bedchamber. We use only the area around the bed and entrance to the room.

After last line, fade out stage lights quickly.

IV-1:   As soon as furniture is in place and actors are onstage, bring up stage lights.

Late afternoon interior. Friar Laurence's cell. We use only the area around the furniture.

After last line, fade stage lights out quickly.

IV-2:   As soon as Friar Laurence's furniture is removed, bring up stage lights.

Evening interior. Hall in Capulet's house. We use only a small area.

IV-3:   As soon as actors are onstage, bring up stage lights on bed and surrounding area.

Night interior. Juliet's bedchamber.

After Juliet collapses, black out.

IV-4:   Slowly bring up dim stage lights.

Daybreak interior. Hall in Capulet house. Same as IV-2.

After last line, fade stage lights out quickly.

IV-5:   Immediately bring up lights on bed and surrounding area.

Morning interior. Juliet's bedchamber.

After Friar's last line, fade stage lights out quickly.

V-1:   After bed is removed, bring up stage lights.

Daytime exterior. Street in Mantua. We use only small area around apothecary shop.

On Romeo's exit, fade stage lights out quickly.

FIGURE 4-7: **continued**

V-2:   After cross is in place, bring up stage lights.

Evening exterior. Outside Friar Laurence's cell. We use only small area around cross.

After last line, fade stage lights out quickly.

V-3:   After Juliet and bier are in place, bring up stage lights.

Before dawn. Churchyard and Capulet's tomb. We use full stage. Lighting should be dim.

After Prince's last line, actors freeze. Use overhead spot on Romeo and Juliet bier as all other stage lights fade out. Hold for about three seconds and then black out.

Curtain call: Director's decision.

FIGURE 4-7: **continued**

Curtain Call

Here are three possible choices for the director to select from: (l) no curtain call; (2) a posed curtain call with the entire cast in character focusing on the dead bodies of Romeo, Juliet and Paris; (3) a conventional curtain call with everyone walking onstage for a bow. It is possible, of course, to use both (2) and (3).

If you do decide on (2) or (3) or both, rehearse until the cast can perform the curtain call(s) smoothly and quickly.

Script of Romeo and Juliet

Following is a complete script of *The Most Excellent and Lamentable Tragedy of Romeo and Juliet.* In the first col-

umn is the text with suggested blocking, sound and light cues in italics and suggested cuts in brackets. In the second column are notes on meanings of unusual words and other points about the script.

At the end of the complete play you will find an Alternate Cut Ending which begins after the death of Juliet in Act V, Scene 3. Why make this drastic cut in the ending? These are the reasons: (1) We have had the climax of the show, now we need a fast denouement. (2) The plot is merely rehashed. (3) No new information is introduced except for the reconciliation of Capulet and Montague, which is shown in the cut version. But as stated several times before, it is the director's decision to take the cut or not.

Script of *Romeo and Juliet*

Cast of Characters for Cut Version*

Escalus, Prince of Verona
Mercutio, kinsman to Prince, friend to Romeo
Paris, young nobleman, kinsman to Prince
Page to Paris

Montague, head of his house
Lady Montague, wife to Montague
Romeo, son to Montagues
Benvolio, nephew to Montague
Balthasar, servant to Romeo
Abraham, servant to Montague

Friar Laurence, a Franciscan
Friar John, a Franciscan
Apothecary

Capulet, head of his house
Lady Capulet, wife to Capulet
Juliet, daughter to Capulets
Tybalt, nephew to Lady Capulet
Old Capulet, cousin to Capulet
Nurse to Juliet
Peter, attendant to Nurse
Sampson, servant to Capulet
Gregory, servant to Capulet

Chorus
Three watchmen
Rosaline, ladies, gentlemen
Citizens of Verona
Vendors, soldiers

Place: Verona with one scene (Act V, Scene 1) in Mantua.
Time: From Sunday morning till the dawn of Friday in July.

The uncut version needs three musicians for Act I, Scene 5, and Act IV, Scenes 4 and 5 and two more Capulet servants for Act I, Scene 5 and Act IV, Scene 4.

PROLOGUE

Text, Blocking, Lights, Sound, Cuts

(Start one minute of music on cue from stage manager. Houselights down. Stage lights up. Set: A public place in Verona. A fountain dresses the stage. Two vendors selling fruit and scarves , two gentlemen and two ladies enter, some through the audience. Benvolio wanders in. Old Capulet and Peter enter. On the opposite side of the stage, Romeo and Mercutio, followed by Balthasar and Abraham, enter and they play at a game of dice. Benvolio joins them. Rosaline and Tybalt, followed by Sampson and Gregory, enter and join Old Capulet. She buys a scarf. A playful Mercutio throws Romeo into Rosaline; she drops the scarf; Rosaline and Romeo kneel to pick it up. Tybalt draws his sword and puts it over Romeo's hand. All actors freeze. Music is out and stage lights are out as spotlight hits Chorus, who comes to center to speak to the audience:)
CHORUS: Two households, both alike in dignity,

NOTES
Suggested blocking is not precise so that the director may adapt it to the type of stage used: proscenium, arena or thrust.

Suggested lines to be cut are enclosed in brackets.

Note that the lines form a sonnet.

In fair Verona, where we lay our scene,
From ancient grudge break to new mutiny,
Where civil blood makes civil hands unclean.

civil blood—civil war

From forth the fatal loins of these two foes
A pair of star-cross'd lovers take their life;

star-cross'd—fated

Whose misadventur'd piteous overthrows

misadventur'd—ill fortuned

Doth, with their death, bury their parents' strife.
The fearful passage of their death-mark'd love,
And the continuance of their parents' rage,
Which, but their children's end, nought could remove,
Is now the two hours' traffic of our stage;
The which if you with patient ears attend,
What here shall miss, our toil shall strive to mend.

miss—lacking

(Blackout. Everyone leaves stage except Sampson and Gregory. Sound: Clock strikes nine. Stage lights come up on six.)

ACT I, SCENE 1

(Set: Same as Prologue. Time: 9 A.M. on Sunday. Sampson and Gregory, who are wearing swords, are sitting center.)

SAM: Gregory, on my word, we'll not carry coals.

carry coals—take insults

GRE: No, for then we should be colliers.

SAM: I mean, and we be in choler, we'll draw.

choler—anger

(Sampson rises and draws his sword.)

GRE: Ay, while you live, draw your neck out o' the collar.

(Sampson makes a jab in the air with sword.)

SAM: I strike quickly, being moved.

(Sampson struts around.)

GRE: But thou art not quickly moved to strike.

SAM: A dog of the house of Montague moves me.

[GRE: To move is to stir, and to be valiant, is to stand: therefore, if thou art moved, thou runn'st away.

Suggested cut begins.

SAM: A dog of that house shall move me to stand: I will take the wall of any man or maid of Montague's.

take the wall—keep to the preferred side of the path

GRE: That shows thee a weak slave; for the weakest goes to the wall.

SAM: 'Tis true; and therefore women, being the weaker vessels, are ever thrust to the wall: therefore I will push Montague's men from the wall and thrust his maids to the wall.]

Suggested cut ends.

GRE: The quarrel is between our masters and us their men.

SAM: 'Tis all one, I will show myself a tyrant: when I have fought with the men, I will be cruel with the maids; I will cut off their heads.

GRE: The heads of the maids?

SAM: Ay, the heads of the maids, or their maidenheads; take it in what sense thou wilt. *(He puts sword away and sits.)*

maidenheads—virginities

GRE: They must take it in sense that feel it.

SAM: Me they shall feel, while I am able to stand: and 'tis known I am a pretty piece of flesh.

[GRE: 'Tis well thou art not fish; if thou hadst, thou hadst been poor John.]

Suggested cut begins and ends.

(Enter Abraham and Balthasar, two servants of Montague. They stop and draw their swords. Gregory and Sampson rise and do the same.)

GRE: Draw thy tool; here comes two of the house of Montagues.

SAM: My naked weapon is out: quarrel, I will back thee. *(He moves in back of Gregory.)*

GRE: How! turn thy back and run?

SAM: Fear me not.

GRE: No, marry; I fear thee!

SAM: Let us take the law of our sides; let them begin.

GRE: I will frown as I pass by, and let them take it as they list.

SAM: Nay, as they dare. I will bite my thumb at them; which is a disgrace to them, if they bear it.

bite my thumb—an insulting gesture

(Sampson, who has been hiding behind Gregory, runs closer to Abraham and Balthasar, "bites his thumb" and returns to his position behind Gregory.)

ABR: Do you bite your thumb at us, sir?

SAM: I do bite my thumb, sir.

ABR: Do you bite your thumb at us, sir?

SAM: *(Aside to Gregory.)* Is the law of our side, if I say ay?

GRE: No.

SAM: *(Stepping toward Abraham.)* No, sir, I do not bite my thumb at you, sir, but I bite my thumb, sir. *(He does the gesture again and returns to behind Gregory.)*

GRE: Do you quarrel, sir?

ABR: Quarrel, sir! No, sir.

SAM: If you do, sir, I am for you: I serve as good a man as you. *(Bravely stepping in front of Gregory.)*

ABR: *(Aggressively.)* No better.

SAM: Well, sir. *(Retreats to behind Gregory.)*

GRE: *(Seeing Tybalt entering.)* Say "better:" here comes one of my master's kinsmen.

SAM: *(Defiantly.)* Yes, better, sir.

ABR: You lie.

SAM: Draw, if you be men. Gregory, remember thy swashing blow.

swashing—smashing

(Sampson fights Abraham on one side of the stage while Gregory fights Balthasar on the other side. After a few moments, Benvolio, with sword drawn, rushes to the center.)

BEN: Part, fools!
Put up your swords; you know not what you do.
(Beats down their swords. Tybalt comes forward, with sword drawn.)

TYB: What, art thou drawn among these heartless hinds?
Turn thee, Benvolio, look upon thy death.

hinds—servants

BEN: I do but keep the peace: put up thy sword,

Or manage it to part these men with me.

TYB: What, drawn, and talk of peace! I hate the word,

As I hate hell, all Montagues, and thee:

Have at thee, coward! *(They fight. Enter citizens, two gentlemen, two ladies, two vendors, Old Capulet and Peter, to watch the fight. Then three watchmen enter, shouting for help.)*

WATCHMEN: Clubs, bills, and partisans! Strike!

Beat them down!

CITIZENS: Down with the Capulets! Down with the Montagues!

(Enter Capulet and Lady Capulet. On other side of stage, enter Montague, with sword in hand, and Lady Montague.)

CAP: What noise is this? Give me my long sword, ho!

L. CAP: A crutch, a crutch! Why call you for a sword?

CAP: My sword, I say! Old Montague is come,

And flourishes his blade in spite of me.

MON: Thou villain Capulet! *(To Lady Montague.)*

Hold me not, let me go.

L. MON: Thou shalt not stir a foot to seek a foe.

(Prince Escalus and two soldiers enter. The crowd is shouting, "Here comes the Prince. Do something!")

PRI: Rebellious subjects, enemies to peace,

Profaners of this neighbour-stainèd steel,—

Will they not hear? [What, ho! you men, you beasts

That quench the fire of your pernicious rage

With purple fountains issuing from your veins,

On pain of torture, from those bloody hands]

Throw your mistemper'd weapons to the ground,

And hear the sentence of your movèd prince.

(The noise abates as the watchmen and soldiers restore order.)

Three civil brawls, bred of an airy word,

By thee, old Capulet, and Montague,

Have thrice disturb'd the quiet of our streets,

[And made Verona's ancient citizens

Cast by their grave beseeming ornaments,

To wield old partisans, in hands as old,

Canker'd with peace, to part your canker'd hate:]

If ever you disturb our streets again,

Your lives shall pay the forfeit of the peace.

For this time, all the rest depart away:

You, Capulet, shall go along with me;

And, Montague, come you this afternoon,

To know our further pleasure in this case,

bills, partisans—weapons

Suggested cut begins.

Suggested cut ends.

airy—slight

Suggested cut begins.

Canker'd—(1) corroded, (2) malignant. Suggested cut ends.

[To old Free-town, our common judgement-place.]   Suggested cut begins and ends.

Once more, on pain of death, all men depart.

(The Prince exits, followed by Capulet and soldiers. Tybalt and Lady Capulet exit. Watch-

men disperse the crowd. Montague, Lady Montague and Benvolio are left onstage.)

MON: Who set this ancient quarrel new abroach?

Speak, nephew, were you by when it began?

BEN: Here were the servants of your adversary,

And yours, close fighting ere I did approach:

I drew to part them: in the instant came

The fiery Tybalt, with his sword prepar'd;

[Which, as he breath'd defiance to my ears,   Suggested cut begins.

He swung about his head, and cut the winds,

Who, nothing hurt withal, hiss'd him in scorn:]   Suggested cut ends.

While we were interchanging thrusts and blows,

Came more and more and fought on part and part,   **part and part**—either side

Till the Prince came, who parted either part.

L. MON: O, where is Romeo? Saw you him today?

Right glad I am he was not at this fray.

BEN: Madam, an hour before the worshipp'd sun

Peer'd forth the golden window of the east,

A troubl'd mind drave me to walk abroad;   **drave**—urged

Where, underneath the grove of sycamore

That westward rooteth from the city's side,

So early walking did I see your son:

Towards him I made, but he was ware of me

And stole into the covert of the wood:

[I, measuring his affections by my own,   Suggested cut begins.

That most are busied when they're most alone,

Pursued my humour not pursuing his,

And gladly shunn'd who gladly fled from me.]   Suggested cut ends.

MON: Many a morning hath he there been seen,

With tears augmenting the fresh morning's dew,

Adding to clouds more clouds with his deep sighs:

[But all so soon as the all-cheering sun   Suggested cut begins.

Should in the furthest east begin to draw

The shady curtains from Aurora's bed,]   Suggested cut ends.

Away from light steals home my heavy son,

And private in his chamber pens himself,   **pens**—confines

Shuts up his windows, locks fair daylight out

And makes himself an artificial night:

Black and portentous must this humour prove,

Unless good counsel may the cause remove.

BEN: My noble uncle, do you know the cause?

MON: I neither know it nor can learn of him.

[BEN: Have you importun'd him by any means?   Suggested cut begins.

MON: Both by myself and many other friends:

But he, his own affections' counsellor,

Is to himself—I will not say how true—

But to himself so secret and so close,

So far from sounding and discovery,

As is the bud bit with an envious worm,

Ere he can spread his sweet leaves to the air,

Or dedicate his beauty to the sun.]   Suggested cut ends.

Could we but learn from whence his sorrows grow,

We would as willingly give cure as know.

(Romeo enters, appearing sad.)

BEN: See, where he comes: so please you step aside,

I'll know his grievance, or be much denied.

MON: [I would thou wert so happy by thy stay,   Suggested cut begins.

To hear true shrift.] Come, madam, let's away.   Suggested cut ends.

(Lady Montague and Montague exit quickly. Romeo looks at his departing parents.)

BEN: Good morrow, cousin.

ROM: Is the day so young?

BEN: But new struck nine.

ROM: Ay me! sad hours seem long.

Was that my father that went hence so fast?

BEN: It was. What sadness lengthens Romeo's hours?

ROM: Not having that, which, having, makes them short.

BEN: In love?

ROM: Out—

BEN: Of love?

ROM: Out of her favour, where I am in love.

[BEN: Alas, that love, so gentle in his view,   Suggested cut begins.

Should be so tyrannous and rough in proof!

ROM: Alas, that love, whose view is muffled still,

Should, without eyes, see pathways to his will!]   Suggested cut ends.

Where shall we dine? O me! What fray was here?

Yet tell me not, for I have heard it all.

Here's much to do with hate, but more with love:

Why, then, O brawling love! O loving hate!   Note the oxymorons.

[O any thing, of nothing first created!   Suggested cut begins.

O heavy lightness! serious vanity!

Mis-shapen chaos of well-seeming forms!

Feather of lead, bright smoke, cold fire, sick health!

Still-waking sleep, that is not what it is!]   Suggested cut ends.

This love feel I, that feel no love in this.

Dost thou not laugh?

BEN: No, coz, I rather weep.

ROM: Good heart, at what?

BEN: At thy good heart's oppression.   Note the rhyming couplets.

ROM: Why, such is love's transgression.

Griefs of mine own lie heavy in my breast,

Which thou wilt propagate, to have it prest   **propagate**—increase

With more of thine: this love that thou hast shown

Doth add more grief to too much of mine own.

[Love is a smoke rais'd with the fume of sighs;   Suggested cut begins.

Being purg'd, a fire sparkling in lovers' eyes;

Being vex'd, a sea nourish'd with lovers' tears:

What is it else? a madness most discreet,

A choking gall and a preserving sweet.]   Suggested cut ends.

Farewell, my coz.

BEN: Soft! I will go along: **Soft**—Wait a minute

An if you leave me so, you do me wrong.

ROM: Tut, I have lost myself; I am not here;

This is not Romeo, he's some other where.

BEN: Tell me in sadness, who is that you love?   **sadness**—seriousness

ROM: What, shall I groan and tell thee?

BEN: Groan! Why no;

But sadly tell me who.

ROM: [Bid a sick man in sadness make his will: Suggested cut begins.

Ah, word ill urg'd to one that is so ill!]   Suggested cut ends.

In sadness, cousin, I do love a woman.

BEN: I aim'd so near when I suppos'd you loved.

ROM: A right good mark-man! And she's fair I love.

BEN: A right fair mark, fair coz, is soonest hit.

ROM: Well, in that hit you miss: she'll not be hit

With Cupid's arrow; she hath Dian's wit;

And in strong proof of chastity well arm'd,

From love's weak childish bow she lives unharm'd.

[She will not stay the siege of loving terms,   Suggested cut begins.

Nor bide the encounter of assailing eyes,

Nor ope her lap to saint-seducing gold:

O, she is rich in beauty, only poor,

That when she dies, with beauty dies her store.]   Suggested cut ends.

BEN: Then she hath sworn that she will still live chaste?

ROM: She hath, and in that sparing makes huge waste

For beauty, starved with her severity,

Cuts beauty off from all posterity.

She is too fair, too wise, wisely too fair,

To merit bliss by making me despair:
She hath forsworn to love, and in that vow
Do I live dead that live to tell it now.
BEN: Be ruled by me, forget to think of her.
ROM: O, teach me how I should forget to think.
BEN: By giving liberty unto thine eyes;
Examine other beauties.
ROM: 'Tis the way
To call hers exquisite, in question more:

[These happy masks that kiss fair ladies' brows,
Being black, put us in mind they hide the fair;
He that is strucken blind cannot forget
The precious treasure of his eyesight lost;
Show me a mistress that is passing fair,
What doth her beauty serve but as a note
Where I may read who pass'd that passing fair?]
Farewell: thou canst not teach me to forget.
BEN: I'll pay that doctrine, or else die in debt.
(Benvolio and Romeo exit. Fade stage lights out, fast. After three seconds of blackout, bring up stage lights quickly.)

in question more—considered more

Suggested cut begins.

Suggested cut ends.

pay that doctrine—give that instruction

ACT I, SCENE 2

(Same set. Later on Sunday. Onstage is First Vendor selling fruit and First Gentleman who is purchasing some. Capulet and Paris enter, followed by Sampson.)
CAP: But Montague is bound as well as I,
In penalty alike; and 'tis not hard, I think,
For men so old as we to keep the peace.
PAR: Of honourable reckoning are you both;
(Paris looks at vendor's fruit. Gentleman exits.)
And pity 'tis you liv'd at odds so long.
(Paris pays vendor and sits at fountain. Vendor exits.)
But now, my lord, what say you to my suit?
CAP: But saying o'er what I have said before:
My child is yet a stranger in the world;
She hath not seen the change of fourteen years;
Let two more summers wither in their pride
Ere we may think her ripe to be a bride.
(He sits near Paris.)
PAR: Younger than she are happy mothers made.
CAP: And too soon marr'd are those so early made.
The earth hath swallow'd all my hopes but she,

reckoning—reputation

She is the hopeful lady of my earth: *(He rises.)*
But woo her, gentle Paris, get her heart,
My will to her consent is but a part;
An she agree, within her scope of choice   **An**—if, **scope**—range
Lies my consent and fair-according voice.   **fair-according voice**—
This night I hold an old accustom'd feast,   approval
Whereto I have invited many a guest,
Such as I love; and you among the store,   **store**—crowd
One more, most welcome, makes my number more.
[At my poor house, look to behold this night   Suggested cut begins.
Earth-treading stars that make dark heaven light:
Such comfort as do lusty young men feel
When well-apparell'd April on the heel
Of limping winter treads, even such delight
Among fresh female buds shall you this night
Inherit at my house; hear all, all see,
And like her most whose merit most shall be:
Which on more view, of many mine being one
May stand in number, though in reckoning none.]   **reckoning**—estimation
                                                            Suggested cut ends.

Come, go with me. Go, sirrah, trudge about
(He hands list of guests to Sampson.)
Through fair Verona; find those persons out
Whose names are written there, and to them say,
My house and welcome on their pleasure stay.
(Capulet and Paris exit. Sampson, who cannot read, stares at the list.)
SAM: Find them out, whose names are written here! It is written that the shoemaker
should meddle with his yard and the tailor with his last, the fisher with his pencil and
the painter with his nets; but I am sent to find those persons whose names are here
writ, and can never find what names the writing person hath here writ. I must to the
learned. In good time.
(Romeo and Benvolio enter.)
[BEN: Tut, man, one fire burns out another's burning.   Suggested cut begins.
One pain is lessen'd by another's anguish;
Turn giddy, and be holp by backward turning;   **holp**—helped
One desperate grief cures with another's languish:
Take thou some new infection to thy eye,
And the rank poison of the old will die.
ROM: Your plantain-leaf is excellent for that.
BEN: For what, I pray thee?
ROM: For your broken shin.]   Suggested cut ends.
BEN: Why, Romeo, art thou mad?
(Benvolio sits at fountain.)

ROM: Not mad, but bound more than a madman is;

Shut up in prison, kept without my food,

Whipp'd and tormented and—*(Sampson tugs on Romeo's sleeve.)* God-den, good fellow.

God-den—God give you good
evening

SAM: God gi' god-den. I pray, sir, can you read?

ROM: Ay, mine own fortune in my misery.

SAM: Perhaps you have learned it without book: but, I pray, can you read anything you see?

ROM: Ay, if I know the letters and the language.

SAM: Ye say honestly: rest you merry!

(Sampson starts to walk away.)

ROM: Stay, fellow; I can read. *(Romeo reads.)*

"Signior Martino and his wife and daughters; County Anselme and his beauteous sisters; the lady widow of Vitruvio; Signior Placentio and his lovely nieces; Mercutio and his brother Valentine; mine uncle Capulet, his wife, and daughters; my fair niece—Rosaline; *(Romeo reacts to Rosaline's name.)* Livia; Signior Valentio and his cousin Tybalt; Lucio and the lively Helena."

A fair assembly: whither should they come?

SAM: Up.

ROM: Whither?

SAM: To supper; to our house.

ROM: Whose house?

SAM: My master's.

ROM: Indeed, I should have ask'd you that before.

SAM: Now I'll tell you without asking: my master is the great rich Capulet; and if you be not of the house of Montagues, I pray, come and crush a cup of wine. Rest you merry! *(Sampson bows and exits.)*

crush a cup—drink a bottle

BEN: At this same ancient feast of Capulet's

Sups the fair Rosaline whom thou so lovest,

With all the admired beauties of Verona:

Go thither; and with unattainted eye,

Compare her face with some that I shall show,

And I will make thee think thy swan a crow.

ROM: [When the devout religion of mine eye

Maintains such falsehood, then turn tears to fires;

And these, who, often drown'd, could never die,—

Transparent heretics,—be burnt for liars!]

One fairer than my love! the all-seeing sun

Ne'er saw her match since first the world begun.

BEN: Tut, you saw her fair, none else being by,

Herself poised with herself in either eye:

But in that crystal scales let there be weigh'd

Your lady's love against some other maid,

That I will show you shining at this feast,

Suggested cut begins.

Suggested cut ends.

poised—weighed

And she shall scant show well that now seems best.

ROM: I'll go along, no such sight to be shown,

But to rejoice in splendour of mine own.

(Fade stage lights out quickly as Romeo and Benvolio exit. As soon as furniture is set and actors are onstage, bring up stage lights.)

scant—barely

ACT I, SCENE 3

(Set: Room in the Capulet house. Time: Later on Sunday. Onstage are a settee, chair and small table. Lady Capulet, who is looking at the guest list, is seated on the settee. The Nurse, who is dozing, is seated in the chair.)

L.CAP: Nurse, where's my daughter? call her forth to me.

NUR: *(Waking up.)* Now, by my maidenhead at twelve year old,

I bade her come. *(Rising.)* What, lamb! what, lady-bird!

God forbid! Where's this girl? *(Calling offstage.)*

What, Juliet!

JUL: *(Offstage.)* How now! who calls?

NUR: Your mother.

JUL: *(Entering.)* Madam, I am here. What is your will?

L.CAP: This is the matter. Nurse, give leave awhile,

We must talk in secret:—*(Nurse starts to leave.)* Nurse, come back again; *(Nurse returns.)*

I have remember'd me, thou's hear our counsel.

Thou know'st my daughter's of a pretty age.

(Juliet sits on settee with her mother. Nurse stands and walks about during the following.)

NUR: Faith, I can tell her age unto an hour.

L.CAP: She's not fourteen.

NUR: I'll lay fourteen of my teeth,—

And yet, to my teen be it spoken, I have but four,—

She is not fourteen. How long is it now

To Lammas-tide?

L.CAP: A fortnight and odd days.

NUR.: Even or odd, of all days in the year,

Come Lammas-eve at night shall she be fourteen.

Susan and she—God rest all Christian souls!—

(Nurse crosses herself.)

Were of an age: well, Susan is with God;

She was too good for me:—but, as I said,

On Lammas-eve at night shall she be fourteen;

That shall she, marry; I remember it well.

'Tis since the earthquake now eleven years;

And she was wean'd—I never shall forget it—

Of all the days of the year, upon that day:

For I had then laid wormwood to my dug,

maidenhead—virginity

thou's—thou shalt

teen—sorrow

Lammas-tide—August 1

dug—teat

Sitting in the sun under the dove-house wall;
My lord and you were then at Mantua:—
Nay, I do bear a brain:—but, as I said,
When it did taste the wormwood on the nipple
Of my dug, and felt it bitter, pretty fool,
To see it tetchy and fall out with the dug!   **tetchy**—fretful
["Shake," quoth the dove-house: 'twas no need, I trow,   Suggested cut begins.
                                                                     trow—believe
To bid me trudge:]   Suggested cut ends.
And since that time it is eleven years;
For then she could stand alone; nay by the rood,   **rood**—holy cross
She could have run and waddled all about;
For even the day before, she broke her brow:
And then my husband,—God be with his soul!
A' was a merry man—took up the child: **A'**—he
"Yea," quoth he, "dost thou fall upon thy face?
Thou wilt fall backward when thou hast more wit;
Wilt thou not, Jule?" and, by my holidame,   **holidame**—sacred relic
The pretty wretch left crying and said "Ay."
To see, now, how a jest shall come about!
I warrant, and I should live a thousand years,
I never should forget it: *(Nurse laughs.)*
"Wilt thou not, Jule?" quoth he;
And, pretty fool, it stinted and said "Ay."   **stinted**—stopped
L.CAP: *(Irritated.)* Enough of this; I pray thee, hold thy peace.
NUR: Yes, madam: yet I cannot choose but laugh,
To think it should leave crying, and say "Ay":
And yet, I warrant, it had upon its brow
A bump as big as a young cockerel's stone;   **stone**—testicle
A perilous knock; and it cried bitterly: **perilous**—awful
"Yea," quoth my husband, "fall'st upon thy face?
Thou wilt fall backward when thou comest to age;
Wilt thou not, Jule?" it stinted, and said "Ay."
JUL: And stint thou too, I pray thee, Nurse, say I.
(Juliet rises. Nurse stops laughing and sits in chair.)
NUR: Peace, I have done. God mark thee to his grace!
Thou wast the prettiest babe that e'er I nurs'd:
(Nurse takes Juliet on her lap.)
An I might live to see thee married once,
I have my wish.
L.CAP: Marry, that "marry" is the very theme
I came to talk of. Tell me, daughter Juliet,
How stands your disposition to be married?

JUL: It is an honour that I dream not of.

(Juliet rises to sit next to mother on settee.)

NUR: An honour! Were not I thine only nurse,

I would say thou hadst suck'd wisdom from thy teat.

L.CAP: Well, think of marriage now; younger than you,

Here in Verona, ladies of esteem,

Are made already mothers: by my count,

I was your mother much upon these years

That you are now a maid. Thus then in brief:

The valiant Paris seeks you for his love.

(No reaction from Juliet. Nurse rises and crosses to Juliet.)

NUR: A man, young lady! lady, such a man

As all the world—why, he's a man of wax   **man of wax**—faultless

L.CAP: Verona's summer hath not such a flower.

NUR: Nay, he is a flower; in faith, a very flower.

L.CAP: What say you? can you love the gentleman?

This night you shall behold him at our feast:

Read o'er the volume of young Paris' face,

And find delight writ there with beauty's pen;

[Examine every married lineament,   Suggested cut begins.

    married—harmonious

    lineament—feature

And see how one another lends content;

And what obscur'd in this fair volume lies

Fine written in the margent of his eyes.]   **margent**—margin

    Suggested cut ends.

This precious book of love, this unbound lover,   **unbound**—unattached

To beautify him, only lacks a cover;   **cover**—wife

[The fish lives in the sea; and 'tis much pride   Suggested cut begins.

For fair without the fair within to hide:

That book in many's eyes doth share the glory,

That in gold clasps locks in the golden story;]   Suggested cut ends.

So shall you share all that he doth possess,

By having him making yourself no less.

NUR: No less! Nay, bigger: women grow by men.

L.CAP: Speak briefly, can you like of Paris' love?

(Juliet rises.)

JUL: I'll look to like, if looking liking move: **look to**—expect

But no more deep will I endart mine eye

Than your consent gives strength to make it fly.

(Nurse kisses Juliet. Sampson enters, bowing.)

SAM: Madam, the guests are come, supper served up, you called, my young lady asked

for, the nurse curs'd in the pantry, and every thing in extremity. I must hence to wait;
I beseech you, follow straight.

L.CAP: *(Rising.)* We follow thee. *(Sampson bows and exits.)* Juliet, the County stays.

NUR: Go, girl, seek happy nights to happy days.

(They exit as stage lights fade out quickly.)

County stays—Count waits

ACT I, SCENE 4

*(After Capulet furniture is removed or concealed, bring up dim stage lights. Set: Same as
Act I, Scene 2, street in Verona. Time: Sunday night. Drum beats are heard as Abraham
strikes a tabor with a stick. Balthasar, carrying two lanterns, is the first onstage, followed
by First and Second Gentlemen, who are masked and carrying torches, and Abraham, who
carries Mercutio's mask. They are happily laughing and having fun. Romeo and Benvolio
enter after them, carrying masks. Romeo is in a sad mood.)*

[ROM: What, shall this speech be spoke for our excuse?

Or shall we on without apology?

BEN: The date is out of such prolixity:

We'll have no Cupid hoodwink'd with a scarf,

Bearing a Tartar's painted bow of lath,

Scaring the ladies like a crow-keeper;

Nor no without-book prologue, fairly spoke

After the prompter, for our entrance:

But let them measure us by what they will,

We'll measure them a measure, and be gone.]

ROM: *(To Balthasar.)* Give me a torch: I am not for this ambling; *(Mercutio enters.)*

Being but heavy, I will bear the light.*(He takes a lantern from Balthasar.)*

MER: Nay, gentle Romeo, we must have you dance.

ROM: Not I, believe me: you have dancing shoes

With nimble soles: I have a soul of lead

So stakes me to the ground I cannot move.

MER: You are a lover; borrow Cupid's wings,

And soar with them above a common bound.

ROM: I am too sore enpierced with his shaft

To soar with his light feathers, and so bound,

I cannot bound a pitch above dull woe:

Under love's heavy burden do I sink.

(Romeo sits on steps.)

MER: And, to sink in it, should you burden love:

Too great oppression for a tender thing.

ROM: Is love a tender thing? it is too rough,

Too rude, too boisterous, and it pricks like thorn.

MER: If love be rough with you, be rough with love;

Suggested cut begins.

prolixity—unduly prolonged

hoodwink'd—blindfolded

crow-keeper—one who scares
crows

measure—(1) judge (2-3)
dance

Suggested cut ends.

heavy—sad

Prick love for pricking, and you beat love down.

(Getting his mask from Abraham.)

Give me a case to put my visage in:

A visor for a visor! What care I

What curious eye doth quote deformities?

(Showing his mask.)

Here are the beetle-brows shall blush for me.

(All laugh.)

BEN: Come, knock and enter, and no sooner in

But every man betake him to his legs.

ROM: A torch for me: [let wantons light of heart

Tickle the senseless rushes with their heels;

For I am proverb'd with a grandsire phrase;]

(Romeo rises.) I'll be a candle-holder, and look on.

[The game was ne'er so fair, and I am done.

MER: Tut, dun's the mouse, the constable's own word:

If thou art dun, we'll draw thee from the mire

Of this sir-reverence love, wherein thou stick'st

Up to the ears. Come, we burn daylight, ho!

ROM: Nay, that's not so.

MER: I mean, sir, in delay

We waste our lights in vain, like lamps by day.

Take our good meaning, for our judgement sits

Five times in that ere once in our five wits.]

ROM: And we mean well, in going to this mask;

But 'tis no wit to go.

MER: Why, may one ask?

ROM: I dreamt a dream tonight.

MER: And so did I.

ROM: Well, what was yours?

MER: That dreamers often lie.

ROM: In bed asleep, while they do dream things true.

MER: O, then I see Queen Mab hath been with you.

(Reaction from listeners, "Who?" "Who is Queen Mab?" Mercutio delivers the following
lightly and quickly. He acts out many of the lines.)

She is the fairies' midwife, *(All laugh.)* and she comes

In shape no bigger than an agate-stone

On the fore-finger of an alderman,

Drawn with a team of little atomies

Athwart men's noses as they lie asleep:

Her waggon-spokes made of long spinners' legs;

The cover of the wings of grasshoppers;

The traces of the smallest spider's web,

Prick love for pricking—
diminish lust by satisfying

case—mask

visor for a visor—mask for a face

quote—note

Suggested cut begins.

rushes—floor covering

Suggested cut ends.

Suggested cut begins.

dun's the mouse—keep still as
a mouse

sir-reverence—irreverent

burn daylight—waste time

Suggested cut ends.

wit—wisdom

Queen Mab—Fairy Queen

atomies—tiny animals

spinners'—spiders'

The collars of the moonshine's watery beams,
Her whip of cricket's bone, the lash of film,

film—gossamer

Her waggoner, a small grey-coated gnat,

waggoner—coachman

Not half so big as a round little worm
Prick'd from the lazy finger of a maid;
Her chariot is an empty hazel-nut
[Made by the joiner squirrel or old grub,

Suggested cut begins.

Time out o' mind the fairies' coachmakers.]

Suggested cut ends.

And in this state she gallops night by night
Through lovers' brains, and then they dream of love;
O'er courtiers' knees, that dream on curtsies straight;

curtsies—respectful gestures

straight—immediately

O'er lawyers' fingers, who straight dream on fees;
O'er ladies' lips, who straight on kisses dream,
Which oft the angry Mab with blisters plagues,
Because their breaths with sweetmeats tainted are:
Sometimes she gallops o'er a courtier's nose,
And then dreams he of smelling out a suit;
And sometime comes she with a tithe-pig's tail

tithe-pig—the parson received

Tickling a parson's nose as a' lies asleep,

a tenth of a litter of pigs

Then dreams he of another benefice:
Sometime she driveth o'er a soldier's neck,
And then dreams he of cutting foreign throats,
Of breaches, ambuscados, Spanish blades,

ambuscados—ambushes

Of healths five fathom deep; and then anon
Drums in his ear, at which he starts and wakes,
And being thus frighted swears a prayer or two
And sleeps again. This is that very Mab
That plats the manes of horses in the night,

plats—plaits

[And bakes the elf-locks in foul-sluttish hairs,

Suggested cut begins.

elf-locks—tangled hair

Which once untangled much misfortune bodes:]

Suggested cut ends.

This is the hag, when maids lie on their backs,

hag—witch

That presses them and learns them first to bear,
(Yelling.) Making them women of good carriage:
This is she—
ROM: *(Comforting him.)* Peace, peace, Mercutio, peace!
Thou talk'st of nothing.
MER: True, I talk of dreams;
Which are the children of an idle brain,
Begot of nothing but vain fantasy,

vain—foolish

Which is as thin of substance as the air,
And more inconstant than the wind, who wooes

Even now the frozen bosom of the north,

And, being anger'd, puffs away from thence,

Turning his face to the dew-dropping south.

BEN: This wind, you talk of, blows us from ourselves;

Supper is done, and we shall come too late.

ROM: I fear, too early: for my mind misgives

Some consequence, yet hanging in the stars,

Shall bitterly begin his fearful date

With this night's revels, and expire the term

Of a despisèd life clos'd in my breast,

By some vile forfeit of untimely death:

But He, that hath the steerage of my course,

Direct my sail! On lusty gentlemen.

BEN: Strike, drum. *(Gentlemen put on masks. Abraham leads the way beating his drum. All, except Romeo, are enjoying themselves. Balthasar is last with lanterns. Fade out stage lights quickly.)*

ACT I, SCENE 5

(Set: Room in the Capulet house—same as Act I, Scene 3. Time: Sunday night. Onstage are a settee, chair and small table. As soon as furniture is set, bring up downstage lights. If following cut is taken, bring up lights on full stage.) [*(Enter Sampson followed by Gregory, who is carrying a stool, and Peter with a plate of food.)*

SAM: Where's Potpan, that he helps not to take away? He shift a trencher! he scrape a trencher!

GRE: When good manners shall lie all in one or two men's hands, and they unwashed too, 'tis a foul thing.

SAM: Away with the joint-stools, remove the court-cupboard, look to the plate. *(Gregory exits with stool. To Peter.)* Good thou, save me a piece of marchpane; and, as thou lovest me, let the porter let in Susan Grindstone and Nell. *(Peter exits.)* Antony and Potpan! *(Enter two servants, Antony and Potpan, running.)*

ANT: Ay, boy, ready.

POT: You are looked for and called for; asked for and sought for, in the great chamber.

SAM: We cannot be here and there too. Cheerly, boys; be brisk a while, and the longer liver take all. *(They exit.)*]

(Bring up lights on full stage. Juliet and Lady Capulet enter followed by Nurse. On other side of stage guests enter: First and Second Gentlemen, who are masked, First and Second Ladies, Tybalt and Rosaline. Lady Capulet greets them. Juliet crosses to welcome Paris. Capulet and Old Capulet enter followed by masked Mercutio, Benvolio and Romeo. The servants, Abraham and Balthasar, stay near the entrance.)

CAP: Welcome, gentlemen! ladies that have their toes

Unplagu'd with corns will have a bout with you:

Ah ha, my mistresses! Which of you all

Suggested cut begins.

trencher—plate

court-cupboard—sideboard

marchpane—marzipan

longer liver—survivor

Suggested cut ends.

Will now deny to dance? She that makes dainty

She, I'll swear, hath corns; *(Laughs)* am I come near ye now?

Welcome, gentlemen! I have seen the day

That I have worn a visor, and could tell

A whispering tale in a fair lady's ear,

Such as would please: *(Laughs.)* 'tis gone, 'tis gone, 'tis gone:

You are welcome, gentlemen! *(To offstage musicians.)* Come, musicians, play.

A hall, a hall! Give room! And—foot it, girls.

(Benvolio and Mercutio ask the First and Second Ladies to dance. The other couples are Tybalt and Rosaline, First Gentleman and Lady Capulet and Juliet and Paris. Second Gentleman crosses to talk with Nurse. Music and dancing begin.)

[More light, you knaves; and turn the tables up,   Suggested cut begins.

And quench the fire, the room is grown too hot.]   Suggested cut ends.

Ah, sirrah, this unlook'd-for sport comes well.

(Taking Old Capulet to chair.)

Nay, sit, nay, sit, good cousin Capulet;

For you and I are past our dancing days:

(Capulet sits on settee.)

How long is't now since last yourself and I

Were in a mask?

(Romeo has been looking for Rosaline, but suddenly he sees Juliet.

O. CAP: *(Somewhat deaf.)* By'r lady, thirty years.   **By'r**—by our

(Sampson, Gregory and Peter enter with small trays of food to offer to guests.)

CAP: What, man! 'tis not so much, 'tis not so much;

'Tis since the nuptial of Lucentio,

Come Pentecost as quickly as it will,

Some five and twenty years; and then we mask'd.

O. CAP: 'Tis more, 'tis more: his son is elder, sir;

His son is thirty.

CAP: Will you tell me that?

His son was but a ward two years ago.   **ward**—minor

ROM: *(To Balthasar.)* What lady's that, which doth enrich the hand

Of yonder knight?

BAL: I know not, sir.

ROM: O, she doth teach the torches to burn bright!

It seems she hangs upon the cheek of night

Like a rich jewel in an Ethiope's ear;   **Ethiope**—native of Ethiopia

Beauty too rich for use, for earth too dear!

[So shows a snowy dove trooping with crows,   Suggested cut begins.

As yonder lady o'er her fellows shows.]   Suggested cut ends.

(Music ends and dancers walk about. First Gentleman returns Lady Capulet to settee. Juliet and Paris walk to settee also.)

The measure done, I'll watch her place of stand,

And, touching hers, make blessèd my rude hand.
Did my heart love till now? Forswear it, sight!
For I ne'er saw true beauty till this night.
TYB: This, by his voice, should be a Montague.
(Crossing to Sampson.) Fetch me my rapier, boy.
(Sampson exits.) What dares the slave
Come hither, cover'd with an antic face,
To fleer and scorn at our solemnity?
Now, by the stock and honour of my kin,
To strike him dead I hold it not a sin.
CAP: *(Crossing to Tybalt.)* Why, how now, kinsman! wherefore storm you so?
TYB: Uncle, this is a Montague, our foe;
A villain, that is hither come in spite,
To scorn at our solemnity this night.
CAP: Young Romeo is it?
TYB: 'Tis he, that villain Romeo.
(Sampson returns with Tybalt's rapier.)
CAP: Content thee, gentle coz, let him alone,
He bears him like a portly gentleman;
And, to say truth, Verona brags of him
To be a virtuous and well-govern'd youth:
I would not for the wealth of all this town
Here in my house do him disparagement:
Therefore be patient, take no note of him:
It is my will, the which if thou respect,
Show a fair presence and put off these frowns,
An ill-beseeming semblance for a feast.
TYB: It fits, when such a villain is a guest:
I'll not endure him. *(Tybalt takes rapier from Sampson and starts after Romeo. Capulet stops him, takes rapier and hands it to Sampson, who exits with rapier. Everyone stops and watches. Juliet crosses to Capulet.)*
CAP: *(To Tybalt.)* He shall be endur'd:
What, goodman boy! I say, he shall: go to:
Am I the master here or you? go to.
You'll not endure him! God shall mend my soul!
You'll make a mutiny among my guests!
You will set cock-a-hoop! you'll be the man!
TYB: Why, uncle, 'tis a shame.
CAP: Go to, go to;
You are a saucy boy: is't so, indeed?
This trick may chance to scathe you, I know what:
You must contrary me! *(To his guests.)* Marry, 'tis
time—*(Mercutio raises his hand to lips to indicate it is time for a drink. Everyone laughs.)*

antic—absurd
fleer—sneer, solemnity—celebration
portly—dignified
goodman boy—an insulting remark
cock-a-hoop—disorder
saucy—insolent
scathe—injure

Well said, my hearts! *(To Tybalt.)* You are a princox; go: **princox**—insolent youth

(Tybalt starts to speak.) Be quiet, or— *(To Gregory.)* More light, more light! *(Gregory exits. To Tybalt.)* For shame! I'll make you quiet. *(To Old Capulet who takes Capulet away from Tybalt.)* What, cheerly, my hearts! *(Most of the guests follow Capulet offstage to another room. Juliet crosses to Tybalt.)*

TYB: [Patience perforce with wilful choler meeting   Suggested cut begins.

Makes my flesh tremble in their different greeting.]   Suggested cut ends.

I will withdraw: but this intrusion shall,

Now seeming sweet convert to bitter gall.

(Tybalt exits, leaving only Romeo, Juliet, Lady Capulet and Nurse onstage. The latter two are seated some distance away on the settee, quietly talking in pantomime and not watching Romeo and Juliet. Seeing Juliet alone, Romeo quickly moves to her. Music begins softly. Romeo removes his mask and takes her hand.)

ROM: If I profane with my unworthiest hand   Note that the line forms a

This holy shrine, the gentle fine is this;   sonnet.

My lips, two blushing pilgrims, ready stand

To smooth that rough touch with a tender kiss.

(Romeo kisses her hand.)

JUL: Good pilgrim, you do wrong your hand too much,

Which mannerly devotion shows in this;

For saints have hands that pilgrims' hands do touch   **saints**—statues of saints

(Juliet and Romeo's palms touch.)

And palm to palm is holy palmers' kiss.

ROM: Have not saints lips, and holy palmers too?

JUL: Ay, pilgrim, lips that they must use in prayer.

ROM: O, then, dear saint, let lips do what hands do;

They pray, grant thou, lest faith turn to despair.

JUL: Saints do not move, though grant for prayers' sake   **move**—take the initiative

ROM: Then move not, while my prayer's effect I take.

Thus from my lips, by yours, my sin is purg'd.   **purg'd**—cleansed away

(They kiss. Lady Capulet sees this and sends Nurse to intervene.)

JUL: Then have my lips the sin that they have took.

ROM: Sin from my lips? O trespass sweetly urg'd!

Give me my sin again. *(They kiss again.)*

JUL: You kiss by the book.   **book**—book of etiquette

(Music: Out.)

NUR: *(Approaching.)* Madam, your mother craves a word with you. *(Juliet goes to mother on settee. Romeo puts on his mask.)*

ROM: What is her mother?

NUR: Marry, bachelor,

Her mother is the lady of the house,

And a good lady, and a wise and virtuous:

I nurs'd her daughter, that you talk'd withal;

I tell you, he that can lay hold of her

Shall have the chinks. *(Nurse follows Juliet.)*   **chinks**—money

ROM: Is she a Capulet?

O, dear account: My life is my foe's debt.   **my foe's debt**—due to my foe

(Benvolio enters and crosses quickly to Romeo.)

BEN: Away, be gone; the sport is at the best.

ROM: Ay, so I fear; the more is my unrest.

(Guests enter to leave party. Mercutio joins Benvolio and others who are departing.)

CAP: *(Entering.)* Nay, gentlemen, prepare not to be gone;

We have a trifling foolish banquet towards.   **foolish**—trivial, **towards**—

  (The guests indicate that they must depart.)   ready

Is it e'en so? Why, then, I thank you all;   **Is it e'en so?**—Must you leave?

I thank you, honest gentlemen; good night.

(To servants.) More torches here!

Come on then, let's to bed.

Ah, sirrah, by my fay, it waxes late: **fay**—faith

I'll to my rest. *(Capulet and Lady Capulet exit.)*

JUL: *(To Nurse, pointing to Second Gentleman.)*

Come hither, Nurse. What is yond gentleman?

NUR: The son and heir of old Tiberio.

JUL: *(Pointing to First Gentleman.)*

What's he that now is going out of door?

NUR: Marry, that, I think, be young Petruchio.

(Romeo is moving slowly to the exit.)

JUL: What's he that follows there, that would not dance?

NUR: I know not.

JUL: Go ask his name. If he be married,

My grave is like to be my wedding bed.

NUR: *(Not moving; she knows who he is.)*

His name is Romeo, and a Montague,

The only son of your great enemy.

(Nurse crosses to watch departing guests.)

JUL: My only love sprung from my only hate!

Too early seen unknown, and known too late!

Prodigious birth of love it is to me,   **prodigious**—portentous

That I must love a loathèd enemy.

NUR: *(Returning.)* What's this? What's this?

JUL: A rhyme I learn'd even now

Of one I danc'd withal.

L.CAP: *(Offstage.)* Juliet!

NUR: Anon, anon!   **anon**—right away

Come, let's away; the strangers all are gone.

(They exit as stage lights fade out quickly.)

ACT II PROLOGUE

[(Chorus enters in spotlight.)

Suggested cut begins. Note that the lines form a sonnet.

CHO: Now old desire doth in his death-bed lie,
And young affection gapes to be his heir;
That fair for which love groan'd for and would die,
With tender Juliet match'd, is now not fair.
Now Romeo is belov'd and loves again,
Alike bewitchèd by the charm of looks,
But to his foe suppos'd he must complain,
And she steal love's sweet bait from fearful hooks:
Being held a foe, he may not have access
To breathe such vows as lovers use to swear;
And she as much in love, her means much less
To meet her new beloved any where:
But passion lends them power, time means, to meet,
Tempering extremities with extreme sweet.

old desire—i.e., Rosaline

(Blackout as Chorus exits.)]

Suggested cut ends.

ACT II, SCENE 1

(Set: Capulet's orchard. Juliet's balcony and a garden bench are onstage. Time: Later on Sunday night. As the stage lights come up, the Nurse is heard calling from offstage balcony, "Juliet." Offstage on the opposite side, Benvolio and Mercutio are yelling "Romeo." Enter Romeo.)

ROM: Can I go forward when my heart is here?
Turn back, dull earth, and find thy centre out.
(Romeo runs off away from Benvolio and Mercutio.)
BEN: *(Calling as he and Mercutio enter.)* Romeo!
My cousin Romeo!
MER: He is wise;
And, on my life, hath stol'n him home to bed.
BEN: He ran this way, [and leap'd this orchard wall:]
Call, good Mercutio.
MER: Nay, I'll conjure too.
Romeo! Humours! Madman! Passion! Lover!
[Appear thou in the likeness of a sigh:
Speak but one rhyme, and I am satisfi'd;
Cry but "Ay me!" pronounce but "love" and "dove";
Speak to my gossip Venus one fair word,

dull earth—Romeo, **centre**—Juliet

Suggested cut begins and ends.

conjure—call up a spirit

Suggested cut begins.

gossip—intimate friend

One nick-name for her purblind son and heir,
Young Adam Cupid, he that shot so trim
When King Cophetua lov'd the beggar-maid!]
(*Mercutio looks left and right.*)
He heareth not, he stirreth not, he moveth not;
The ape is dead, and I must conjure him.
I conjure thee by Rosaline's bright eyes,
By her high forehead and her scarlet lip,
By her fine foot, straight leg and quivering thigh,
And the demesnes that there adjacent lie,
That in thy likeness thou appear to us!
[BEN: And if he hear thee, thou wilt anger him.
MER: This cannot anger him: 'twould anger him
To raise a spirit in his mistress' circle
Of some strange nature, letting it there stand
Till she had laid it and conjur'd it down;
That were some spite: my invocation
Is fair and honest, and in his mistress' name
I conjure only but to raise up him.]
BEN: Come, he hath hid himself among these trees,
To be consorted with the humorous night:
Blind is his love and best befits the dark.
MER: If love be blind, love cannot hit the mark.
[Now will he sit under a medlar tree,

And wish his mistress were that kind of fruit
As maids call medlars when they laugh alone.
O, Romeo, that she were, O, that she were
An open-arse, thou a poperin pear!]

Romeo, good night: I'll to my truckle-bed;
This field-bed is too cold for me to sleep:
Come, shall we go?
BEN: Go then, for 'tis in vain
To seek him here that means not to be found.
(*They exit and we are in Scene 2 immediately.*)

ACT II, SCENE 2

(*Romeo enters.*)
ROM: He jests at scars that never felt a wound.
(*Juliet appears at her balcony window.*)
But, soft! What light through yonder window breaks?

purblind—very blind
trim—strongly
Suggested cut ends.

demesnes—regions

Suggested cut begins.

spite—annoyance

Suggested cut ends.

consorted with—an associate of

Suggested cut begins.
medlar—fruit resembling female genitalia

poperin pear—male genitals
Suggested cut ends.

field-bed—the ground

He—i.e., Mercutio

It is the east, and Juliet is the sun!

Arise, fair sun, and kill the envious moon,

Who is already sick and pale with grief,

That thou her maid are far more fair than she:

Be not her maid, since she is envious;

Her vestal livery is but sick and green   **vestal livery**—virgin's costume

And none but fools do wear it; cast it off.

(Juliet comes out on the balcony.)

It is my lady; O, it is my love!

O, that she knew she were!

(Juliet sighs, then whispers, "Romeo.")

She speaks,—yet she says nothing: what of that?

Her eye discourses; I will answer it.

I am too bold, 'tis not to me she speaks:

Two of the fairest stars in all the heaven,

Having some business, do entreat her eyes

To twinkle in their spheres till they return.

[What if her eyes were there, they in her head?   Suggested cut begins.

The brightness of her cheek would shame those stars,

As daylight doth a lamp; her eyes in heaven

Would through the airy region stream so bright

That birds would sing and think it were not night.]   Suggested cut ends.

(Juliet leans her cheek upon her hand.)

See, how she leans her cheek upon her hand!

O, that I were a glove upon that hand,

That I might touch that cheek!

JUL: Ay me!

ROM: She speaks:

O, speak again, bright angel! for thou art

As glorious to this night, being o'er my head,

As is a wingèd messenger of heaven

Unto the white-upturnèd wondering eyes

Of mortals that fall back to gaze on him,

When he bestrides the lazy-pacing clouds

And sails upon the bosom of the air.

JUL: O Romeo, Romeo! wherefore art thou Romeo?   **wherefore**—why

Deny thy father and refuse thy name;

Or, if thou wilt not, be but sworn my love,

And I'll no longer be a Capulet.

ROM: *(Aside.)* Shall I hear more, or shall I speak at this?

JUL: 'Tis but thy name that is my enemy;

Thou art thyself, though not a Montague.

What's Montague? It is nor hand, nor foot,

Nor arm, nor face, nor any other part
Belonging to a man. O, be some other name!
What's in a name? That which we call a rose
By any other name would smell as sweet;
So Romeo would, were he not Romeo call'd,
Retain that dear perfection which he owes   **owes**—possesses
Without that title. Romeo, doff thy name,   **doff**—get rid of
And for that name, which is no part of thee,
Take all myself.

ROM: *(Stepping forward.)* I take thee at thy word:
(Juliet draws back.)
Call me but love, and I'll be new baptiz'd;
Henceforth I never will be Romeo.

JUL: What man art thou, that, thus bescreen'd in night,
So stumblest on my counsel?   **counsel**—intimate thoughts

ROM: By a name
I know not how to tell thee who I am:
My name, dear saint, is hateful to myself,
Because it is an enemy to thee;
Had I it written, I would tear the word.

JUL: My ears have not yet drunk a hundred words
Of that tongue's utterance, yet I know the sound:
Art thou not Romeo, and—a Montague?

ROM: Neither, fair saint, if either thee dislike.

JUL: How camest thou hither, tell me, and wherefore?
The orchard walls are high and hard to climb,
And the place death, considering who thou art,
If any of my kinsmen find thee here.

ROM: With love's light wings did I o'er-perch these walls,   **o'er-perch**—overcome
For stony limits cannot hold love out,
And what love can do, that dares love attempt;
Therefore thy kinsmen are no let to me.   **let**—hindrance

JUL: If they do see thee, they will murder thee.

ROM: Alack, there lies more peril in thine eye
Than twenty of their swords: look thou but sweet,
And I am proof against their enmity.   **proof**—protected

JUL: I would not for the world they saw thee here.

ROM: I have night's cloak to hide me from their sight;
And but thou love me, let them find me here:
My life were better ended by their hate,
Than death proroguèd, wanting of thy love.   **proroguèd**—postponed

JUL: By whose direction found'st thou out this place?

ROM: By love, who first did prompt me to inquire;

He lent me counsel, and I lent him eyes.
[I am no pilot; yet, wert thou as far

Suggested cut begins.

As that vast shore wash'd with the farthest sea,
I would adventure for such merchandise.]

Suggested cut ends.

JUL: Thou know'st the mask of night is on my face,
Else would a maiden blush bepaint my cheek
For that which thou hast heard me speak tonight.
Fain would I dwell on form, fain, fain deny
What I have spoke: but farewell compliment!

fain—gladly
compliment—ceremony

Dost thou love me? I know thou wilt say "Ay,"
And I will take thy word: yet, if thou swear'st,
Thou mayst prove false; at lovers' perjuries,
They say, Jove laughs. O gentle Romeo,
If thou dost love, pronounce it faithfully:
Or if thou think'st I am too quickly won,
I'll frown and be perverse and say thee nay,
So thou wilt woo; but else, not for the world.
In truth, fair Montague, I am too fond,

fond—foolish

And therefore thou mayst think my 'haviour light:
But trust me, gentleman, I'll prove more true
Than those that have more cunning to be strange.

strange—reserved

I should have been more strange, I must confess,
But that thou overheard'st, ere I was ware,
My true love's passion; therefore pardon me,
And not impute this yielding to light love,
Which the dark night hath so discovered.
ROM: Lady, by yonder blessed moon I swear,
That tips with silver all these fruit-tree tops—
JUL: O, swear not by the moon, the inconstant moon,
That monthly changes in her circled orb,
Lest that thy love prove likewise variable.
ROM: What shall I swear by?
(Romeo starts to climb up to balcony.)
JUL: Do not swear at all;
Or, if thou wilt, swear by thy gracious self,
Which is the god of my idolatry,
And I'll believe thee.
ROM: If my heart's dear love—
(They kiss.)
JUL: Well, do not swear: although I joy in thee,
I have no joy of this contract tonight:

contract—betrothal

It is too rash, too unadvised, too sudden,
Too like the lightning, which doth cease to be

Ere one can say "It lightens." Sweet, good night!
This bud of love, by summer's ripening breath,
May prove a beauteous flower when next we meet.
Good night, good night! As sweet repose and rest
Come to thy heart as that within my breast!
(Juliet starts to leave.)
ROM: O, wilt thou leave me so unsatisfied?
JUL: What satisfaction canst thou have tonight?
ROM: The exchange of thy love's faithful vow for mine.
JUL: I gave thee mine before thou didst request it:
And yet I would it were to give again.
ROM: Wouldst thou withdraw it? for what purpose, love?
JUL: But to be frank, and give it thee again.
(They kiss again.)
And yet I wish but for the thing I have:
My bounty is as boundless as the sea,
My love as deep; the more I give to thee,
The more I have, for both are infinite.
(Offstage the Nurse calls, "Juliet!")
I hear some noise within; dear love, adieu!
Anon, good Nurse! Sweet Montague, be true.
Stay but a little, I will come again.
(Juliet exits into her home.)
ROM: O blessèd, blessèd night! I am afeard,
Being in night, all this is but a dream,
Too flattering-sweet to be substantial.
(Juliet returns.)
JUL: Three words, dear Romeo, and good night indeed.
If that thy bent of love be honourable,
(Romeo enthusiastically nods "Yes.")
Thy purpose marriage, send me word tomorrow,
By one that I'll procure to come to thee,
Where and what time thou wilt perform the rite,
And all my fortunes at thy foot I'll lay,
And follow thee my lord throughout the world.
NUR: *(Within.)* Madam!
JUL: I come, anon—But if thou mean'st not well,
I do beseech thee—
NUR: *(Within.)* Madam!
JUL: By and by, I come:—   **By and by**—at once
To cease thy suit, and leave me to my grief:
Tomorrow will I send.
ROM: So thrive my soul—

JUL: A thousand times good night!

(Juliet exits into her home.)

ROM: A thousand times the worse, to want thy light.

Love goes toward love, as schoolboys from their books,

But love from love, toward school with heavy looks.

(He returns to the ground. Juliet enters the balcony.)

JUL: Hist!—Romeo,—hist! [O, for a falconer's voice.—

To lure this tassel-gentle back again!

Bondage is hoarse, and may not speak aloud;

Else would I tear the cave where Echo lies,

And make her airy tongue more hoarse than mine,

With repetition of my Romeo's name.]

ROM: It is my soul that calls upon my name:

How silver-sweet sound lovers' tongues by night,

Like softest music to attending ears!

JUL: Romeo!

ROM: My dear?

JUL: At what o'clock tomorrow

Shall I send to thee?

ROM: At the hour of nine.

JUL: I will not fail: 'tis twenty years till then.

I have forgot why I did call thee back.

ROM: Let me stand here till thou remember it.

JUL: I shall forget, to have thee still stand there,

Remembering how I love thy company.

ROM: And I'll still stay, to have thee still forget,

Forgetting any other home but this.

(Romeo climbs up again to the balcony.)

JUL: 'Tis almost morning; I would have thee gone:

[And yet no further than a wanton's bird,

Who lets it hop a little from her hand,

Like a poor prisoner in his twisted gyves

And with a silk thread plucks it back again,

So loving-jealous of his liberty.

ROM: I would I were thy bird.

JUL: Sweet, so would I:

Yet I should kill thee with much cherishing.]

Good night, good night! *(They kiss.)* Parting is such sweet sorrow

That I shall say good night till it be morrow.

ROM: Sleep dwell upon thine eyes, peace in thy breast!

Would I were sleep and peace, so sweet to rest!

(Juliet exits. Romeo returns to ground.)

Hence will I to my ghostly father's cell,

Suggested cut begins.

tassel-gentle—male hawk

Suggested cut ends.

Suggested cut begins.

gyves—shackles

Sugested cut ends.

ghostly—spiritual

His help to crave, and my dear hap to tell.   **hap**—fortune
(Romeo exits as stage lights fade out quickly.)

ACT II, SCENE 3

(Sound in blackout: Distant clock strikes four. Set: Outside Friar Laurence's cell. Large standing cross is onstage. Time: 4 A.M., Monday. Stage lights up as Friar Laurence enters with a basket of flowers and herbs.)

FR.L: The grey-eyèd morn smiles on the frowning night,
Chequering the eastern clouds with streaks of light,   **chequering**—variegating
[And fleckèd darkness like a drunkard reels   Suggested cut begins.
                                                             fleckèd—dappled

From forth day's path and Titan's fiery wheels:]   Suggested cut ends.
Now, ere the sun advance his burning eye,
The day to cheer and night's dank dew to dry,
I must up-fill this osier cage of ours   **osier cage**—wicker basket
With baleful weeds and precious-juicèd flowers.   **baleful**—full of evil
[The earth that's nature's mother is her tomb;   Suggested cut begins.
What is her burying grave that is her womb,
And from her womb children of divers kind
We sucking on her natural bosom find,
Many for many virtues excellent,
None but for some and yet all different.]   Suggested cut ends.
O, mickle is the powerful grace that lies   **mickle**—much
In herbs, plants, stones, and their true qualities:
[For nought so vile that on the earth doth live   Suggested cut begins.
But to the earth some special good doth give,
Nor aught so good but strain'd from that fair use
Revolts from true birth, stumbling on abuse:
Virtue itself turns vice, being misapplied;
And vice sometimes by action dignified.]   Suggested cut ends.
(Looking at small flower.)
Within the infant rind of this small flower
Poison hath residence and medicine power:
For this, being smelt, with that part cheers each part;
Being tasted, slays all senses with the heart.
[Two such opposèd kings encamp them still   Suggested cut begins.
In man as well as herbs, grace and rude will;
And where the worser is predominant,
Full soon the canker death eats up that plant.]   Suggested cut ends.
(Enter Romeo.)
ROM: Good morrow, father. *(He kneels.)*

FR.L: Benedicite!   **Benedicite**—blessing be upon

(Romeo rises.)   you

What early tongue so sweet saluteth me?

Young son, it argues a distemper'd head   **distemper'd**—diseased

So soon to bid good morrow to thy bed:

[Care keeps his watch in every old man's eye,   Suggested cut begins.

And where care lodges, sleep will never lie;

But where unbruisèd youth with unstuff'd brain

Doth couch his limbs, there golden sleep doth reign:

Therefore thy earliness doth me assure

Thou art up-roused by some distemperature;]   Suggested cut ends.

Or if not so, then here I hit it right,

Our Romeo hath not been in bed tonight.

ROM: That last is true; the sweeter rest was mine.

FR.L: God pardon sin! wast thou with Rosaline?

ROM: With Rosaline, my ghostly father? no;

I have forgot that name, and that name's woe.

FR.L: That's my good son: but where hast thou been, then?

ROM: *(Happily.)* I'll tell thee, ere thou ask it me again.

I have been feasting with mine enemy,

Where on a sudden one hath wounded me,

That's by me wounded: both our remedies

Within thy help and holy physic lies: **physic**—art of healing

[I bear no hatred, blessed man, for, lo,   Suggested cut begins.

My intercession likewise steads my foe.]   Suggested cut ends.

FR.L: Be plain, good son, and homely in thy drift;   **drift**—meaning

Riddling confession finds but riddling shrift.   **riddling**—uncertain

                                                                                    shrift—absolution

ROM: Then plainly know my heart's dear love is set

On the fair daughter of rich Capulet:

As mine on hers, so hers is set on mine;

And all combined, save what thou must combine

By holy marriage: when and where and how

We met, we woo'd and made exchange of vow,

I'll tell thee as we pass; but this I pray,   **pass**—go along

That thou consent to marry us today.

FR.L: *(Kindly.)* Holy Saint Francis, what a change is here!

Is Rosaline, whom thou didst love so dear,

So soon forsaken? young men's love then lies

Not truly in their hearts, but in their eyes.

Jesu Maria, what a deal of brine

Hath wash'd thy sallow cheeks for Rosaline!

[How much salt water thrown away in waste,   Suggested cut begins.

To season love, that of it doth not taste!
The sun not yet thy sighs from heaven clears,
Thy old groans ring yet in my ancient ears;
Lo, here upon thy cheek the stain doth sit
Of an old tear that is not wash'd off yet:
If e'er thou wast thyself and these woes thine,
Thou and these woes were all for Rosaline:
And art thou changed? pronounce this sentence then,
Women may fall, when there's no strength in men.] *Suggested cut ends.*
ROM: Thou chid'st me oft for loving Rosaline.
FR.L: For doting, not for loving, pupil mine.
[ROM: And bad'st me bury love. *Suggested cut begins.*
FR.L: Not in a grave,
To lay one in, another out to have.] *Suggested cut ends.*
ROM: I pray thee, chide not; she whom I love now
Doth grace for grace and love for love allow;
The other did not so.
FR.L: O, she knew well
Thy love did read by rote and could not spell. **rote**—memorized repetition
But come, young waverer, come, go with me,
(Starts walking offstage with Romeo.)
In one respect I'll thy assistant be;
For this alliance may so happy prove,
To turn your households' rancour to pure love.
ROM: *(Eager to leave.)* O, let us hence; I stand on sudden haste. **stand**—insist
FR.L: *(Pulling Romeo back.)* Wisely and slow; they stumble that run fast.
(They exit as lights fade out.)

ACT II, SCENE 4

(Set: Same as Act I, Scene 4, a street in Verona. Time: Shortly before noon, Monday. Lights come up as Mercutio, with a flower behind his ear, enters followed by Benvolio.)
MER: Where the devil should this Romeo be?
Came he not home tonight?
BEN: Not to his father's; I spoke with his man.
MER: Ah, that same pale hard-hearted wench, that Rosaline,
Torments him so, that he will sure run mad.
BEN: Tybalt, the kinsman of old Capulet,
Hath sent a letter to his father's house.
MER: A challenge, on my life.
BEN: Romeo will answer it.
[MER: Any man that can write may answer a letter. *Suggested cut begins.*
BEN: Nay, he will answer the letter's master, how he dares, being dared.] *Sugested cut ends.*

MER: *(Laughing.)* Alas poor Romeo! he is
already dead; stabbed with a white wench's
black eye; shot through the ear with a
love-song; the very pin of his heart cleft
with the blind bow-boy's butt-shaft: and

pin—center of target
bow-boy's—Cupid's, **butt-shaft**—arrow for shooting at butts

is he a man to encounter Tybalt?
BEN: Why, what is Tybalt?
MER: More than prince of cats, I can tell

prince of cats—refers to Tibert,
prince of cats in Reynard the Fox

you. O, he is the courageous captain of
compliments. He fights as you sing prick-song,
[keeps time, distance, and proportion; rests
me his minim rest, one, two, and the third in
your bosom: the very butcher of a silk button,]
a duellist, a duellist; a gentleman of the
very first house, of the first and second

prick-song—printed music
Suggested cut begins.
minim rest—rest equal to half-note. Suggested cut ends.

cause: ah, the immortal passado!
(He demonstrates these with his sword.)
the punto reverso! the hai!

first and second cause—rules
of dueling
passado—forward thrust with
sword
punto reverso—backhanded
stroke, hai—thrust home

BEN: The what?
MER: The pox of such antic, lisping, affecting
fantasticoes; these new tuners of accents!
"By Jesu, a very good blade! A very tall man!
a very good whore!" Why, is not this a
lamentable thing, grandsire, that we should be
thus afflicted with these strange flies,
these fashion-mongers, these perdona-mi's,

antic—absurd
fantasticoes—affected fellows

strange flies—parasites
perdona-mi's—affected
speakers of foreign words
stand—insist

who stand so much on the new form, that they
cannot sit at ease on the old bench? O,
their bones, their bones!
(Enter Romeo, who appears thoughtful.)
BEN: Here comes Romeo, here comes Romeo.
MER: [Without his roe, like a dried herring:
O flesh, flesh, how art thou fishified!
Now is he for the numbers that Petrarch

bones—pun on French *bon* and
English *bone*

Suggested cut begins.

Petrarch—fourteenth-century
Italian poet
Laura—love of Petrarch

flowed in: Laura to his lady was but a
kitchen-wench; marry, she had a better love
to be-rhyme her; Dido a dowdy; Cleopatra a

Dido—queen of Carthage

gipsy; Helen and Hero hildings and harlots;

Thisbe a grey eye or so, but not to the

purpose.] Signior Romeo, bon jour! there's

a French salutation to your French slop.

You gave us the counterfeit fairly last night.

ROM: Good morrow to you both. What counterfeit did I give you?

MER: The slip, sir, the slip; can you not conceive?

ROM: Pardon, good Mercutio, my business was great; and in such a case as mine a man may strain courtesy.

MER: That's as much as to say, such a case as yours constrains a man to bow in the hams.

ROM: Meaning, to court'sy.

MER: Thou hast most kindly hit it.

ROM: A most courteous exposition.

MER: Nay, I am the very pink of courtesy.

ROM: *(Taking flower from behind Mercutio's ear.)* Pink for flower.

MER: Right.

ROM: *(Putting flower on his shoe.)* Why, then is my pump well flowered.

MER: Well said: follow me this jest now till thou hast worn out thy pump, that when the single sole of it is worn, the jest may remain after the wearing sole singular.

ROM: O single-soled jest, solely singular for the singleness.

MER: Come between us, good Benvolio; my wits faint.

[ROM: Switch and spurs, switch and spurs; or I'll cry a match.

MER: Nay, if thy wits run the wild-goose chase, I have done, for thou hast more of the wild-goose in one of thy wits than, I am sure, I have in my whole five: was I with you there for the goose?

ROM: Thou wast never with me for any thing when thou wast not there for the goose.

MER: I will bite thee by the ear for that jest.

ROM: Nay, good goose, bite not.

MER: Thy wit is a very bitter sweeting; it is a most sharp sauce.

ROM: And is it not well served in to a sweet goose?

MER: O here's a wit of cheveril, that stretches from an inch narrow to an ell broad!

ROM: I stretch it out for that word "broad;" which added to the goose, proves thee far and wide a broad goose.

MER: Why, is not this better now than groaning for love? now art thou sociable, now art thou Romeo; now art thou what thou art, by art as well as by nature: for this drivelling love is like a great natural, that runs lolling up and down to hide his bauble in a hole.

hildings—worthless women

Thisbe—beloved by Pyramus

Suggested cut ends.

slop—loosely-cut trousers

counterfeit—name for counterfeit coin was *slip*

hams—hips

court'sy—bow

pink—perfection

pump—shoe

single-soled—contemptible

singleness—silliness

Suggested cut begins.

cry a match—claim victory

cheveril—kid leather, ell—45 inches

natural—idiot, bauble—jester's stick

BEN: Stop there, stop there.

MER: Thou desirest me to stop in my tale against the hair.

BEN: Thou wouldst else have made thy tale large.

MER: O, thou art deceived; I would have made it short: for I was come to the whole depth of my tale; and meant, indeed, to occupy the argument no longer.]

ROM: Here's goodly gear!

(Enter the Nurse and Peter. Her veil is billowing out in back of her. Peter carries two shopping bags and her fan.)

MER: A sail, a sail!

BEN: Two, two; a shirt and a smock.

NUR: Peter!

PET: Anon!

NUR: My fan, Peter.

MER: Good Peter, to hide her face; for her fan's the fairer face.

NUR: God ye good morrow, gentlemen.

MER: God ye good den, fair gentlewoman.

NUR: [Is it good den?

MER: 'Tis no less, I tell you, for the bawdy hand of the dial is now upon the prick of noon.

NUR: Out upon you! what a man are you!

ROM: One, gentlewoman, that God hath made for himself to mar.

NUR: By my troth, it is well said; "for himself to mar," quoth a'?]
Gentlemen, can any of you tell me where I may find the young Romeo?

ROM: I can tell you; but young Romeo will be older when you have found him than he was when you sought him: I am the youngest of that name, for fault of a worse.

NUR: You say well.

MER: Yea, is the worst well? very well took, i' faith; wisely, wisely.

NUR: If you be he, sir, I desire some confidence with you.

(All laugh at her misuse of a word.)

BEN: She will indite him to some supper.

MER: A bawd, a bawd, a bawd! So ho!

ROM: What hast thou found?

MER: No hare, sir; unless a hare, sir, in a
lenten pie, that is something stale and
hoar ere it be spent. *(Sings as he turns the
Nurse around.)*

An old hare hoar,
And an old hare hoar,
Is very good meat in Lent
But a hare that is hoar

---

against the hair—against the grain

large—licentious

Suggested cut ends.

gear—matter

shirt—Peter's garb

smock—Nurse's garment

God ye good morrow—God give you good morning

good den—good evening

Suggested cut begins.

prick—point

Suggested cut ends.

fault—for lack of

took—handled

confidence—she means *conference*

indite—he jokingly misuses the word

So ho—hunter's cry

hare—slang for *harlot*

lenten—meatless

hoar—moldy, punning on *whore*

Is too much for a score,

When it hoars ere it be spent.

Romeo, will you come to your father's? We'll to dinner, thither.

ROM: I will follow you.

MER: Farewell, ancient lady; farewell,

(Singing and bowing.)"lady, lady, lady."

(Exit Mercutio followed by Benvolio.)

NUR: Marry, farewell! I pray you, sir, what saucy merchant was this, that was so full of his ropery?

ROM: A gentleman, nurse, that loves to hear himself talk, and will speak more in a minute than he will stand to in a month.

NUR: *(Very agitated.)* An a' speak any thing against me, I'll take him down, an a' were lustier than he is, and twenty such Jacks; and if I cannot, I'll find those that shall. Scurvy knave! I am none of his flirt-gills; I am none of his skains-mates.

(To Peter.) And thou must stand by too and suffer every knave to use me at his pleasure?

PET: I saw no man use you at his pleasure; if I had, my weapon should quickly have been out, I warrant you: I dare draw as soon as another man, if I see occasion in a good quarrel, and the law on my side.

NUR: Now, afore God, I am so vexed, that every part about me quivers. Scurvy knave! *(To Romeo.)* Pray you, sir, a word: and as I told you, my young lady bade me inquire you out; what she bade me say, I will keep to myself: but first let me tell ye, if ye should lead her into a fool's paradise, as they say, it were a very gross kind of behavior, as they say: for the gentlewoman is young; and, therefore, if you should deal double with her, truly it were an ill thing to be offered to any gentlewoman, and very weak dealing.

ROM: *(Kindly.)* Nurse, commend me to thy lady and mistress. I protest unto thee—

NUR: *(Relieved.)* Good heart, and, i' faith, I will tell her as much: Lord, Lord, she will be a joyful woman. *(She is crying.)*

ROM: What wilt thou tell her, Nurse? thou dost not mark me.

NUR: I will tell her, sir, that you do protest; which, as I take it, is a gentlemanlike offer.

ROM: Bid her devise

Some means to come to shrift this afternoon;

And there she shall at Friar Laurence' cell

Be shrived and married. Here is for thy pains.

(He offers her money.)

NUR: No truly sir; not a penny.

ROM: Go to; I say you shall.

(She takes a coin.)

NUR: This afternoon, sir? well, she shall be there.

ROM: And stay, good nurse, behind the abbey wall:

Within this hour my man shall be with thee

And bring thee cords made like a tackled stair;

Which to the high top-gallant of my joy

---

for a score—to pay for

ropery—her error for roguery

stand to—abide by

Jacks—peasants from France

flirt-gills—prostitutes

skains-mates—cut-throat companions

protest—vow

mark—pay attention to

shrift—confession

tackled stair—rope ladder

top-gallant—summit

Must be my convoy in the secret night.

Farewell; be trusty, and I'll quit thy pains:

Farewell; commend me to thy mistress.

(Romeo starts to leave.)

NUR: Now God in heaven bless thee! Hark you, sir.

ROM: What say'st thou, my dear Nurse?

NUR: Is your man secret? Did you ne'er hear say,

Two may keep counsel, putting one away?

ROM: I warrant thee, my man's as true as steel.

NUR: Well, sir; my mistress is the sweetest

lady—Lord, Lord! when 'twas a little prating

thing:—O, there is a nobleman in town, one

Paris, that would fain lay knife aboard; but

she, good soul, had as lief see a toad, a very

toad, as see him. I anger her sometimes and

tell her that Paris is the properer man; but,

I'll warrant you, when I say so, she looks as

pale as any clout in the versal world.

[Doth not rosemary and Romeo begin both with a letter?

ROM: Ay, Nurse; what of that? both with an R.

NUR: Ah, mocker! that's the dog's name; R is

for the—No; I know it begins with some other

letter:—and she hath the prettiest

sententious of it, of you and rosemary, that

it would do you good to hear it.]

ROM: Commend me to thy lady.

NUR: Ay, a thousand times.

(Romeo exits.) Peter!

PET: Anon! *(He crosses to her.)*

NUR: Peter, take my fan, and go before and apace.

(They exit as stage lights fade out.)

convoy—conveyance

quit—reward

fain—gladly

lay knife aboard—lay claim

properer—handsomer

clout—cloth, **versal**—universal
Suggested cut begins.

sententious—her mistake for
sentences. Suggested cut ends.

ACT II, SCENE 5

(Set: Capulet's orchard, same as Act II, Scenes 1 and 2. A bench is onstage. Time: A little after noon on Monday. As lights come up, Juliet enters, anxious and impatient.)

JUL: The clock struck nine when I did send the Nurse;

In half an hour she promised to return.

Perchance she cannot meet him: that's not so.

O, she is lame! love's heralds should be thoughts,

Which ten times faster glide than the sun's beams,
[Driving back shadows over louring hills:

Therefore do nimble-pinion'd doves draw love,
And therefore hath the wind-swift Cupid wings.]
Now is the sun upon the highmost hill
Of this day's journey, and from nine till twelve
Is three long hours, yet she is not come.
Had she affections and warm youthful blood,
She would be as swift in motion as a ball;
My words would bandy her to my sweet love,
And his to me:
But old folks, many feign as they were dead;
Unwieldy, slow, heavy and pale as lead.
(Enter Nurse, with shopping bag, and Peter,
with shopping bag and fan.)
O God, she comes! O honey Nurse, what news?
Hast thou met with him? Send thy man away.
NUR: Peter, stay at the gate.
(Peter gives fan to Nurse and exits with bags.
Nurse sits on bench.)
JUL: Now, good sweet Nurse,—O Lord, why look'st thou sad?
Though news be sad, yet tell them merrily;
If good, thou shamest the music of sweet news
By playing it to me with so sour a face.
NUR: I am a-weary, give me leave awhile:
Fie, how my bones ache! what a jaunt have I had!
JUL: I would thou hadst my bones, and I thy news:
Nay, come, I pray thee, speak; good, good Nurse, speak. *(Juliet sits by Nurse.)*
NUR: Jesu, what haste? can you not stay awhile?
Do you not see that I am out of breath?
JUL: How art thou out of breath, when thou hast breath
To say to me that thou art out of breath?
The excuse that thou dost make in this delay
Is longer than the tale thou dost excuse.
Is thy news good, or bad? answer to that;
Say either, and I'll stay the circumstance:
Let me be satisfied, is't good or bad?
NUR: Well, you have made a simple choice; you know not how to choose a man: Romeo!
no, not he; though his face be better than any man's, yet his leg excels all men's; and
for a hand, and a foot, and a body, though they be not to be talked on, yet they are
past compare: he is not the flower of courtesy, but, I'll warrant him, as gentle as a lamb.
Go thy ways, wench; serve God. What, have you dined at home?

Suggested cut begins.
louring—dark

Suggested cut ends.

bandy—volley

stay the circumstance—wait
for details

JUL: *(Rises.)* No, no: but all this did I know before.

What says he of our marriage? what of that?

NUR: Lord, how my head aches! what a head have I!

(From behind the bench, Juliet massages the Nurse's forehead.)

It beats as it would fall in twenty pieces.

My back o' t' other side,—O, my back, my back!

(Juliet rubs one side of her back, then moves to the other side.)

Beshrew your heart for sending me about,   **beshrew**—shame upon

To catch my death with jaunting up and down!

JUL: I' faith, I am sorry that thou art not well.

(Juliet puts her arms around the Nurse.)

Sweet, sweet, sweet nurse, tell me, what says my love?

NUR: Your love says, like an honest gentleman, and a courteous, and a kind, and a

handsome, and, I warrant, a virtuous,—Where is your mother?

JUL: Where is my mother! why, she is within;

Where should she be? How oddly thou repliest!

"Your love says, like an honest gentleman,

Where is your mother?"

NUR: *(Rising, sharply.)* O God's lady dear!

Are you so hot? marry, come up, I trow;   **trow**—believe

Is this the poultice for my aching bones?

Henceforward do your messages yourself.

JUL: Here's such a coil! *(Demanding an answer.)* Come, what says Romeo?   **coil**—fuss

NUR: *(Kindly)* Have you got leave to go to shrift today?

JUL: I have.

NUR: Then hie you hence to Friar Laurence' cell;   **hie**—hurry

There stays a husband to make you a wife:

Now comes the wanton blood up in your cheeks,

They'll be in scarlet straight at any news.

Hie you to church; I must another way,

To fetch a ladder, by the which your love

Must climb a bird's nest soon when it is dark:

I am the drudge and toil in your delight,

But you shall bear the burden soon at night.

Go; I'll to dinner: hie you to the cell.

JUL: Hie to high fortune! Honest Nurse, farewell.

(Juliet exits as Nurse watches happily. Stage lights fade out.)

ACT II, SCENE 6

(Set: Outside Friar Laurence's cell, same set as Act II, Scene 3. Large cross is onstage. Time: 1 P.M., Monday. Stage lights up as Friar Laurence and Romeo enter.)

FR.L: So smile the heavens upon this holy act,

That after hours with sorrow chide us not!

ROM: Amen, amen! but come what sorrow can,

It cannot countervail the exchange of joy

That one short minute gives me in her sight:

Do thou but close our hands with holy words,

Then love-devouring death do what he dare;

It is enough I may but call her mine.

FR.L: These violent delights have violent ends

And in their triumph die, like fire and powder,

Which as they kiss consume: the sweetest honey

Is loathsome in his own deliciousness

And in the taste confounds the appetite:

Therefore love moderately; long love doth so;

Too swift arrives as tardy as too slow.

(Juliet enters, breathless, happy. Romeo rushes

to embrace her but Friar Laurence steps between them.)

Here comes the lady: [O, so light a foot

Will ne'er wear out the everlasting flint:

A lover may bestride the gossamer

That idles in the wanton summer air,

And yet not fall; so light is vanity.]

JUL: *(Kneeling.)* Good even to my ghostly confessor.

FR.L: Romeo shall thank thee, daughter, for us both.

JUL: *(Rising.)* As much to him, else is his thanks too much.

ROM: Ah, Juliet, if the measure of thy joy

Be heap'd like mine and that thy skill be more

To blazon it, then sweeten with thy breath

This neighbour air, and let rich music's tongue

Unfold the imagined happiness that both

Receive in either by this dear encounter.

(Friar Laurence is still between them.)

JUL: Conceit, more rich in matter than in words,

Brags of his substance, not of ornament:

They are but beggars that can count their worth;

But my true love is grown to such excess

I cannot sum up sum of half my wealth.

FR.L: Come, come with me, and we will make short work;

(He has Romeo on one side and Juliet on the other as they start to exit.)

For, by your leaves, you shall not stay alone

Till holy church incorporate two in one.

(The three move to cross where Romeo and Juliet kneel to Friar Laurence. Music of about twenty

seconds begins as they start to move. Fade out lights so that they are out by the end of the music.)

Intermission: Ten Minutes

countervail—equal

his—its

confounds—destroys

tardy—ineffectual

Suggested cut begins.

gossamer—spiders' webs

Suggested cut ends.

ghostly—spiritual

blazon—proclaim

conceit—imagination

sum up—add

ACT III, SCENE 1

(On stage manager's cue, start music, which lasts one minute. At thirty seconds, start fading out houselights. By sixty seconds there should be a blackout. Immediately bring up stage lights. It is a hot afternoon. Set: Same as Act I Prologue, a street in Verona with fountain onstage. Time: Later, Monday afternoon. As lights come up, Peter and Sampson, carrying shopping bags, cross stage and exit. Mercutio and Benvolio enter with Abraham following. Mercutio crosses to fountain where he dips his handkerchief into water and wipes his face and neck.)

BEN: I pray thee, good Mercutio, let's retire:
The day is hot, the Capulets abroad,
And, if we meet, we shall not 'scape a brawl;
For now, these hot days, is the mad blood stirring. *(Benvolio sits at fountain.)*

MER: Thou art like one of those fellows that
when he enters the confines of a tavern claps
me his sword upon the table and says "God send
me no need of thee!" and by the operation of
the second cup draws it on the drawer, when

operation—intoxicating influence
draws—draws his sword
drawer—waiter

indeed there is no need.

BEN: Am I like such a fellow?

MER: [Come, come, thou art as hot a Jack in thy mood as any in Italy, and as soon
moved to be moody, and as soon moody to be moved.

Suggested cut begins.
moved—provoked

BEN: And what to?

MER: Nay, an there were two such, we should have none shortly, for one would kill the
other.]

Suggested cut ends.

Thou! why, thou wilt quarrel with a man that hath a hair more, or a hair less, in his
beard, than thou hast: thou wilt quarrel with a man for cracking nuts, having no other
reason but because thou hast hazel eyes.

(Benvolio laughs and rises. Mercutio follows.)

[What eye, but such an eye, would spy out such
a quarrel? Thy head is as full of quarrels
as an egg is full of meat, and yet thy head
hath been beaten as addle as an egg for
quarrelling.]

Suggested cut begins.

addle—rotten
Suggested cut ends.

Thou hast quarrelled with a man for coughing
in the street, because he hath wakened thy
dog that hath lain asleep in the sun: didst
thou not fall out with a tailor for wearing
his new doublet before Easter? with another,
for tying his new shoes with old riband? and
yet thou wilt tutor me from quarrelling!

doublet—jacket
riband—ribbon

[BEN: An I were so apt to quarrel as thou art,

Suggested cut begins.

any man should buy the fee-simple of my life
for an hour and a quarter.
MER: The fee-simple! O simple!]

(Tybalt enters, followed by Sampson and Gregory.)
BEN: By my head, here come the Capulets.
MER: *(Sitting at fountain.)* By my heel, I care not.
TYB: *(To Gregory.)* Follow me close, for I will speak to them.
Gentlemen, good den: a word with one of you.
MER: *(Rising.)* And but one word with one of us? couple it with something; make it a
word and a blow.
TYB: You shall find me apt enough to that, sir, an you will give me occasion.
MER: Could you not take some occasion without giving?
TYB: Mercutio, thou consort'st with Romeo,—
MER: *(Angry.)* Consort! what, dost thou make
us minstrels? An thou make minstrels of us,
look to hear nothing but discords: here's my
fiddlestick; *(Indicating sword.)* here's that
shall make you dance. 'Zounds, consort!
BEN: *(Crossing between Tybalt and Mercutio.)*
We talk here in the public haunt of men:
Either withdraw unto some private place,
And reason coldly of your grievances,
Or else depart; here all eyes gaze on us.
MER: Men's eyes were made to look, and let them gaze;
I will not budge for no man's pleasure, I.
(Enter Romeo and Balthasar.)
TYB: Well, peace be with you, sir: here comes my man.
MER: But I'll be hanged, sir, if he wear your livery:
Marry, go before to field, he'll be your follower;
Your worship in that sense may call him "man."
TYB: Romeo, the hate I bear thee can afford
No better term than this,—thou art a villain.
ROM: *(Calmly.)* Tybalt, the reason that I have to love thee
Doth much excuse the appertaining rage
To such a greeting: villain am I none;
Therefore farewell; I see thou know'st me not.
(Romeo starts to leave.)
TYB: Boy, this shall not excuse the injuries
That thou hast done me; therefore turn and draw.
ROM: *(Romeo turns back but he does not want to
fight with his wife's relative.)*
I do protest, I never injured thee,

fee-simple—property
Suggested cut ends.

consort'st—are a close companion
consort—group of hired
musicians

'Zounds—by God's wounds

But love thee better than thou canst devise,
Till thou shalt know the reason of my love:
And so, good Capulet,—which name I tender
As dearly as my own,—be satisfied.
(Romeo pats Tybalt's shoulder. The latter pulls
away and looks disgusted, which throws Mercutio into a rage.)
MER: O calm, dishonourable, vile submission!
(Mercutio draws his sword.)
Alla stoccata carries it away.

Tybalt, you rat-catcher, will you walk?
TYB: What wouldst thou have with me?
MER: Good king of cats, nothing but one of
your nine lives; that I mean to make bold
withal, and as you shall use me hereafter,
drybeat the rest of the eight. Will you

pluck your sword out of his pilcher by the
ears? make haste, lest mine be about your
ears ere it be out.
TYB: *(Drawing his sword.)* I am for you.
(Romeo crosses to Mercutio.)
ROM: Gentle Mercutio, put thy rapier up.
(Mercutio pushes Romeo away.)
MER: Come, sir, your passado.
(Tybalt and Mercutio fight.)
ROM: Draw, Benvolio; beat down their weapons.
Gentlemen, for shame, forbear this outrage!
Tybalt, Mercutio, the prince expressly hath
Forbidden bandying in Verona streets:
Hold, Tybalt! *(Trying to separate them, Romeo stands with his arms out between Tybalt*
and Mercutio. Tybalt thrusts under Romeo's arm and stabs Mercutio, who drops his sword
and sinks to his knees.)
Good Mercutio!
SAM: Away, Tybalt.
(Tybalt, Sampson and Gregory exit quickly.)
MER: I am hurt.
A plague o' both your houses! I am sped.
Is he gone, and hath nothing?
BEN: What, art thou hurt?
(Benvolio and Romeo help Mercutio to rise.)
MER: Ay, ay, a scratch, a scratch; marry, 'tis enough. Where is my page?
(Abraham crosses to Mercutio.)

Alla stoccata—a thrust
carries it away—wins the day
rat-catcher—because he is the
king of cats

drybeat—beat without drawing
blood
pilcher—scabbard

passado—thrust

bandying—dueling

sped—done for

Go, villain, fetch a surgeon.

(Abraham exits quickly.)

ROM: Courage, man; the hurt cannot be much.

MER: No, 'tis not so deep as a well, nor so wide as a church-door; but 'tis enough, 'twill
serve: ask for me tomorrow, and you shall find me a grave man. I am peppered, I
warrant, for this world. A plague o' both your houses! 'Zounds, a dog, a rat, a mouse,
a cat, to scratch a man to death! a braggart, a rogue, a villain, that fights by the book
of arithmetic! Why the devil came you between us? I was hurt under your arm.

ROM: I thought all for the best.

MER: Help me into some house, Benvolio,
Or I shall faint. A plague o' both your houses!
They have made worms' meat of me: I have it,
And soundly too: your houses!

(Mercutio and Benvolio exit.)

ROM: *(Dazed; sitting at fountain.)*
This gentleman, the prince's near ally,
My very friend, hath got his mortal hurt
In my behalf; my reputation stain'd
With Tybalt's slander,—Tybalt, that an hour
Hath been my kinsman! O sweet Juliet,
Thy beauty hath made me effeminate
And in my temper soften'd valour's steel!

(Benvolio returns quickly.)

BEN: O Romeo, Romeo, brave Mercutio's dead!
That gallant spirit hath aspired the clouds,
Which too untimely here did scorn the earth.

ROM: This day's black fate on more days doth depend;
This but begins the woe others must end.

BEN: Here comes the furious Tybalt back again.

ROM: Alive, in triumph! and Mercutio slain!
Away to heaven, respective lenity,
And fire-eyed fury be my conduct now!

(Tybalt enters followed by Sampson.)

Now, Tybalt, take the "villain" back again,
That late thou gavest me; for Mercutio's soul
Is but a little way above our heads,
Staying for thine to keep him company:
Either thou, or I, or both, must go with him.

TYB: Thou, wretched boy, that didst consort him here,
Shalt with him hence.

ROM: This shall determine that.

*(Romeo and Tybalt engage in a short but
vigorous fight. Tybalt is stabbed, falls,*

peppered—finished

book of arithmetic—fencing
manual

aspired—risen up to

depend—impend

respective lenity—careful
gentleness

consort—attend

dies. Sampson exits quickly to get help.)

BEN: Romeo, away, be gone!

The citizens are up, and Tybalt slain.

Stand not amazed: the prince will doom thee death,

If thou art taken: hence, be gone, away!

ROM: O, I am fortune's fool!

BEN: Why dost thou stay?

(Romeo exits quickly. Enter Sampson with three watchmen. Also two ladies, two gentlemen, two vendors, Rosaline, Old Capulet, Peter and Citizens enter.)

FIRST WATCH: Which way ran he that kill'd Mercutio?

Tybalt, that murderer, which way ran he?

BEN: There lies that Tybalt.

(Benvolio and Second Watchman kneel to examine Tybalt.)

FIRST WATCH: *(To Benvolio.)* Up, sir, go with me;

I charge thee in the Prince's name, obey.

(Enter Prince, attended by two soldiers, Montague, Capulet, their wives and Nurse.)

PRI: Where are the vile beginners of this fray?

BEN: O noble Prince, I can discover all

The unlucky manage of this fatal brawl: **manage**—conduct

There lies the man, slain by young Romeo,

That slew thy kinsman, brave Mercutio.

L. CAP: *(Kneeling at body.)* Tybalt, my cousin! O my brother's child!

O Prince! O cousin! husband! O, the blood is spilt

Of my dear kinsman! *(Rising.)* Prince, as thou art true,

For blood of ours, shed blood of Montague.

O cousin, cousin! *(She cries in arms of Capulet.)*

PRI: Benvolio, who began this bloody fray?

BEN: Tybalt, here slain, whom Romeo's hand did slay;

Romeo that spoke him fair, bade him bethink

How nice the quarrel was, and urged withal   **nice**—trivial

Your high displeasure: all this uttered

With gentle breath, calm look, knees humbly bow'd,

Could not take truce with the unruly spleen   **take truce**—make peace

                                                                                 spleen—anger

Of Tybalt deaf to peace, but that he tilts

With piercing steel at bold Mercutio's breast,

Who all as hot, turns deadly point to point,

And, with a martial scorn, with one hand beats

Cold death aside, and with the other sends

It back to Tybalt, whose dexterity,

Retorts it: Romeo he cries aloud,

"Hold, friends! friends, part!" and, swifter than his tongue,

His agile arm beats down their fatal points,

And 'twixt them rushes; underneath whose arm
An envious thrust from Tybalt hit the life

envious—spiteful

Of stout Mercutio, and then Tybalt fled;
But by and by comes back to Romeo,

by and by—immediately

Who had but newly entertain'd revenge,
And to 't they go like lightning, for, ere I
Could draw to part them, was stout Tybalt slain.
And, as he fell, did Romeo turn and fly.
This is the truth, or let Benvolio die.
L.CAP: He is a kinsman to the Montague;
Affection makes him false; he speaks not true:
Some twenty of them fought in this black strife,
And all those twenty could but kill one life.
I beg for justice, which thou, prince, must give;
Romeo slew Tybalt, Romeo must not live.
PRI: Romeo slew him, he slew Mercutio;
Who now the price of his dear blood doth owe?
MON: Not Romeo, Prince, he was Mercutio's friend;
His fault concludes but what the law should end,
The life of Tybalt.
PRI: And for that offence
Immediately we do exile him hence:
I have an interest in your hate's proceeding,
My blood for your rude brawls doth lie a-bleeding;

My blood—i.e., Mercutio

But I'll amerce you with so strong a fine

amerce—punish

That you shall all repent the loss of mine:
I will be deaf to pleading and excuses;
Nor tears nor prayers shall purchase out abuses:

purchase—atone for

Therefore use none: let Romeo hence in haste,
Else, when he's found, that hour is his last.
(Indicating Tybalt.)
Bear hence this body and attend our will:
Mercy but murders, pardoning those that kill.
(The Prince immediately exits, followed by the soldiers. Lady Capulet looks again at Tybalt, then Capulet escorts her offstage. The three watchmen are preparing to remove Tybalt's body. The crowd is slowly exiting as the lights fade out.)

ACT III, SCENE 2

(Set: Capulet's orchard, same as Act II, Scene 5, with bench onstage. Time: Later, Monday. Juliet enters and looks offstage eagerly.)
JUL: [Gallop apace, you fiery-footed steeds,

Suggested cut begins.

Towards Phoebus' lodging: such a waggoner

Phoebus' lodging—west

As Phaethon would whip you to the west,
And bring in cloudy night immediately.
Spread thy close curtain, love-performing night,
That runaways' eyes may wink and Romeo

runaways'—steeds', **wink**—close

Leap to these arms, untalk'd of and unseen.
Lovers can see to do their amorous rites
By their own beauties; or, if love be blind,
It best agrees with night. Come, civil night,

civil—friendly

Thou sober-suited matron, all in black,
And learn me how to lose a winning match,
Play'd for a pair of stainless maidenhoods:

maidenhoods—being maidens

Hood my unmann'd blood, bating in my cheeks,

Hood—cover, **unmann'd**—
untrained, **bating**—fluttering

With thy black mantle; till strange love, grown bold,

strange—unfamiliar

Think true love acted simple modesty.
Come, night; come, Romeo; come, thou day in night;
For thou wilt lie upon the wings of night
Whiter than new snow on a raven's back.]

Suggested cut ends.

Come, gentle night, come, loving, black-brow'd night,
Give me my Romeo; and, when he shall die,
Take him and cut him out in little stars,
And he will make the face of heaven so fine
That all the world will be in love with night
And pay no worship to the garish sun.
(Juliet sits on bench.)
O, I have bought the mansion of a love,
But not possess'd it, and, though I am sold,
Not yet enjoy'd: so tedious is this day
As is the night before some festival
To an impatient child that hath new robes
And may not wear them. *(Juliet rises.)*
O, here comes my Nurse,
And she brings news; and every tongue that speaks
But Romeo's name speaks heavenly eloquence.
(Enter Nurse, with cords, followed by Peter. The Nurse is very upset.)

cords—rope ladder

Now, Nurse, what news? What hast thou there? the cords
That Romeo bid thee fetch?
NUR: Ay, ay, the cords.
(She throws them down and wrings her hands.)
JUL: Ay me! what news? why dost thou wring thy hands?
NUR: *(Crossing to bench.)* Ah, well-a-day! he's dead, he's dead, he's dead!
We are undone, lady, we are undone!

Alack the day! he's gone, he's kill'd, he's dead!

(Nurse, crying, sits on bench.)

JUL: Can heaven be so envious?

NUR: Romeo can,

Though heaven cannot: O Romeo, Romeo!

Who ever would have thought it? Romeo!

JUL: What devil art thou, that dost torment me thus?

This torture should be roar'd in dismal hell.

Hath Romeo slain himself? say thou but "Ay,"

And that bare vowel "I" shall poison more

Than the death-darting eye of cockatrice:

[I am not I, if there be such an "I",

Or those eyes shut, that make thee answer "Ay."]

If he be slain, say "Ay"; or if not, "No":

Brief sounds determine of my weal or woe.

NUR: I saw the wound, I saw it with mine eyes,—

God save the mark!—here on his manly breast:

A piteous corse, a bloody piteous corse;

Pale, pale as ashes, all bedaub'd in blood,

All in gore-blood; I swounded at the sight.

JUL: O, break, my heart! poor bankrupt, break at once!

To prison, eyes, ne'er look on liberty!

[Vile earth, to earth resign; end motion here;

And thou and Romeo press one heavy bier!]

NUR: O Tybalt, Tybalt, the best friend I had!

O courteous Tybalt! honest gentleman!

That ever I should live to see thee dead!

JUL: *(Bewildered, she looks at Nurse.)*

What storm is this that blows so contrary?

Is Romeo slaughter'd, and is Tybalt dead?

My dear-loved cousin, and my dearer lord?

Then, dreadful trumpet, sound the general doom!

For who is living, if those two are gone?

NUR: Tybalt is gone, and Romeo banishèd;

Romeo that kill'd him, he is banishèd.

JUL: O God! did Romeo's hand shed Tybalt's blood?

(Juliet sits on bench with Nurse.)

NUR: It did, it did; alas the day, it did!

JUL: *(Rising and crossing away from Nurse.)*

O serpent heart, hid with a flowering face!

Did ever dragon keep so fair a cave?

Beautiful tyrant! fiend angelical!

cockatrice—serpent
Suggested cut begins.
Suggested cut ends.

weal—wealth

God save the mark—an oath to divert an ill omen
corse—corpse

Suggested cut begins.
Suggested cut ends.

Note the oxymorons.

[Dove-feather'd raven! wolvish-ravening lamb!   Suggested cut begins.
Despisèd substance of divinest show!]   Suggested cut ends.
Just opposite to what thou justly seem'st,
A damnèd saint, an honourable villain!
[O nature, what hadst thou to do in hell,   Suggested cut begins.
When thou didst bower the spirit of a fiend   **bower**—lodge
In mortal paradise of such sweet flesh?
Was ever book containing such vile matter
So fairly bound? O that deceit should dwell
In such a gorgeous palace!]   Suggested cut ends.
NUR: There's no trust,
No faith, no honesty in men; all perjured,
All forsworn, all naught, all dissemblers.   **forsworn**—breakers of promises
Ah, where's my man? give me some aqua vitae: **aqua vitae**—alcoholic drink
*(Peter brings her a flask from which she takes
a drink and hands it back to him. Peter exits.)*
These griefs, these woes, these sorrows make me old.
Shame come to Romeo!
JUL: *(Crossing to Nurse.)* Blister'd be thy tongue
For such a wish! he was not born to shame:
Upon his brow shame is ashamed to sit;
For 'tis a throne where honour may be crown'd
Sole monarch of the universal earth.
O, what a beast was I to chide at him!
(Juliet sits on bench.)
NUR: Will you speak well of him that kill'd your cousin?
JUL: Shall I speak ill of him that is my husband?
Ah, poor my lord, what tongue shall smooth thy name,
When I, thy three-hours wife, have mangled it?
(Rising and crossing away from Nurse.)
But, wherefore, villain, didst thou kill my cousin? *(She is crying.)*
That villain cousin would have kill'd my husband:
[Back, foolish tears, back to your native spring;   Suggested cut begins.
Your tributary drops belong to woe,
Which you, mistaking, offer up to joy.]   Suggested cut ends.
My husband lives, that Tybalt would have slain;
And Tybalt's dead, that would have slain my husband:
All this is comfort; wherefore weep I then?
Some word there was, worser than Tybalt's death,
That murder'd me: I would forget it fain;   **fain**—gladly
But, O, it presses to my memory,
Like damnèd guilty deeds to sinners' minds:
"Tybalt is dead, and Romeo—banishèd;"

That "banishèd," that one word "banishèd,"
Hath slain ten thousand Tybalts. [Tybalt's death   Suggested cuts begins.
Was woe enough, if it had ended there:
Or, if sour woe delights in fellowship
And needly will be rank'd with other griefs,   **needly**—of necessity
Why follow'd not, when she said "Tybalt's dead,"
Thy father, or thy mother, nay, or both,
Which modern lamentation might have moved?
But with a rear-ward following Tybalt's death,   **rear-ward**—rear guard
"Romeo is banishèd," to speak that word,
Is father, mother, Tybalt, Romeo, Juliet,
All slain, all dead. "Romeo is banishèd!"]   Suggested cut ends.
(Juliet, weeping, sits next to Nurse who comforts her.)
There is no end, no limit, measure, bound,
In that word's death; no words can that woe sound.
Where is my father, and my mother, Nurse?
NUR: Weeping and wailing over Tybalt's corse:
Will you go to them? I will bring you thither.
(Nurse helps Juliet to rise.)
JUL: Wash they his wounds with tears: mine shall be spent,
When theirs are dry, for Romeo's banishment.
Take up those cords: poor ropes, you are beguiled,
(Nurse picks up cords.)
Both you and I; for Romeo is exiled:
[He made you for a highway to my bed;   Suggested cut begins.
But I, a maid, die maiden-widowèd.]   Suggested cut ends.
(Juliet takes cords.)
Come, cords, come, Nurse; I'll to my wedding-bed;
And death, not Romeo, take my maidenhead!
NUR: Hie to your chamber: I'll find Romeo
To comfort you: I wot well where he is.
Hark ye, your Romeo will be here at night:
I'll to him; he is hid at Laurence' cell.
JUL: O, find him! give this ring to my true knight,
And bid him come to take his last farewell.
(They exit in opposite directions as lights fade out.)

ACT III, SCENE 3

(Sound: On blackout for Scene 2, begin rain and thunder sounds of a mild summer rain. Continue rain sounds through one minute of dialogue, then gradually fade out. Set: Friar

Laurence's cell with desk, chair, candle in holder, matches, books, writing materials. Time: Monday evening. Bring up stage lights as Friar Laurence enters, closes and bolts door, throws back his wet hood, lights the candle, then calls to Romeo.)

FR.L: Romeo, come forth; come forth, thou fearful man:

(Friar Laurence is exhausted and sits in chair.)

[Affliction is enamour'd of thy parts,   Suggested cut begins.

And thou art wedded to calamity.]   Suggested cut ends.

*(Romeo enters from the Friar's study where
he has been hiding.)*

ROM: Father, what news? what is the Prince's doom?   **doom**—decree

[What sorrow craves acquaintance at my hand,   Suggested cut begins.

That I yet know not?

FR.L: Too familiar

Is my dear son with such sour company: **sour**—painful

I bring thee tidings of the Prince's doom.

ROM: What less than dooms-day is the Prince's doom?

FR.L: A gentler judgment vanish'd from his lips,]   **vanish'd**—issued

                                                         Suggested cut ends.

Not body's death, but body's banishment.

ROM: Ha, banishment! be merciful, say "death;"

For exile hath more terror in his look,

Much more than death: do not say "banishment."

FR.L: Hence from Verona art thou banishèd:

Be patient, for the world is broad and wide.

ROM: *(Emotionally.)* There is no world without Verona walls,

But purgatory, torture, hell itself.

Hence banishèd is banish'd from the world,

And world's exile is death: [then banishèd,   Suggested cut begins.

Is death mis-term'd: calling death banishment,

Thou cut'st my head off with a golden axe,

And smilest upon the stroke that murders me.]   Suggested cut ends.

FR.L: *(Crossing to Romeo.)*

O deadly sin! O rude unthankfulness!

Thy fault our law calls death; but the kind Prince,

Taking thy part, hath rush'd aside the law,   **rush'd**—brushed

And turn'd that black word death to banishment:

This is dear mercy, and thou seest it not.

ROM: *(Walking away.)*

'Tis torture, and not mercy: heaven is here,

Where Juliet lives; and every cat and dog

And little mouse, every unworthy thing,

Live here in heaven and may look on her;

[But Romeo may not: more validity,   Suggested cut begins.
                                                                            validity—value

More honourable state, more courtship lives
In carrion-flies than Romeo: they may seize
On the white wonder of dear Juliet's hand
And steal immortal blessing from her lips,
Who even in pure and vestal modesty,
Still blush, as thinking their own kisses sin;]   Suggested cut ends.
But Romeo may not; he is banishèd:
[Flies may do this, but I from this must fly: Suggested cut begins.
They are free men, but I am banishèd.
And say'st thou yet that exile is not death?
Hadst thou no poison mix'd, no sharp-ground knife,
No sudden mean of death, though ne'er so mean,   **mean**—means, **mean**—base
But "banishèd" to kill me?] "Banishèd"?   Suggested cut ends.
(Crossing to Friar Laurence.)
O friar, the damnèd use that word in hell;
Howlings attend it: how hast thou the heart,
Being a divine, a ghostly confessor,
A sin-absolver, and my friend profess'd,
To mangle me with that word "banishèd"?
FR.L: Thou fond mad man, hear me but speak a word.   **fond**—foolish
ROM: O, thou wilt speak again of banishment.
FR.L: I'll give thee armour to keep off that word:
Adversity's sweet milk, philosophy,
To comfort thee, though thou art banishèd.
ROM: Yet "banishèd"? Hang up philosophy!
Unless philosophy can make a Juliet,
Displant a town, reverse a prince's doom,   **displant**—move
It helps not, it prevails not: talk no more.
FR.L: O, then I see that madmen have no ears.
ROM: How should they, when that wise men have no eyes?
FR.L: Let me dispute with thee of thy estate.   **dispute**—discuss, **estate**—affairs
ROM: Thou canst not speak of that thou dost not feel:
Wert thou as young as I, Juliet thy love,
An hour but married, Tybalt murdered,
Doting like me and like me banishèd,
Then mightst thou speak, then mightst thou tear thy hair,
And fall upon the ground, as I do now,
(Romeo falls to his knees and then lies on the floor. He is crying.)
Taking the measure of an unmade grave.
(There is knocking on door to outside.)
FR.L: Arise; one knocks; good Romeo, hide thyself.

ROM: Not I; [unless the breath of heartsick groans,

Mist-like, infold me from the search of eyes.]

(More knocking.)

FR.L: Hark, how they knock! *(To door.)* Who's there? *(To Romeo.)* Romeo, arise;

Thou wilt be taken. *(To door.)* Stay awhile!

(To Romeo.) Stand up; Run to my study.

(More knocking. To door.) By and by! God's will

What simpleness is this! I come, I come!

(More knocking. Friar Laurence crosses to door.)

Who knocks so hard? whence come you? what's your will?

NUR: *(Offstage.)* Let me come in, and you shall know my errand;

I come from Lady Juliet.

FR.L: *(Opening door.)* Welcome, then.

(Nurse enters.)

NUR: O holy Friar, O, tell me, holy Friar,

Where is my lady's lord, where's Romeo?

FR.L: There on the ground, with his own tears made drunk.

NUR: O, he is even in my mistress' case,

Just in her case! O woeful sympathy!

Piteous predicament! Even so lies she,

Blubbering and weeping, weeping and blubbering.

(Nurse crosses to Romeo.)

Stand up, stand up; stand, and you be a man:

For Juliet's sake, for her sake, rise and stand;

Why should you fall into so deep an O?

ROM: Nurse!

NUR: Ah sir! ah sir! Well, death's the end of all. *(She sits in chair.)*

ROM: *(Kneeling to Nurse.)*

Spakest thou of Juliet? how is it with her?

Doth she not think me an old murderer,

Now I have stain'd the childhood of our joy

With blood removed but little from her own?

Where is she? and how doth she? and what says

My conceal'd lady to our cancell'd love?

NUR: O, she says nothing, sir, but weeps and weeps;

And now falls on her bed; and then starts up,

And Tybalt calls; and then on Romeo cries,

And then down falls again.

ROM: As if that name,

Shot from the deadly level of a gun,

Did murder her; as that name's cursèd hand

Murder'd her kinsman. *(Violently he crosses to the Friar.)* O, tell me, Friar, tell me,

In what vile part of this anatomy

Suggested cut begins.

Suggested cut ends.

By and by—wait a moment

O—exclamation of grief

anatomy—body

Doth my name lodge? tell me, that I may sack

The hateful mansion.

(Romeo draws his dagger to stab himself.)

FR.L: Hold thy desperate hand:

(Friar struggles with him and gets the dagger. Romeo collapses to his knees.)

Art thou a man? thy form cries out thou art:

Thy tears are womanish; thy wild acts denote

The unreasonable fury of a beast:

Unseemly woman in a seeming man!

Or ill-beseeming beast in seeming both!

Thou hast amazed me: by my holy order,

I thought thy disposition better temper'd.

Hast thou slain Tybalt? wilt thou slay thyself?

And slay thy lady too that lives in thee,

By doing damnèd hate upon thyself?

[Why rail'st thou on thy birth, the heaven, and earth?   Suggested cut begins.

Since birth, and heaven, and earth, all three do meet

In thee at once; which thou at once wouldst lose.

Fie, fie, thou shamest thy shape, thy love, thy wit;

Which, like a usurer, abound'st in all,

And usest none in that true use indeed

Which should bedeck thy shape, thy love, thy wit:

Thy noble shape is but a form of wax,

Digressing from the valour of a man;

Thy dear love sworn but hollow perjury,

Killing that love which thou hast vow'd to cherish;

Thy wit, that ornament to shape and love,

Mis-shapen in the conduct of them both,

Like powder in a skilless soldier's flask,

Is set afire by thine own ignorance,

And thou dismember'd with thine own defence.]   Suggested cut ends.

What, rouse thee, man! thy Juliet is alive,

For whose dear sake thou wast but lately dead;

There art thou happy: Tybalt would kill thee,

But thou slew'st Tybalt; there art thou happy.

The law that threaten'd death becomes thy friend

And turns it to exile; there art thou happy:

A pack of blessings lights upon thy back;

Happiness courts thee in her best array;

But, like a misbehaved and sullen wench,

Thou pout'st upon thy fortune and thy love:

Take heed, take heed, for such die miserable.

(Friar helps Romeo to rise.)

Go, get thee to thy love, as was decreed,
Ascend her chamber—hence and comfort her.
But look thou stay not till the watch be set,
For then thou canst not pass to Mantua,
Where thou shalt live, till we can find a time
To blaze your marriage, reconcile your friends,   **blaze**—make public
Beg pardon of the Prince and call thee back
With twenty hundred thousand times more joy
Than thou went'st forth in lamentation.
(Friar crosses to outside door and unlocks it.)
Go before, Nurse: commend me to thy lady;
And bid her hasten all the house to bed,
Which heavy sorrow makes them apt unto:
Romeo is coming.
NUR: *(Crossing to outside door.)* O Lord,
I could have stay'd here all the night
To hear good counsel: O, what learning is!
My lord, I'll tell my lady you will come.
ROM: Do so, and bid my sweet prepare to chide.
NUR: *(Giving Romeo ring.)* Here, sir, a ring she bid me give you, sir:
Hie you, make haste, for it grows very late.
(Nurse exits.)
ROM: How well my comfort is revived by this!
FR.L: Go hence; good night; and here stands all your state: **stands**—depends, **state**—fortune
Either be gone before the watch be set,
Or by the break of day disguised from hence:
Sojourn in Mantua; I'll find out your man,
And he shall signify from time to time
Every good hap to you that chances here: **hap**—fortune
Give me thy hand; 'tis late: farewell;
good night. *(Friar gives dagger to Romeo.)*
ROM: But that a joy past joy calls out on me,
It were a grief, so brief to part with thee:
Farewell.
(Romeo cautiously looks out the door, then exits quickly. Friar latches it again as the lights fade out.)

ACT III, SCENE 4

(Set: A room in Capulet's house, same as Act I, Scenes 3 and 5, with settee, chair, table, but if easier, it can be played without furniture. Time: Later Monday night. As stage lights come up, Capulet enters with Paris, followed by Lady Capulet and Sampson with candle.)
CAP: Things have fall'n out, sir, so unluckily,
That we have had no time to move our daughter: **move**—persuade

Look you, she loved her kinsman Tybalt dearly,
And so did I:—Well, we were born to die.
'Tis very late, she'll not come down tonight:
I promise you, but for your company,
I would have been a-bed an hour ago.
PAR: These times of woe afford no time to woo.
Madam, good night: commend me to your daughter.
(Paris bows and kisses Lady Capulet's hand.)
L.CAP: I will, and know her mind early tomorrow;
Tonight she is mew'd up to her heaviness.

mew'd up—cooped up

CAP: Sir Paris, I will make a desperate tender
Of my child's love: I think she will be ruled
In all respects by me; nay, more, I doubt it not.
Wife, go you to her ere you go to bed;
Acquaint her here of my son Paris' love;
And bid her, mark you me, on Wednesday next—
But, soft! what day is this?

soft—wait a minute

PAR: Monday, my lord,
CAP: Monday! ha, ha! Well, Wednesday is too soon,
O' Thursday let it be: o' Thursday, tell her,
She shall be married to this noble earl.
Will you be ready? do you like this haste?
We'll keep no great ado,—a friend or two;

ado—fuss

For, hark you, Tybalt being slain so late,
It may be thought we held him carelessly,

carelessly—with little regard

Being our kinsman, if we revel much:
Therefore we'll have some half a dozen friends,
And there an end. But what say you to Thursday?
PAR: My lord, I would that Thursday were tomorrow.
CAP: Well get you gone: o' Thursday be it, then.
(To Lady Capulet.) Go you to Juliet ere you go to bed,
Prepare her, wife, against this wedding-day.
Farewell, my lord. *(Paris bows and exits.)*
(To Sampson.) Light to my chamber, ho!
Afore me! it is so very very late,
That we may call it early by and by.
Good night.
(Sampson, Capulet and Lady Capulet exit as stage lights fade out.)

ACT III, SCENE 5

(Sound: On blackout for Scene 4, begin faint bird [lark] sounds. Fade out after dialogue begins. Set: Juliet's chamber with her bed. Time: Dawn, Tuesday. Romeo and Juliet are

sleeping. He wakes up, kisses her, rises, puts on his clothes, kisses her again. She wakes up.)

JUL: Wilt thou be gone? it is not yet near day:
It was the nightingale, and not the lark,
That pierced the fearful hollow of thine ear;
Nightly she sings on yon pomegranate-tree:
Believe me, love, it was the nightingale.

ROM: It was the lark, the herald of the morn,
No nightingale: look, love, what envious streaks
Do lace the severing clouds in yonder east:
Night's candles are burnt out, and jocund day   jocund—marked by high spirits
Stands tiptoe on the misty mountain tops.
I must be gone and live, or stay and die.

JUL: Yond light is not day-light, I know it, I:
It is some meteor that the sun exhales,
To be to thee this night a torch-bearer,
And light thee on thy way to Mantua:
Therefore stay yet; thou need'st not to be gone.

ROM: Let me be ta'en, let me be put to death;
(He kisses her again then sits on bed.)
I am content, so thou wilt have it so.
I'll say yon grey is not the morning's eye,
'Tis but the pale reflex of Cynthia's brow;   Cynthia's—the moon's
Nor that is not the lark, whose notes do beat
The vaulty heaven so high above our heads:
I have more care to stay than will to go:
Come, death, and welcome! Juliet wills it so.
How is 't, my soul? let's talk; it is not day.

JUL: *(She rises, distressed, and pulls him up.)*
It is, it is: hie hence, be gone, away!
It is the lark that sings so out of tune,
Straining harsh discords and unpleasing sharps.
Some say the lark makes sweet division;
This doth not so, for she divideth us:
[Some say the lark and loathèd toad change eyes,   Suggested cut begins.
O, now I would they had changed voices too!
Since arm from arm that voice doth us affray,   affray—frighten
Hunting thee hence with hunt's-up to the day.]   hunt's-up—song to arouse
                                                         hunters. Suggested cut ends.

O, now be gone; more light and light it grows.

ROM: More light and light: more dark and dark our woes!
(Nurse enters quickly. She speaks softly and urgently.)

NUR: Madam!

JUL: Nurse? *(Juliet puts on dressing gown.)*

NUR: Your lady mother is coming to your chamber:
The day is broke; be wary, look about.
(Nurse exits.)
JUL: Then, window, let day in, and let life out.
ROM: Farewell, farewell! one kiss, and I'll descend. *(They kiss.)*
JUL: Art thou gone so? love, lord, ay, husband, friend! *(She helps him dress.)*
I must hear from thee every day in the hour,
For in a minute there are many days:
O, by this count I shall be much in years
Ere I again behold my Romeo!
ROM: Farewell!
I will omit no opportunity
That may convey my greetings, love, to thee.
(They kiss.)
JUL: O, think'st thou we shall ever meet again?
ROM: I doubt it not; and all these woes shall serve
For sweet discourses in our time to come.
JUL: O God, I have an ill-divining soul!   **ill-divining**—prophetic of evil
Methinks I see thee, now thou art below,
As one dead in the bottom of a tomb:
Either my eyesight fails, or thou look'st pale.
ROM: And trust me, love, in my eye so do you:
Dry sorrow drinks our blood. Adieu, adieu!   **drinks our blood**—makes one
(Romeo exits.)   pale
JUL: O fortune, fortune! all men call thee fickle: *(She is crying.)*
[If thou art fickle, what dost thou with him.   Suggested cut begins.
That is renown'd for faith?]   Suggested cut ends.
Be fickle, fortune;
For then, I hope, thou wilt not keep him long,
But send him back.
L.CAP: *(Offstage.)* Ho, daughter! are you up?
JUL: *(Straightening up the bed.)*
Who is 't that calls? is it my lady mother?
Is she not down so late, or up so early?
What unaccustom'd cause procures her hither?
(Lady Capulet enters as Juliet sits on bed trying to stop crying.)
L.CAP: Why, how now, Juliet!
JUL: Madam, I am not well.
L.CAP: Evermore weeping for your cousin's death?
What, wilt thou wash him from his grave with tears?
An if thou couldst, thou couldst not make him live;
Therefore, have done: some grief shows much of love;
But much of grief shows still some want of wit.   **wit**—wisdom

JUL: Yet let me weep for such a feeling loss.

[L.CAP: So shall you feel the loss, but not the friend

Which you weep for.

Suggested cut begins.

JUL: Feeling so the loss,

I cannot choose but ever weep the friend.]

Suggested cut ends.

L.CAP: Well, girl, thou weep'st not so much for his death,

As that the villain lives which slaughter'd him.

JUL: What villain, madam?

L.CAP: That same villain, Romeo.

JUL: [Villain and he be many miles asunder.

Suggested cut begins.

God Pardon him! I do, with all my heart;

And yet no man like he doth grieve my heart.

L.CAP: That is, because the traitor murderer lives.

JUL: Ay, madam, from the reach of these my hands:]

Suggested cut ends.

Would none but I might venge my cousin's death!

L.CAP: We will have vengeance for it, fear thou not:

(Comforting Juliet.)

Then weep no more. I'll send to one in Mantua,

Where that same banish'd runagate doth live,

runagate—fugitive

Shall give him such an unaccustom'd dram,

dram—small amount

That he shall soon keep Tybalt company:

And then, I hope, thou wilt be satisfied.

JUL: Indeed, I never shall be satisfied

With Romeo, till I behold him—dead—

Is my poor heart so for a kinsman vex'd.

Madam, if you could find out but a man

To bear a poison, I would temper it;

temper—mix

That Romeo should, upon receipt thereof,

Soon sleep in quiet. O, how my heart abhors

To hear him named, and cannot come to him.

To wreak the love I bore my cousin

wreak—revenge

Upon his body that hath slaughter'd him!

L.CAP: Find thou the means, and I'll find

such a man. *(Sitting beside Juliet on bed.)*

But now I'll tell thee joyful tidings, girl.

JUL: And joy comes well in such a needy time:

What are they, I beseech your ladyship?

L.CAP: Well, well, thou hast a careful father, child;

One who, to put thee from thy heaviness,

Hath sorted out a sudden day of joy,

sorted out—selected

That thou expect'st not nor I look'd not for.

JUL: Madam, in happy time, what day is that?

L.CAP: Marry, my child, early next Thursday morn,

The gallant, young and noble gentleman,

The County Paris, at Saint Peter's Church, **County**—Count

Shall happily make thee there a joyful bride.

JUL: *(Very upset, she rises.)* Now, by Saint Peter's Church and Peter too,

He shall not make me there a joyful bride.

I wonder at this haste; that I must wed

Ere he, that should be husband, comes to woo.

I pray you, tell my lord and father, madam,

I will not marry yet; and, when I do, I swear,

It shall be Romeo, whom you know I hate,

Rather than Paris. These are news indeed!

(Juliet is crying and collapses on bed.)

L.CAP: *(Rising.)* Here comes your father; tell him so yourself,

And see how he will take it at your hands.

(Capulet and Nurse enter.)

CAP: When the sun sets, the air doth drizzle dew;

But for the sunset of my brother's son

It rains downright.

How now! a conduit, girl? what, still in tears? **conduit**—fountain

Evermore showering? [In one little body Suggested cut begins.

Thou counterfeit'st a bark, a sea, a wind;

For still thy eyes, which I may call the sea,

Do ebb and flow with tears; the bark thy body is,

Sailing in this salt flood; the winds, thy sighs;

Who, raging with thy tears, and they with them,

Without a sudden calm, will overset

Thy tempest-tossèd body.] How now, wife! Suggested cut ends.

Have you deliver'd to her our decree?

L.CAP: Ay, sir; but she will none, she gives you thanks.

I would the fool were married to her grave!

CAP: Soft! take me with you, take me with you, wife. **take me with you**—let me

How! will she none? doth she not give us thanks? understand you

Is she not proud? doth she not count her blest,

Unworthy as she is, that we have wrought **wrought**—procured

So worthy a gentleman to be her bridegroom?

JUL: Not proud, you have; but thankful, that you have:

Proud can I never be of what I hate;

But thankful even for hate, that is meant love.

CAP: How now, how now, chop-logic! What is this? **chop-logic**—sophistical arguer

"Proud," and "I thank you," and "I thank you not;"

And yet "not proud," mistress minion, you,

Thank me no thankings, nor proud me no prouds,

But fettle your fine joints 'gainst Thursday next, **fettle**—prepare

To go with Paris to Saint Peter's Church,

(He pulls Juliet up from bed.)

Or I will drag thee on a hurdle thither.   hurdle—a sled

Out, you green-sickness carrion! Out, you baggage!   green-sickness—anemic

You tallow-face!   tallow-face—pale face

L.CAP: *(Crossing to help Juliet.)*

Fie, fie! what, are you mad?

JUL: *(Falling on knees.)* Good father, I beseech you on my knees,

Hear me with patience but to speak a word.

CAP: Hang thee, young baggage! disobedient wretch!

I tell thee what: get thee to church o' Thursday,

Or never after look me in the face:

(Juliet starts to reply.)

Speak not, reply not, do not answer me;

My fingers itch. Wife, we scarce thought us blest

That God had lent us but this only child;

But now I see this one is one too much,

And that we have a curse in having her:

Out on her, hilding!   hilding—good-for-nothing

(Lady Capulet and Nurse help Juliet to sit on bed.)

NUR: God in heaven bless her!

You are to blame, my lord, to rate her so.   rate—berate

CAP: And why, my lady wisdom? hold your tongue,

Good prudence; smatter with your gossips, go.   smatter—chatter

NUR: I speak no treason.

CAP: O, God ye god-den.

NUR: May not one speak?

CAP: Peace, you mumbling fool!

Utter your gravity o'er a gossip's bowl;   gravity—advice

For here we need it not.

L.CAP: You are too hot.

CAP: God's bread! it makes me mad:

Day, night, hour, tide, time, work, play,

Alone, in company, still my care hath been

To have her match'd: and having now provided

A gentleman of noble parentage,

Of fair demesnes, youthful, and nobly train'd,   demesnes—estates

Stuff'd, as they say, with honourable parts,

Proportion'd as one's thought would wish a man;

And then to have a wretched puling fool,   puling—whimpering

A whining mammet, in her fortune's tender,   mammet—doll

                                                                 fortune's tender—fortunate offer

To answer "I'll not wed; I cannot love,

I am too young; I pray you, pardon me."
But, and you will not wed, I'll pardon you:
Graze where you will, you shall not house with me:
Look to 't, think on 't, I do not use to jest.
Thursday is near; lay hand on heart, advise:
And you be mine, I'll give you to my friend;
And you be not, hang, beg, starve, die in the streets,
For, by my soul, I'll ne'er acknowledge thee,
Nor what is mine shall never do thee good:
Trust to't, bethink you; I'll not be forsworn.   **forsworn**—break my word
(Capulet exits.)
JUL: Is there no pity sitting in the clouds,
That sees into the bottom of my grief?
(Crossing to Lady Capulet.)
O, sweet my mother, cast me not away!
Delay this marriage for a month, a week;
Or, if you do not, make the bridal bed
In that dim monument where Tybalt lies.
L.CAP: *(Crossing to exit.)*
Talk not to me, for I'll not speak a word:
Do as thou wilt, for I have done with thee.
(Lady Capulet exits.)
JUL: *(Running to Nurse's arms.)*
O God!—O Nurse, how shall this be prevented?
My husband is on earth, my faith in heaven;
[How shall that faith return again to earth,   Suggested cut begins.
Unless that husband send it me from heaven
By leaving earth? comfort me, counsel me.
Alack, alack, that heaven should practise stratagems   **stratagems**—tricks of war
Upon so soft a subject as myself!]   Suggested cut ends.
What say'st thou? hast thou not a word of joy?
Some comfort, Nurse. *(Both sit on bed.)*
NUR: Faith, here it is.
Romeo is banish'd; and all the world to nothing,
That he dares ne'er come back to challenge you;   **challenge**—lay claim to
Or, if he do, it needs must be by stealth.
Then, since the case so stands as now it doth,
I think it best you married with the County.
(Juliet pulls away from Nurse.)
O, he's a lovely gentleman!
Romeo's a dishclout to him: an eagle, madam,   **dishclout**—dishcloth
Hath not so green, so quick, so fair an eye
As Paris hath. Beshrew my very heart,   **Beshrew**—curse

I think you are happy in this second match,
For it excels your first: or if it did not,
Your first is dead; or 'twere as good he were,
As living here and you no use of him.

JUL: Speakest thou from thy heart?

NUR: And from my soul too;
Or else beshrew them both.

JUL: Amen!

NUR: What?

JUL: Well, thou hast comforted me marvellous much. *(Juliet and Nurse rise.)*
Go in: and tell my lady I am gone,
Having displeased my father, to Laurence' cell,
To make confession and to be absolved.

NUR: Marry, I will; and this is wisely done.

(Nurse exits.)

JUL: *(Angrily.)* Ancient damnation! O most wicked fiend!   **Ancient damnation**—wicked old woman
Is it more sin to wish me thus forsworn,
Or to dispraise my lord with that same tongue
Which she hath praised him with above compare
So many thousand times? Go, counsellor;
Thou and my bosom henceforth shall be twain.   **twain**—two
I'll to the Friar, to know his remedy:
If all else fail, myself have power to die.

(Juliet begins to dress as the lights fade out.)

ACT IV, SCENE 1

(Set: Friar Laurence's cell, same as Act III, Scene 3, with desk, chair, candle in holder, books, writing materials. Time: Late afternoon, Tuesday. Stage lights come up as Friar Laurence and Paris enter through door.)

FR.L: On Thursday, sir? the time is very short.

PAR: My father Capulet will have it so;
And I am nothing slow to slack his haste.

FR.L: You say you do not know the lady's mind:
Uneven is the course, I like it not.

PAR: Immoderately she weeps for Tybalt's death,
And therefore have I little talk'd of love;
For Venus smiles not in a house of tears.
Now, sir, her father counts it dangerous
That she doth give her sorrow so much sway,
And in his wisdom hastes our marriage,

To stop the inundation of her tears;

[Which, too much minded by herself alone,   Suggested cut begins.

May be put from her by society:]   Suggested cut ends.

Now do you know the reason of this haste.

FR.L: *(Aside)* I would I knew not why it should be slow'd. *(Looking out the open door.)*

Look, sir, here comes the lady towards my cell.

(Juliet enters. Paris bows to her.)

PAR: Happily met, my lady and my wife!

JUL: That may be, sir, when I may be a wife.

PAR: That may be must be, love, on Thursday next.

JUL: What must be shall be.

FR.L: That's a certain text.

PAR: Come you to make confession to this father?

JUL: To answer that, I should confess to you.

PAR: Do not deny to him that you love me.

JUL: I will confess to you that I love him.

PAR: So will ye, I am sure, that you love me.

JUL: If I do so, it will be of more price,

Being spoke behind your back, than to your face.

[PAR: Poor soul, thy face is much abused with tears.   Suggested cut begins.

JUL: The tears have got small victory by that;

For it was bad enough before their spite.

PAR: Thou wrong'st it more than tears with that report.

JUL: That is no slander, sir, which is a truth;

And what I spake, I spake it to my face.

PAR: Thy face is mine, and thou hast slander'd it.

JUL: It may be so, for it is not mine own.]   Suggested cut ends.

Are you at leisure, holy father, now;

Or shall I come to you at evening mass?

FR.L: My leisure serves me, pensive daughter, now. *(To Paris.)*

My lord, we must entreat the time alone.

PAR: God shield I should disturb devotion!

Juliet, on Thursday early will I rouse ye:

Till then, adieu; and keep this holy kiss.

(Paris kisses Juliet on the forehead, then he exits.)

JUL: O shut the door! and when thou hast done so,

Come weep with me; past hope, past cure, past help! *(As Friar Laurence closes the door,*
Juliet wearily sinks into chair, crying.)

FR.L: Ah, Juliet, I already know thy grief;

It strains me past the compass of my wits:

I hear thou must, and nothing may prorogue it,   **prorogue**—postpone

On Thursday next be married to this County.

JUL: Tell me not, Friar, that thou hear'st of this,

Unless thou tell me how I may prevent it:
If, in thy wisdom, thou canst give no help,
Do thou but call my resolution wise,
(Juliet pulls out a dagger.)
And with this knife I'll help it presently.
God join'd my heart and Romeo's, thou our hands;
And ere this hand, by thee to Romeo seal'd,
Shall be the label to another deed,
Or my true heart with treacherous revolt
Turn to another, this shall slay them both:
[Therefore, out of thy long-experienced time,   Suggested cut begins.
Give me some present counsel, or, behold,
'Twixt my extremes and me this bloody knife   **extremes**—intense difficulties
Shall play the umpire, arbitrating that
Which the commission of thy years and art   **commission**—authority
Could to no issue of true honour bring.]   Suggested cut ends.
Be not so long to speak; I long to die,
If what thou speak'st speak not of remedy.
FR.L: *(Taking the dagger from her.)*
Hold, daughter: I do spy a kind of hope,
Which craves as desperate an execution.
As that is desperate which we would prevent.
If, rather than to marry County Paris,
Thou hast the strength of will to slay thyself,
Then it is likely thou wilt undertake
A thing like death to chide away this shame,   **chide**—scold
That copest with death himself to scape from it;   **copest**—contends
And, if thou dar'st, I'll give thee remedy.
JUL: O, bid me leap, rather than marry Paris,
From off the battlements of yonder tower,
Or walk in thievish ways; or bid me lurk
Where serpents are; chain me with roaring bears;
[Or shut me nightly in a charnel-house,   Suggested cut begins.
                                                                 charnel-house—where bodies
O'er-cover'd quite with dead men's rattling bones,   or bones are put
With reeky shanks and yellow chapless skulls;]   Suggested cut ends.
Or bid me go into a new-made grave
And hide me with a dead man in his shroud;
Things that, to hear them told, have made me tremble;
And I will do it without fear or doubt,
To live an unstain'd wife to my sweet love.
FR.L: *(Crossing to desk, he puts down dagger and gets vial.)*
Hold, then; go home, be merry, give consent

To marry Paris: *(Juliet shakes head No!)*
Wednesday is to-morrow;
Tomorrow night look that thou lie alone;
Let not thy Nurse lie with thee in thy chamber:
Take thou this vial, being then in bed,
And this distillèd liquor drink thou off;
When presently through all thy veins shall run
A cold and drowsy humour, for no pulse
Shall keep his native progress, but surcease:
No warmth, no breath, shall testify thou livest;
[The roses in thy lips and cheeks shall fade
To paly ashes, thy eyes' windows fall,
Like death, when he shuts up the day of life;
Each part, deprived of supple government,
Shall, stiff and stark and cold, appear like death:]
And in this borrow'd likeness of shrunk death
Thou shalt continue two and forty hours,
And then awake as from a pleasant sleep.
Now, when the bridegroom in the morning comes
To rouse thee from thy bed, there art thou dead:
Then, as the manner of our country is,
In thy best robes uncover'd on the bier
Thou shalt be borne to that same ancient vault
Where all the kindred of the Capulets lie.
In the mean time, against thou shalt awake,
Shall Romeo by my letters know our drift,
And hither shall he come: and he and I
Will watch thy waking, and that very night
Shall Romeo bear thee hence to Mantua.
And this shall free thee from this present shame;
If no inconstant toy, nor womanish fear,
Abate thy valour in the acting it.
JUL: *(Taking the vial.)* Give me, give me!
O, tell not me of fear!
FR.L: *(He gives her back the dagger and opens the door.)*
Hold; get you gone, be strong and prosperous
In this resolve: I'll send a friar with speed
To Mantua, with my letters to thy lord.
JUL: *(She kneels and kisses his hand.)* Love give me strength! and strength shall help afford.
Farewell, dear father! *(She rises and exits as lights fade out.)*

Glossary:
humour—fluid
native—customary, surcease—cease
Suggested cut begins.
Suggested cut ends.
against—in anticipation of when
drift—intention
toy—fickle whim

ACT IV, SCENE 2

(Set: Hall in Capulet's house. No furniture needed. Time: Tuesday evening. As lights come up,
Capulet enters, holding a list of guests. He is followed by Lady Capulet, Nurse, Sampson and Gregory.)

CAP: *(To Sampson.)* So many guests invite as here are writ.

(Sampson exits with list.)

(To Gregory.) Sirrah, go hire me twenty cunning cooks.

[GRE: You shall have none ill, sir; for   Suggested cut begins.
I'll try if they can lick their fingers.

CAP: How canst thou try them so?

GRE: Marry, sir, 'tis an ill cook that cannot lick his own fingers: therefore he that cannot
lick his fingers goes not with me.]   Suggested cut ends.

CAP: Go, be gone.

(Gregory exits.)

We shall be much unfurnished for this time.   **unfurnished**—unprepared

What, is my daughter gone to Friar Laurence?

NUR: Ay, forsooth.

CAP: Well, he may chance to do some good on her:

A peevish self-will'd harlotry it is.   **harlotry**—good-for-nothing

NUR: See where she comes from shrift with merry look.

(Juliet enters.)

CAP: How now, my headstrong! where have you been gadding?

JUL: Where I have learn'd me to repent the sin

Of disobedient opposition

To you and your behests, and am enjoin'd   **behests**—commands

By holy Laurence to fall prostrate here,

(Juliet kneels to Capulet.)

And beg your pardon: pardon, I beseech you!

Henceforward I am ever ruled by you.

CAP: Send for the County; go tell him of this:

I'll have this knot knit up tomorrow morning.

JUL: I met the youthful lord at Laurence' cell;

And gave him what becomèd love I might,   **becomèd**—becoming

Not stepping o'er the bounds of modesty.

CAP: Why, I am glad on't; this is well: stand up: *(Juliet rises.)*

This is as 't should be. Let me see the county;

Ay, marry, go, I say, and fetch him hither.

Now, afore God! this reverend holy friar,

All our whole city is much bound to him.

JUL: Nurse, will you go with me into my closet,   **closet**—private room

To help me sort such needful ornaments

As you think fit to furnish me tomorrow?

L.CAP: No, not till Thursday; there is time enough.

CAP: Go, Nurse, go with her: we'll to church tomorrow.

(Juliet and Nurse exit.)

L.CAP: We shall be short in our provision:

'Tis now near night.

CAP: Tush, I will stir about,

And all things shall be well, I warrant thee, wife:

Go thou to Juliet, help to deck up her;

I'll not to bed tonight; let me alone;

I'll play the housewife for this once.

(Calling for servants.) What, ho!

They are all forth. Well, I will walk myself

To County Paris, to prepare him up

Against tomorrow: my heart is wondrous light,

Since this same wayward girl is so reclaim'd.

(Capulet exits as lights fade out.)

ACT IV, SCENE 3

(Set: Juliet's bedchamber, same as Act III, Scene 5. Time: Tuesday night. As stage lights come up, Juliet is sitting on the bed and the Nurse is showing her a dress.)

JUL: Ay, those attires are best: but, gentle Nurse,

I pray thee, leave me to myself tonight,

For I have need of many orisons   orisons—prayers

To move the heavens to smile upon my state,

Which, well thou know'st, is cross, and full of sin.

(Lady Capulet enters.)

L.CAP: What, are you busy, ho? need you my help?

JUL: No, madam; we have cull'd such necessaries

As are behoveful for our state tomorrow: behoveful—necessary

                                                state—celebration

So please you, let me now be left alone,

And let the Nurse this night sit up with you;

For, I am sure, you have your hands full all,

In this so sudden business.

L.CAP: *(Kissing Juliet on cheek.)* Good night:

Get thee to bed, and rest; for thou hast need.

(Lady Capulet and Nurse, with dress, exit.)

JUL: Farewell! God knows when we shall meet again. *(She rises.)*

I have a faint cold fear thrills through my veins,

That almost freezes up the heat of life:

I'll call them back again to comfort me:

Nurse! What should she do here?

My dismal scene I needs must act alone.
(She takes vial from under a pillow.)
Come, vial.
What if this mixture do not work at all?
Shall I be married then tomorrow morning?
No, no: *(Takes dagger out from under pillow.)* this shall forbid it: lie thou there.
(Puts dagger on bed. She holds vial.)
What if it be a poison, which the Friar
Subtly hath minister'd to have me dead,
Lest in this marriage he should be dishonour'd,
Because he married me before to Romeo?
I fear it is: and yet, methinks, it should not,
For he hath still been tried a holy man.   **still**—always
How if, when I am laid into the tomb,
I wake before the time that Romeo
Come to redeem me? there's a fearful point!
Shall I not, then, be stifled in the vault,
To whose foul mouth no healthsome air breathes in,
And there die strangled ere my Romeo comes?
Or, if I live, is it not very like,
The horrible conceit of death and night,   **conceit**—idea
Together with the terror of the place,—
As in a vault, an ancient receptacle,
Where for these many hundred years, the bones
Of all my buried ancestors are packed:
Where bloody Tybalt, yet but green in earth,   **green in earth**—newly buried
Lies festering in his shroud; where, as they say,
At some hours in the night spirits resort;—
(She sits on bed as she is beginning to cry.)
Alack, alack, is it not like that I,
So early waking, what with loathsome smells,
And shrieks like mandrakes' torn out of the earth,   **mandrakes'**—plant that was
That living mortals, hearing them, run mad:—   supposed to shriek when
(She abruptly rises.)   uprooted
O, if I wake, shall I not be distraught,
Environèd with all these hideous fears?
(She kneels as though playing in a tomb.)
And madly play with my forefathers' joints?
And pluck the mangled Tybalt from his shroud?
And, in this rage, with some great kinsman's bone,
As with a club, dash out my desperate brains?
(She rises.)
O, look! methinks I see my cousin's ghost

Seeking out Romeo, that did spit his body
Upon a rapier's point: stay, Tybalt, stay!
Romeo, I come! this do I drink to thee.
(She drinks from the vial, sways slightly, then falls upon her bed as the lights black out.)

ACT IV, SCENE 4

*(Set: Hall in Capulet's house, same as Act IV, Scene 2. No furniture is onstage. Time: 3
A.M., Wednesday. Stage lights come up. [Lady Capulet and Nurse enter.])*

L.CAP: Hold, take these keys, and fetch more spices, Nurse.
NUR: They call for dates and quinces in the pastry.

(Capulet enters.)

CAP: Come, stir, stir, stir! the second cock hath crow'd,
The curfew-bell hath rung, 'tis three o'clock:
Look to the baked meats, good Angelica:
Spare not for cost.
NUR: Go, you cot-quean, go,
Get you to bed; faith, you'll be sick tomorrow
For this night's watching.
CAP: No, not a whit: what! I have watch'd ere now
All night for lesser cause, and ne'er been sick.
L.CAP: Ay, you have been a mouse-hunt in your time;
But I will watch you from such watching now.
(Lady Capulet and Nurse exit.)
CAP: A jealous hood, a jealous hood!
(Enter Sampson, Gregory and two other servants with spits, logs, and baskets.)
                        Now, fellow,
What's there?
SAM: Things for the cook, sir; but I know not what.
CAP: Make haste, make haste.
(Sampson exits.)
                        Sirrah, fetch drier logs:
Call Peter, he will show thee where they are.
GRE: I have a head, sir, that will find out logs,
And never trouble Peter for the matter.
(Gregory and other servants exit.)
CAP: Mass, and well said; a merry whoreson, ha!
Thou shalt be logger-head.]

                        Good faith, 'tis day:
The County will be here with music straight,
For so he said he would: *(Music offstage.)*

Suggested cut begins.

quinces—a fruit
pastry—where pastry is made

Angelica—Nurse's name

cot-quean—man who acts as a housewife

mouse-hunt—hunter of women

jealous hood—jealous person

whoreson—bastard
logger-head—blockhead
Suggested cut ends.

I hear him near.

Nurse! Wife! What, ho! What, Nurse, I say!

(Nurse enters.)

Go waken Juliet, go and trim her up;

I'll go and chat with Paris: hie, make haste,

Make haste; the bridegroom he is come already:

Make haste, I say.

(They exit in opposite directions as the stage lights fade out.)

ACT IV, SCENE V

(Set: Juliet's bedchamber, same as Act IV, Scene 3. Time: immediately following the previous scene. As the stage lights come up, the Nurse is calling from offstage.)

NUR: Mistress! what, mistress! Juliet! fast, I warrant her, she:

Why, lamb! why, lady! fie, you slug-a-bed!

Why, love, I say! madam! sweet-heart! why, bride!

(Nurse is now onstage and walking around the bed.)

What, not a word? you take your pennyworths now;

Sleep for a week; for the next night, I warrant,

The County Paris hath set up his rest,

That you shall rest but little. God forgive me,

Marry, and amen, how sound is she asleep!

I must needs wake her. Madam, madam, madam!

Ay, let the County take you in your bed;

He'll fright you up, i' faith. Will it not be?

What, dress'd! and in your clothes! and down again!

I must needs wake you: Lady! lady! lady!

Alas, alas! Help, help! my lady's dead!

O, well-a-day, that ever I was born!

Some aqua vitae, ho! My lord! my lady!

(Lady Capulet enters.)

L.CAP: What noise is here?

NUR: *(She is crying.)*   O lamentable day!

L.CAP: What is the matter?

NUR: Look, look! O heavy day!

L.CAP: O me, O me! My child, my only life,

Revive, look up, or I will die with thee!

Help, help! Call help.

(Capulet enters.)

CAP: For shame, bring Juliet forth; her lord is come.

NUR: She's dead, deceased, she's dead; alack the day!

L.CAP: Alack the day, she's dead, she's dead, she's dead!

CAP: Ha! let me see her: *(Puts hand on her body.)* out, alas! she's cold;

pennyworths—small allowances

Her blood is settled, and her joints are stiff;
Life and these lips have long been separated:
Death lies on her like an untimely frost
Upon the sweetest flower of all the field.

NUR: O lamentable day!

L.CAP: O woeful time!

CAP: Death, that hath ta'en her hence to make me wail,
Ties up my tongue, and will not let me speak.

(Friar Laurence and Paris enter.)

FR.L: Come, is the bride ready to go to church?

CAP: Ready to go, but never to return.
(To Paris.) O son! the night before thy wedding-day
Hath Death lain with thy wife. There she lies,
Flower as she was, deflowered by him.
Death is my son-in-law, Death is my heir;
My daughter he hath wedded: I will die,
And leave him all; life, living, all is Death's.

PAR: Have I thought long to see this morning's face,
And doth it give me such a sight as this?

L.CAP: Accursed, unhappy, wretched, hateful day!
Most miserable hour that e'er time saw
In lasting labour of his pilgrimage!
But one, poor one, one poor and loving child,
But one thing to rejoice and solace in,   solace—find comfort
And cruel death hath catch'd it from my sight!

NUR: O woe! woeful, woeful, woeful day!

[Most lamentable day, most woeful day,   Suggested cut begins.
That ever, ever, I did yet behold!
O day! O day! O day! O hateful day!
Never was seen so black a day as this:
O woeful day, O woeful day!

PAR: Beguiled, divorced, wronged, spited, slain!
Most detestable death, by thee beguil'd,   thee—death
By cruel, cruel thee quite overthrown!]   Suggested cut ends.
O love! O life! not life, but love in death!

CAP: [Despised, distressed, hated, martyr'd, kill'd!   Suggested cut begins.
Uncomfortable time, why camest thou now
To murder, murder our solemnity?]   solemnity—ceremony
                                                     Suggested cut ends.

O child! O child! my soul, and not my child!
Dead art thou! Alack! my child is dead;
And with my child my joys are buried.

FR.L: Peace, ho, for shame! confusion's cure lives not

In these confusions. Heaven and yourself
Had part in this fair maid; now heaven hath all,
And all the better is it for the maid:
Your part in her you could not keep from death,
But heaven keeps his part in eternal life.
The most you sought was her promotion;
For 'twas your heaven she should be advanced:
And weep ye now, seeing she is advanced
Above the clouds, as high as heaven itself?
O, in this love, you love your child so ill,
That you run mad, seeing that she is well:
[She's not well married that lives married long;   Suggested cut begins.
But she's best married that dies married young.
Dry up your tears, and stick your rosemary
On this fair corse; and, as the custom is,   **corse**—corpse
In all her best array bear her to church:
For though fond nature bids us an lament,
Yet nature's tears are reason's merriment.
CAP: All things that we ordainèd festival,
Turn from their office to black funeral;
Our instruments to melancholy bells,
Our wedding cheer to a sad burial feast,
Our solemn hymns to sullen dirges change,
Our bridal flowers serve for a buried corse,
And all things change them to the contrary.]   Suggested cut ends.
FR.L: Sir, go you in; and, madam, go with him;
And go, Sir Paris; every one prepare
To follow this fair corse unto her grave:
The heavens do lour upon you for some ill;   **lour**—frown
Move them no more by crossing their high will.
(*Capulet escorts his weeping wife offstage. They are followed by Paris. The Friar makes the sign of the cross over Juliet and exits. The Nurse is left alone grieving. It is suggested that stage lights now fade out and the rest of this scene be cut.*)
[(*Three musicians enter.*)   Suggested cut begins.
FIRST M: Faith, we may put up our pipes, and be gone.
NUR: Honest good fellows, ah, put up, put up;
For, well you know, this is a pitiful case.
(*Nurse exits.*)
FIRST M: Ay, by my troth, the case may be amended.
(*Peter enters.*)
PET: Musicians, O, musicians, "Heart's ease, Heart's ease:" O, an you will have me live, play "Heart's ease."
FIRST M: Why "Heart's ease?"

PET: O, musicians, because my heart itself plays "My heart is full of woe:" O, play me some merry dump, to comfort me.

FIRST M: Not a dump we; 'tis no time to play now.

PET: You will not, then?

FIRST M: No.

PET: I will then give it you soundly.

FIRST M: What will you give us?

PET: No money, on my faith, but the gleek; I will give you the minstrel.

FIRST M: Then I will give you the serving-creature.

PET: Then will I lay the serving-creature's dagger on your pate. I will carry no crotchets: I'll re you, I'll fa you; do you note me?

FIRST M: An you re us and fa us, you note us.

SECOND M: Pray you, put up your dagger, and put out your wit.

PET: Then have at you with my wit! I will dry-beat you with an iron wit, and put up my iron dagger. Answer me like men:
"When griping grief the heart doth wound,
And doleful dumps the mind oppress,
Then music with her silver sound"—
why "silver sound"? why "music with her silver sound"? What say you, Simon Catling?

FIRST M: Marry, sir, because silver hath a sweet sound.

PET: Pretty! What say you, Hugh Rebeck?

SECOND M: I say "silver sound," because musicians sound for silver.

PET: Pretty too! What say you, James Soundpost?

THIRD M: Faith, I know not what to say.

PET: O, I cry you mercy; you are the singer: I will say for you. It is "music with her silver sound," because musicians have no gold for sounding:
"Then music with her silver sound
With speedy help doth lend redress."
(Peter exits.)

FIRST M: What a pestilent knave is this same!

SECOND M: Hang him, Jack! Come, we'll in here, tarry for the mourners, and stay dinner.
(The three musicians exit as the stage lights fade out.)]

dump—dismal tune

gleek—gibe

carry no crotchets—endure no quirks

dry-beat—beat soundly

Suggested cut ends.

ACT V, SCENE 1

(Set: In front of an apothecary shop on a street in Mantua. Time: Thursday, daytime. As the stage lights come up, a happy Romeo enters.)

ROM: If I may trust the flattering truth of sleep,
My dreams presage some joyful news at hand:
[My bosom's lord sits lightly in his throne;

And all this day an unaccustom'd spirit
Lifts me above the ground with cheerful thoughts.]

presage—foretell
Suggested cut begins.
bosom's lord—heart

Suggested cut ends.

I dreamt my lady came and found me dead—
Strange dream, that gives a dead man leave to think!—
And breathed such life with kisses in my lips,
That I revived, and was an emperor.
Ah me! how sweet is love itself possess'd,
When but love's shadows are so rich in joy!
(Enter Balthasar, dressed in riding clothes.)
News from Verona!—How now, Balthasar!
Dost thou not bring me letters from the Friar?
How doth my lady? Is my father well?
How fares my Juliet? that I ask again;
For nothing can be ill, if she be well.
BAL: *(Kneeling.)* Then she is well, and nothing can be ill:
Her body sleeps in Capel's monument,

Capel's—Capulet's

And her immortal part with angels lives.
I saw her laid low in her kindred's vault,
And presently took post to tell it you:

post—post-horses

O, pardon me for bringing these ill news,
Since you did leave it for my office, sir.
(Balthasar rises.)
ROM: Is it even so? then I defy you, stars!
Thou know'st my lodging: get me ink and paper,
And hire post-horses; I will hence tonight.
BAL: I do beseech you, sir, have patience:
Your looks are pale and wild, and do import
Some misadventure.
ROM: Tush, thou art deceived:
Leave me, and do the thing I bid thee do.
Hast thou no letters to me from the Friar?
BAL: No, my good lord.
ROM: No matter: get thee gone,
And hire those horses; I'll be with thee straight.
(Balthasar exits.)
Well, Juliet, I will lie with thee tonight.
Let's see for means: O mischief, thou art swift
To enter in the thoughts of desperate men!
I do remember an apothecary,—
And hereabouts he dwells,—which late I noted
In tatter'd weeds, with overwhelming brows,

weeds—clothes

Culling of simples; meagre were his looks,

simples—common herbs

Sharp misery had worn him to the bones:
[And in his needy shop a tortoise hung,

Suggested cut begins.

An alligator stuff'd, and other skins

Of ill-shaped fishes; and about his shelves
A beggarly account of empty boxes,
Green earthen pots, bladders and musty seeds,
Remnants of packthread and old cakes of roses,
Were thinly scatter'd, to make up a show.]
Noting this penury, to myself I said
"An if a man did need a poison now,
Whose sale is present death in Mantua,
Here lives a caitiff wretch would sell it him."

[O, this same thought did but forerun my need;
And this same needy man must sell it me.]
As I remember, this should be the house.
Being holiday, the beggar's shop is shut.
What, ho! apothecary!
(Apothecary enters.)

APO: Who calls so loud?
ROM: Come hither, man. I see that thou art poor: *(Showing him bag of coins.)*
Hold, there is forty ducats: let me have
A dram of poison, such soon-speeding gear
As will disperse itself through all the veins
That the life-weary taker may fall dead,
[And that the trunk may be discharged of breath
As violently as hasty powder fired
Doth hurry from the fatal cannon's womb.]
APO: Such mortal drugs I have; but Mantua's law
Is death to any he that utters them.
ROM: Art thou so bare and full of wretchedness,
And fear'st to die? famine is in thy cheeks,
Need and oppression starveth in thine eyes,
Contempt and beggary hangs upon thy back;
The world is not thy friend nor the world's law;
The world affords no law to make thee rich;
Then be not poor, but break it, and take this.
(Romeo opens bag and shows him gold coins.)
APO: My poverty, but not my will, consents.
(Apothecary crosses to door of his shop.)
ROM: I pay thy poverty, and not thy will.
(Apothecary enters shop and returns with vial.)
APO: Put this in any liquid thing you will,
And drink it off; and, if you had the strength
Of twenty men, it would dispatch you straight.
ROM: *(Giving bag of coins to Apothecary and accepting the vial.)*

packthread—twine
Suggested cut ends.
penury—poverty

caitiff wretch—miserable
creature
Suggested cut begins.
Suggested cut ends.

ducats—gold coins
gear—stuff

Suggested cut begins.

Suggested cut ends.

utters—issues

There is thy gold, worse poison to men's souls,

Doing more murders in this loathsome world,

Than these poor compounds that thou mayst not sell.

I sell thee poison; thou hast sold me none.

Farewell: buy food, and get thyself in flesh.

(Apothecary enters his shop.)

Come, cordial and not poison, go with me   **cordial**—stimulant

To Juliet's grave; for there must I use thee.

(Romeo exits as stage lights fade out.)

ACT V, SCENE 2

(Set: Outside Friar Laurence's cell, same as Act II, Scene 6, with large cross onstage.

Time: Thursday evening. As the stage lights come up, a breathless Friar John enters quickly,

shouting.)

FR.J: Holy Franciscan Friar! Brother, ho!

(From the opposite side of the stage, Friar Laurence enters with a basket of flowers.)

FR.L: This same should be the voice of Friar John.

Welcome from Mantua: what says Romeo?

Or, if his mind be writ, give me his letter.

FR.J: Going to find a bare-foot brother out,

One of our order, to associate me,   **associate**—accompany

Here in this city visiting the sick,

And finding him, the searchers of the town,

Suspecting that we both were in a house

Where the infectious pestilence did reign,

Seal'd up the doors, and would not let us forth;

So that my speed to Mantua there was stay'd.

FR.L: Who bare my letter, then, to Romeo?

FR.J: I could not send it—here it is again—

(He gives letter to Friar Laurence.)

Nor get a messenger to bring it thee,

So fearful were they of infection.

FR.L: Unhappy fortune! by my brotherhood,

The letter was not nice but full of charge   **nice**—trivial

Of dear import, and the neglecting it   **import**—important

May do much danger. Friar John, go hence;   significance

Get me an iron crow, and bring it straight   **iron crow**—crowbar

Unto my cell.

FR.J: Brother, I'll go and bring it thee.

(Friar John exits.)

FR.L: Now must I to the monument alone;

Within this three hours will fair Juliet wake:

She will beshrew me much that Romeo

Hath had no notice of these accidents;

But I will write again to Mantua,

And keep her at my cell till Romeo come;

Poor living corse, closed in a dead man's tomb!

(As the lights fade out, Friar Laurence exits.)

beshrew—scold

ACT V, SCENE 3

(Set: Part of the stage is a churchyard which leads to the Capulet tomb where Juliet is lying on a bier with hands crossed over her chest. Time: Before dawn on Friday. As the dim stage lights come up, Paris enters the churchyard with a Page who is carrying flowers and a torch.)

PAR: Give me thy torch, boy: hence, and stand aloof:

Yet put it out, for I would not be seen.

(Page extinguishes the torch.)

Under yond yew-trees lay thee all along,

Holding thine ear close to the hollow ground;

So shall no foot upon the churchyard tread,

Being loose, unfirm, with digging up of graves,

But thou shalt hear it: whistle then to me,

As signal that thou hear'st something approach.

Give me those flowers. *(Page hands him flowers.)* Do as I bid thee, go.

PAGE: *(Aside.)* I am almost afraid to stand alone

Here in the churchyard; yet I will adventure.

(Page exits with torch. Paris approaches tomb.)

PAR: Sweet flower, with flowers thy bridal bed I strew,—

O woe! thy canopy is dust and stones;—

Which with sweet water nightly I will dew,

Or, wanting that, with tears distill'd by moans:

The obsequies that I for thee will keep

Nightly shall be to strew thy grave and weep.

(Paris places flowers at foot of bier.

There is a whistle from offstage.)

The boy gives warning something doth approach.

What cursèd foot wanders this way tonight,

To cross my obsequies and true love's rite?

What, with a torch! muffle me, night, awhile.

(Paris hides from view as Romeo and Balthasar

enter with a torch, [mattock and crowbar.)

ROM: Give me that mattock and the wrenching iron.]

Hold, take this letter; *(Gives Balthasar a letter.)* early in the morning

See thou deliver it to my lord and father.

Give me the light:

obsequies—funeral rites

cross—thwart

Suggested cut begins.

Suggested cut ends.

(Romeo takes the torch and puts it in a bracket on the wall.)
                                    upon thy life, I charge thee,
Whate'er thou hear'st or seest, stand all aloof,
And do not interrupt me in my course.
Why I descend into this bed of death,
Is partly to behold my lady's face;
But chiefly to take thence from her dead finger
A precious ring, a ring that I must use
In dear employment: therefore hence, be gone:
But if thou, jealous, dost return to pry   **jealous**—suspicious
In what I further shall intend to do,
By heaven, I will tear thee joint by joint
And strew this hungry churchyard with thy limbs:
[The time and my intents are savage-wild,   Suggested cut begins.
More fierce and more inexorable far
Than empty tigers or the roaring sea.]   Suggested cut ends.
BAL: I will be gone, sir, and not trouble you.
ROM: So shalt thou show me friendship. Take thou that: *(Romeo gives him a pouch of money.)* Live, and be prosperous: and farewell, good fellow.
BAL: *(Aside.)* For all the same, I'll hide me hereabout:
His looks I fear, and his intents I doubt.
(Balthasar exits.)
[ROM: Thou detestable maw, thou womb of death,   Suggested cut begins.
Gorged with the dearest morsel of the earth,
Thus I enforce thy rotten jaws to open,
And, in despite, I'll cram thee with more food!
(Romeo opens the tomb.)]   Suggested cut ends.
(As Romeo kneels at tomb, Paris emerges from hiding place.)
PAR: This is that banish'd haughty Montague,
That murder'd my love's cousin, with which grief,
It is supposed, the fair creature died;
And here is come to do some villainous shame
To the dead bodies: I will apprehend him.
[Stop thy unhallow'd toil, vile Montague!   Suggested cut begins.
Can vengeance be pursued further than death?]   Suggested cut ends.
(Romeo rises.)
Condemnèd villain, I do apprehend thee:
Obey, and go with me; for thou must die.
ROM: I must indeed; and therefore came I hither.
Good gentle youth, tempt not a desperate man;
Fly hence, and leave me: think upon these gone;
Let them affright thee. I beseech thee, youth,
Put not another sin upon my head,

By urging me to fury: O, be gone!
By heaven, I love thee better than myself;
For I come hither arm'd against myself:
Stay not, be gone; live, and hereafter say,
A madman's mercy bade thee run away.
PAR: I do defy thy conjurations,
And apprehend thee for a felon here.

conjurations—appeals

ROM: Wilt thou provoke me? then have at thee, boy!
(Romeo and Paris draw their swords and fight. Page enters.)
PAGE: O Lord, they fight! I will go call the watch. *(Page exits.)*
PAR: O, I am slain! *(Paris falls.)*
If thou be merciful,
[Open the tomb,] lay me with Juliet.

Suggested cut begins and ends.

(Paris dies.)
ROM: In faith, I will. Let me peruse this face.
Mercutio's kinsman, noble County Paris!
What said my man, when my betossèd soul

betossèd—tossed about

Did not attend him as we rode? I think
He told me Paris should have married Juliet:
Said he not so? or did I dream it so?
[Or am I mad, hearing him talk of Juliet,

Suggested cut begins.

To think it was so? O, give me thy hand,
One writ with me in sour misfortune's book!]

Suggested cut ends.

I'll bury thee in a triumphant grave;
A grave? O no! a lantern, slaughter'd youth,

lantern—lighthouse

For here lies Juliet, and her beauty makes
This vault a feasting presence full of light.

feasting presence—festive chamber

(Romeo lays Paris on ground near Juliet.)
[Death, lie thou there, by a dead man interr'd.

Suggested cut begins.

How oft when men are at the point of death
Have they been merry! which their keepers call
A lightning before death: O, how may I
Call this a lightning?]

Suggested cut ends.

(Romeo bends over Juliet.)
O my love! my wife!
Death, that hath suck'd the honey of thy breath,
Hath had no power yet upon thy beauty:
Thou art not conquer'd; beauty's ensign yet

ensign—flag

Is crimson in thy lips and in thy cheeks,
And death's pale flag is not advancèd there.
[Tybalt, liest thou there in thy bloody sheet?

Suggested cut begins.

O, what more favour can I do to thee,
Than with that hand that cut thy youth in twain

To sunder his that was thine enemy?

Forgive me, cousin!]   Ah, dear Juliet,   Suggested cut ends.

Why art thou yet so fair? shall I believe

That unsubstantial death is amorous,   **unsubstantial**—immaterial

And that the lean abhorrèd monster keeps

Thee here in dark to be his paramour?   **paramour**—lover

(Romeo sits beside Juliet.)

For fear of that, I still will stay with thee;

And never from this palace of dim night

Depart again: here, here will I remain

With worms that are thy chamber-maids; O, here

Will I set up my everlasting rest,

And shake the yoke of inauspicious stars   **inauspicious**—unfriendly

From this world-wearied flesh. Eyes, look your last!

Arms, take your last embrace! and, lips, O you

The doors of breath, seal with a righteous kiss

A dateless bargain to engrossing death!   **dateless**—eternal, **engrossing**—
                                                                  embracing

(Romeo kisses her, then takes out the vial.)

Come, bitter conduct, come, unsavoury guide!   **conduct**—escort

[Thou desperate pilot, now at once run on   Suggested cut begins.

The dashing rocks thy sea-sick weary bark!]   Suggested cut ends.

Here's to my love!

(Romeo drinks from vial of poison.)

O true apothecary!

Thy drugs are quick. Thus with a kiss I die.

(Romeo kisses her, dies and falls next to her on the bier. Friar Laurence enters the churchyard with lantern, crowbar and spade.)

FR.L: Saint Francis be my speed! how oft tonight   **speed**—protector

Have my old feet stumbled at graves! Who's there? *(Balthasar enters.)*

BAL: Here's one, a friend, and one that knows you well.

FR.L: Bliss be upon you! Tell me, good my friend,

What torch is yond, that vainly lends his light

To grubs and eyeless skulls? as I discern,   **grubs**—worms

It burneth in the Capels' monument.

BAL: It doth so, holy sir; and there's my master,

One that you love.

FR.L: Who is it?

BAL: Romeo.

FR.L: How long hath he been there?

BAL: Full half an hour.

FR.L: Go with me to the vault.

BAL: I dare not, sir:

My master knows not but I am gone hence;
And fearfully did menace me with death,
If I did stay to look on his intents.
FR.L: Stay, then; I'll go alone. Fear comes upon me:
O, much I fear some ill unlucky thing.
BAL: As I did sleep under this yew-tree here,
I dreamt my master and another fought,
And that my master slew him.
FR.L: Romeo!
(Looking around.)
Alack, alack, what blood is this, which stains
The stony entrance of this sepulchre?
What mean these masterless and gory swords
To lie discolour'd by this place of peace?
(The Friar crosses to the bier.)
Romeo! O, pale! Who else? what, Paris too?
And steep'd in blood? Ah, what an unkind hour
Is guilty of this lamentable chance!
The lady stirs.
(Juliet wakes.)
JUL: O comfortable Friar! where is my lord?   **comfortable**—comforting
I do remember well where I should be,
And there I am. Where is my Romeo?
(Voices are heard from offstage. Balthasar runs off to investigate. Juliet becomes aware of Romeo lying beside her.)
FR.L: I hear some noise. Lady, come from that nest
Of death, contagion, and unnatural sleep:
A greater power than we can contradict
Hath thwarted our intents. Come, come away.
Thy husband in thy bosom there lies dead;
And Paris too. [Come, I'll dispose of thee   Suggested cut begins.
Among a sisterhood of holy nuns:]   Suggested cut ends.
Stay not to question, for the watch is coming;
Come, go, good Juliet,
(More voices and noise are heard offstage.)
                    I dare no longer stay.
JUL: Go, get thee hence, for I will not away.
(Friar Laurence exits quickly.)
What's here? a cup, closed in my true love's hand?
Poison, I see, hath been his timeless end: **timeless**—ill-timed
O churl! drunk all, and left no friendly drop
To help me after? I will kiss thy lips;
Haply some poison yet doth hang on them,

To make me die with a restorative.

(Juliet kisses him.)

Thy lips are warm.

(The First Watchman calls from offstage.)

FIRST W: Lead, boy: which way?

JUL: *(Seeing Romeo's dagger in scabbard at his waist.)*

Yea, noise? then I'll be brief. O happy dagger!

This is thy sheath; there rust, and let me die.

(She stabs herself and dies beside Romeo. [Enter the Page and three watchmen with lanterns.)

PAGE: This is the place; there, where the torch

doth burn. *(Peter, Sampson, Abraham, two gentlemen enter carrying torches.)*

FIRST W: The ground is bloody; search about the churchyard:

(To the Second and Third Watchmen.)

Go, some of you, whoe'er you find attach.

(Second and Third Watchmen exit. First Watchman crosses to bier.)

Pitiful sight! here lies the County slain,

And Juliet bleeding, warm, and newly dead,

Who here hath lain these two days burièd.

(To the Page.)

Go, tell the Prince: *(Page exits. To Sampson.)*

Run to the Capulets: *(Sampson exits. To Abraham.)*

Raise up the Montagues: *(Abraham exits.)*

(To Peter and two gentlemen.) some others search:

We see the ground whereon these woes do lie;

But the true ground of all these piteous woes

We cannot without circumstance descry.

(Peter and two gentlemen exit. Second Watchman enters with Balthasar.)

SECOND W: Here's Romeo's man; we found him in the churchyard.

FIRST W: Hold him in safety, till the Prince come hither.

(Third Watchman returns with Friar Laurence.)

THIRD W. Here is a Friar, that trembles, sighs and weeps:

We took this mattock and this spade from him,

As he was coming from this churchyard side.

FIRST W: A great suspicion: stay the Friar too.

(Prince, two soldiers, Page and Citizens enter.)

PRI: What misadventure is so early up,

That calls our person from our morning's rest?

(Capulet, Lady Capulet, Nurse, Old Capulet and Sampson enter.)

CAP: What should it be, that they so shriek abroad?

L.CAP: The people in the street cry Romeo,

Some Juliet, and some Paris; and all run

With open outcry toward our monument.

Suggested cut begins here. See end of play for an alternate cut ending.

attach—arrest

circumstance—particulars

descry—determine

PRI: What fear is this which startles in our ears?

FIRST W: Sovereign, here lies the County Paris slain;

And Romeo dead; and Juliet, dead before,

Warm and new kill'd.

PRI: Search, seek, and know how this foul murder comes.

FIRST W: Here is a Friar, and slaughter'd Romeo's man;

With instruments upon them, fit to open

These dead men's tombs.

CAP: O heavens! O wife, look how our daughter bleeds!

This dagger hath mista'en—for, lo, his house

Is empty on the back of Montague,—

And it mis-sheathed in my daughter's bosom!

L.CAP: O me! this sight of death is as a bell,

That warns my old age to a sepulchre.

(Montague, Benvolio and Abraham enter.)

PRI: Come, Montague; for thou art early up,

To see thy son and heir more early down.

MON: Alas, my liege, my wife is dead tonight;

Grief of my son's exile hath stopp'd her breath:

What further woe conspires against mine age?

PRI: Look, and thou shalt see.

MON: O thou untaught! what manners is in this?

To press before thy father to a grave?

PRI: Seal up the mouth of outrage for a while,

Till we can clear these ambiguities,

And know their spring, their head, their true descent;

And then will I be general of your woes,

And lead you even to death: meantime forbear,

And let mischance be slave to patience.

Bring forth the parties of suspicion.

FRI.L: I am the greatest, able to do least,

Yet most suspected, as the time and place

Doth make against me, of this direful murder;

And here I stand, both to impeach and purge

Myself condemnèd and myself excused.

PRI: Then say at once what thou dost know in this.

FR.L: I will be brief, for my short date of breath

Is not so long as is a tedious tale.

Romeo, there dead, was husband to that Juliet;

And she, there dead, that Romeo's faithful wife:

I married them; and their stol'n marriage-day

Was Tybalt's dooms-day, whose untimely death

Banish'd the new-made bridegroom from this city,

house—i.e., scabbard

untaught—ill-mannered

purge—clear of suspicion

date of breath—life expectancy

For whom, and not for Tybalt, Juliet pined.
You, to remove that siege of grief from her,
Betroth'd and would have married her perforce
To County Paris: then comes she to me,
And, with wild looks, bid me devise some mean
To rid her from this second marriage,
Or in my cell there would she kill herself.
Then gave I her, so tutor'd by my art,
A sleeping potion; which so took effect
As I intended, for it wrought on her
The form of death: meantime I writ to Romeo,
That he should hither come as this dire night,
To help to take her from her borrow'd grave,   **borrow'd**—temporary
Being the time the potion's force should cease.
But he which bore my letter, Friar John,
Was stay'd by accident, and yesternight
Return'd my letter back. Then all alone
At the prefixèd hour of her waking,
Came I to take her from her kindred's vault;
Meaning to keep her closely at my cell,   **closely**—secretly
Till I conveniently could send to Romeo:
But when I came, some minute ere the time
Of her awaking, here untimely lay
The noble Paris and true Romeo dead.
She wakes; and I entreated her come forth,
And bear this work of heaven with patience:
But then a noise did scare me from the tomb;
And she, too desperate, would not go with me,
But, as it seems, did violence on herself.
All this I know; and to the marriage
Her Nurse is privy; and, if aught in this
Miscarried by my fault, let my old life
Be sacrificed, some hour before his time,
Unto the rigour of severest law.
PRI: We still have known thee for a holy man.
Where's Romeo's man? what can he say in this?
BAL: I brought my master news of Juliet's death;
And then in post he came from Mantua   **post**—haste
To this same place, to this same monument.
This letter he early bid me give his father,
And threatened me with death, going in the vault,
If I departed not and left him there.
PRI: Give me the letter; I will look on it.

(Balthasar bows to Prince and gives him letter.)

Where is the County's Page, that raised the watch? *(Page comes forward.)*

Sirrah, what made your master in this place?   **made**—was doing

PAGE: He came with flowers to strew his lady's grave;

And bid me stand aloof, and so I did:

Anon comes one with light to ope the tomb;   **ope**—open

And by and by my master drew on him;

And then I ran away to call the watch.

PRI: *(Looking at letter.)* This letter doth make good the Friar's words,

Their course of love, the tidings of her death:

And here he writes that he did buy a poison

Of a poor 'pothecary, and therewithal

Came to this vault to die, and lie with Juliet.

Where be these enemies? Capulet! Montague!

(Capulet and Montague come to the left and right of the Prince.)

See, what a scourge is laid upon your hate,

That heaven finds means to kill your joys with love.

And I for winking at your discords too

Have lost a brace of kinsmen: all are punish'd.

CAP: O brother Montague, give me thy hand:

(Montague and Capulet join hands.)

This is my daughter's jointure, for no more   **jointure**—dowry

Can I demand.

MON: But I can give thee more:

For I will raise her statue in pure gold;

That while Verona by that name is known,

There shall no figure at such rate be set   **rate**—value

As that of true and faithful Juliet.

CAP: As rich shall Romeo's by his lady's lie;

Poor sacrifices of our enmity!

PRI: A glooming peace this morning with it brings;

The sun, for sorrow, will not show his head:

Go hence, to have more talk of these sad things;

Some shall be pardon'd, and some punishèd:

For never was a story of more woe

Than this of Juliet and her Romeo.

(Capulet and Montague embrace. All actors freeze. Sound: Church bells tolling. Lights: Fade out stage lights, spot Romeo and Juliet briefly, then black out and sound out.)

Curtain call: Director's choice.

ALTERNATE CUT ENDING

The following begins in Act V, Scene 3 after Juliet kills herself.
(Sound: Alarm bells and drums, which continue until the Prince speaks. Enter the Page
and three watchmen, with lanterns. Also entering with torches are Peter and Sampson. After
examining the situation, the First Watchman sends the Page to get the Prince. Friar Laurence,
with lantern, enters with Capulet, Lady Capulet, Nurse and Old Capulet. Balthasar, with
lantern, enters with Montague, Benvolio and Abraham. All look at dead bodies and console
each other. The Page enters with the Prince, two gentlemen, two soldiers and citizens. The
Prince crosses to the body of Paris, kneels, then looks at the bier with bodies of Romeo and
Juliet. Sound: Alarm bells and drums are out as the Prince comes to center to speak.)

PRI: Where be these enemies? Capulet! Montague!

(Capulet and Montague come to the left and right of the Prince.)

See, what a scourge is laid upon your hate,

That heaven finds means to kill your joys with love!

And I, for winking at your discords too,

Have lost a brace of kinsmen: all are punish'd.

CAP: O brother Montague, give me thy hand:

(Montague and Capulet join hands.)

This is my daughter's jointure, for no more   **jointure**—dowry

Can I demand.

MON: But I can give thee more:

For I will raise her statue in pure gold;

That while Verona by that name is known,

There shall no figure at such rate be set   **rate**—value

As that of true and faithful Juliet.

CAP: As rich shall Romeo's by his lady's lie;

Poor sacrifices of our enmity!

PRI: A glooming peace this morning with it brings;

The sun for sorrow will not show his head:

Go hence, to have more talk of these sad things

Some shall be pardon'd and some punishèd

For never was a story of more woe

Than this of Juliet and her Romeo.

(Capulet and Montague embrace. All actors freeze. Sound: Church bells tolling. Lights: Fade
out stage lights, spot Romeo and Juliet briefly, then black out and sound out.)

Curtain call: Director's choice.

✦ Appendix ✦

Other Important Plays by Shakespeare

Antony and Cleopatra

Genre: Tragedy

Date of First Performance: 1607

Places Depicted: Rooms in Cleopatra's palace in Alexandria; Caesar's house in Rome; Pompey's house in Messina; house of Lepidus in Rome; a street in Rome; near Misenum; on board Pompey's galley; a plain in Syria; rooms in Antony's house in Athens; Antony's camp near Actium; a plain near Actium; Caesar's camp in Egypt; before Caesar's camp in Alexandria; before Cleopatra's palace; Antony's camp in Alexandria; field of battle between camps; under the walls of Alexandria; a monument; a room in the monument

Characters:

Mark Antony, triumvir

Octavius Caesar, triumvir

M. Aemilius Lepidus, triumvir

Sextus Pompeius

Domitius Enobarbus, friend to Antony

Ventidius, friend to Antony

Eros, friend to Antony

Scarus, friend to Antony

Dercetas, friend to Antony

Demetrius, friend to Antony

Philo, friend to Antony

Mecaenas, friend to Caesar

Agrippa, friend to Caesar

Dolabella friend to Caesar

Proculeius, friend to Caesar

Thyreus, friend to Caesar

Gallus, friend to Caesar

Menas, friend to Pompey

Menecrates friend to Pompey

Varrius, friend to Pompey

Cleopatra, Queen of Egypt

Octavia, sister to Caesar and wife to Antony

Charmian, attendant on Cleopatra

Iras, attendant on Cleopatra

Taurus, lieutenant-general to Caesar

Canidius, lieutenant-general to Antony

Silius, an officer in Ventidius's army

Euphronius, an ambassador from Antony to Caesar

Alexas

Mardian, a Eunuch

Seleucus, attendant on Cleopatra

Diomedes, attendant on Cleopatra

A soothsayer

A clown

Officers, soldiers

Messengers

Other attendants

Antony and Cleopatra

As You Like It

The Comedy of Errors

Hamlet

Henry V

Julius Caesar

King Lear

Macbeth

Measure for Measure

The Merchant of Venice

The Merry Wives of Windsor

A Midsummer Night's Dream

Much Ado About Nothing

Othello

Richard II

Richard III

The Taming of the Shrew

The Tempest

Twelfth Night

Plot: Historically, this play covers about ten years from 40 B.C. to 30 B.C. In Alexandria, Egypt, Mark Antony is enjoying himself with Cleopatra. The news of unrest in Rome, a threat of war by Sextus Pompeius and the death of his wife, Fulvia, force Antony to return to Rome where he is one of the ruling triumvirate. In Rome, Antony and Octavius Caesar mend their relations by a marriage between Caesar's sister, Octavia, and Antony. Later the rivalry between Caesar and Antony flares up again when Antony returns to Egypt and Cleopatra. In the end, Antony falls on a sword and dies in Cleopatra's arms. Then, she kills herself by putting two asps to her breast and arm.

Difficulties:

- This play has a large cast of men with four women.
- There is one song and music called for in Act II, Scene 7, the music of hautboys (oboes) as under the stage in Act IV, Scene 3, as well as flourishes (fanfares), trumpets and drums.
- Music must be found for the above occasions.

As You Like It

Genre: Pastoral comedy

Date of First Performance: 1600

Places Depicted: Orchard of Oliver's house; Duke Frederick's court; lawn before Frederick's palace; room in the palace; the Forest of Arden in the northeast of France

Characters:

Duke Senior, living in banishment	Rosalind, daughter to the banished duke
Frederick, his brother, and usurper of his dukedom	Celia, daughter to Frederick
	Phebe, a shepherdess
Amiens, lord attending on banished duke	Audrey, a country wench
Jaques, lord attending on banished duke	
Le Beau, courtier to Frederick	Touchstone, a clown
Charles, wrestler to Frederick	Sir Oliver Martext, a vicar
Oliver, son to Sir Rowland de Boys	Corin, shepherd
Orlando, son to Sir Rowland	Silvius, shepherd
Jaques de Boys, son to Sir Rowland	William, country fellow
Adam, servant to Oliver	Hymen
Dennis, servant to Oliver	Lords, pages, other attendants

Plot: A Duke of France is banished by his younger brother, the new Duke Frederick, and goes to live in the Forest of Arden. Duke Senior's daughter, Rosalind, stays at court with her best friend, Celia, and becomes interested in Orlando. When Rosalind is banished from the court, Celia and Touchstone leave with her. Rosalind disguises herself as a male named Ganymede and Celia assumes the identity of a woman named Aliena. They go to the Forest of Arden as do Orlando and his servant, Adam. There Orlando meets Ganymede, who asks to be called Rosalind when he comes everyday to woo her. Eventually, the play has four marriages: Rosalind and Orlando, Celia and Oliver, Touchstone and Audrey, Silvius and Phebe. Frederick gets religion and Duke Senior's lands are restored to him.

Difficulties:

- Disguising Rosalind as Ganymede and Celia as Aliena so that nobody recognizes them is difficult.
- Finding suitable tunes to put with the numerous song lyrics in the script may present a problem.
- Two characters, both named Jaques, may be confusing. The first Jaques in the cast list has one of the most famous speeches in all of Shakespeare beginning "All the world's a stage, . . ." (Act II, Scene 7).

The Comedy of Errors

Genre: Farce comedy

Date of First Performance: 1594

Places Depicted: Hall in the Duke's palace in Ephesus; the mart; house of Antipholus of Ephesus; a public place; before the house of Antipholus of Ephesus; a street; before a priory

Characters:

Solinus, Duke of Ephesus

Aegeon, a merchant of Syracuse

Antipholus of Ephesus, twin brother

Antipholus of Syracuse, twin brother

Dromio of Ephesus, twin brother

Dromio of Syracuse, twin brother

Balthazar, a merchant

Angelo, a goldsmith

First Merchant

Second Merchant

Aemilia, wife to Aegeon

Adriana, wife to Antipholus of Ephesus

Luciana, her sister

Luce, servant to Adriana

A courtesan

Pinch, a schoolmaster

Jailer

Officers

Other attendants

Plot: Because Ephesus and Syracuse are enemies, Aegeon, an aged merchant from Syracuse, is arrested in Ephesus and condemned to death. When asked why he came to Ephesus, he tells how his wife bore twin boys and at the same time another woman had twin boys, whom Aegeon bought to serve his two sons. When their ship was wrecked, he escaped with one twin and one little servant, but he saw his wife, Aemilia, and the other two babies taken away by Corinthian fishermen. Eighteen years later, Aegeon's son left him to seek his twin brother. When he did not return, Aegeon spent five years traveling, trying to find him. As it so happens, his son Antipholus of Syracuse and Dromio, his servant, are visiting in Ephesus. Furthermore, his twin Antipholus is married to Adriana and lives in Ephesus with the other Dromio. The first mix-up occurs when Dromio of Ephesus delivers a message to Antipholus of Syracuse that dinner is ready. There are many more mix-ups in the plot until both sons and their servants meet and unravel the errors. Antipholus of Ephesus is reconciled with his wife, his brother woos her sister Luciana, the father is pardoned and finds his long-lost wife, Aemilia.

Difficulties:

- The main problems center on finding two sets of twins or young men who look enough alike to pass for twins.
- Like many farce comedies, this play can be difficult to make funny for modern audiences.

Hamlet

Genre: Tragedy

Date of First Performance: 1601

Places Depicted: A platform before the castle in Elsinore, Denmark; various rooms and a hall in the castle; room in Polonius' house; Queen's room; plain in Denmark; churchyard

Characters:

Claudius, King of Denmark

Hamlet, son to the late King and nephew to Claudius

Polonius, Lord Chamberlain

Horatio, friend to Hamlet

Laertes, son to Polonius

Voltimand, courtier

Cornelius, courtier

Rosencrantz, courtier

Guildenstern, courtier

Osric, courtier

Marcellus, officer

Bernardo, officer

Francisco, a soldier

Reynaldo, servant to Polonius

Gertrude, Queen of Denmark, mother to Hamlet, wife to Claudius

Ophelia, daughter to Polonius

Fortinbras, Prince of Norway

Ghost of Hamlet's father

The players

Two clowns, gravediggers

A gentleman

A priest

A Norwegian captain

English ambassadors

Lords, ladies, officers

Soldiers, sailors, messengers

Other attendants

Plot: In medieval Denmark Hamlet is informed by the Ghost of his father that he was killed by his brother Claudius, who after the murder became king and married Hamlet's mother, Gertrude. The rest of the play is concerned with Hamlet trying to get revenge on Claudius. During this, he kills Polonius by mistake and Ophelia commits suicide. In the ending Laertes stabs Hamlet with a poisoned rapier, Hamlet stabs Laertes with the same weapon, Gertrude drinks poison by mistake and Hamlet kills Claudius. In the denouement we learn that Fortinbras, Prince of Norway, will rule Denmark.

Difficulties:

- The greatest actors in the world have attempted the part of Hamlet because this play—the longest one written by Shakespeare—is generally considered to be the finest tragedy ever written and Hamlet the best male role.

- The fencing match between Laertes and Hamlet at the end can be difficult to stage unless you have excellent fencers.

- Music is needed for Ophelia's songs in Act IV, Scene 5; the First Clown's song in Act V, Scene 1; the dumb-show in Act III, Scene 2; and "a dead march" at the end of the play.

Henry V

Genre: History

Date of First Performance: 1599

Places Depicted: An antechamber in the King's palace in London; the Presence chamber; a street in London; a council-chamber in Southampton; before a tavern in London; the French King's palace in France; before Harfleur in France; the English camp in Picardy; the French camp near Agincourt; the English camp at Agincourt; the field of battle; before King Henry's pavilion

Characters:

King Henry V

Duke of Gloucester, brother to the King

Duke of Bedford, brother to the King

Duke of Exeter, uncle to the King

Duke of York, cousin to the King

Earls of Salisbury, Westmoreland and
    Warwick

Archbishop of Canterbury

Bishop of Ely

Earl of Cambridge

Lord Scroop

Sir Thomas Grey

Sir Thomas Erpingham, Gower, Fluellen,
    Macmorris, Jamy, officers in King
    Henry's army

Bates, Court, Williams, soldiers in same

Pistol, Nym, Bardolph

Boy

A herald

Isabel, Queen of France

Katharine, daughter to Charles and Isabel

Alice, a lady attending on her

Hostess of a tavern in Eastcheap,
    formerly Mistress Quickly, now married
    to Pistol

Charles VI, King of France

Lewis, the Dauphin

Dukes of Burgundy, Orleans and Bourbon

Constable of France

Rambures and Grandpré, French lords

Governor of Harfleur

Montjoy, a French herald

Ambassadors to the King of England

Chorus

Lords, ladies, citizens

Officers, soldiers, messengers

Other attendants

Plot: Historically, this play covers the years 1414 to 1420. Shortly after King Henry V's coronation, he decides to claim certain French dukedoms. The Dauphin of France replies with an insulting gift of tennis balls and Henry prepares for war. The French bribe three English lords to kill Henry, but the plot is discovered. Henry demands the crown and kingdom of France and his forces occupy the French city of Harfleur. At Agincourt the two forces prepare for battle which the English win. The French King gives Henry the hand of his daughter Katharine and acknowledges him as his heir. At the end Henry is more humble and wants peace between France and England.

Difficulties:

- Each act begins and the last act ends with a speech by Chorus. Handling these effectively can be difficult.

- In Act III, Scene 1, Henry has a well-known speech to his troops beginning "Once more unto the breach, dear friends, once more; . . ." This is a difficult speech to do well.
- Most of the history plays need flourishes (fanfares), trumpets, sennets (signal calls on a trumpet or cornet for entrance or exit on the stage) and alarums and excursions (exciting warlike sounds as soldiers move across the stage).

Julius Caesar

Genre: Tragedy

Date of First Performance: 1599

Places Depicted: A street in Rome; a public place; Brutus's orchard; Caesar's house; a street near the Capitol; before the house of Brutus; before the Capitol (the Senate sitting above); the Forum; a house in Rome; before Brutus's tent in camp near Sardis; Brutus's tent; the plains of Philippi

Characters:

Julius Caesar	Messala, friend to Brutus and Cassius
Octavius Caesar, triumvir after death of Julius Caesar	Young Cato, friend to Brutus and Cassius
	Volumnius, friend to Brutus and Cassius
Marcus Antonius, triumvir after death of Julius Caesar	Calpurnia, wife to Caesar
M. Aemilius Lepidus, triumvir after death of Julius Caesar	Portia, wife to Brutus
Cicero, senator	Flavius, tribune
Publius, senator	Marullus, tribune
Popilius Lena, senator	Artemidorus, a Sophist
Marcus Brutus, conspirator against Julius Caesar	A soothsayer
	Cinna, a poet
Cassius, conspirator against Julius Caesar	Another poet
Casca, conspirator against Julius Caesar	Varro, servant to Brutus
Trebonius, conspirator against Julius Caesar	Clitus, servant to Brutus
	Claudius, servant to Brutus
Ligarius, conspirator against Julius Caesar	Strato, servant to Brutus
Decius Brutus, conspirator against Julius Caesar	Lucius, servant to Brutus
	Dardanius, servant to Brutus
Metellus Cimber, conspirator against Julius Caesar	Pindarus, servant to Cassius
	Other senators
Cinna, conspirator against Julius Caesar	Citizens
Lucilius, friend to Brutus and Cassius	Guards
Titinius, friend to Brutus and Cassius	Other servants and attendants

Plot: Shakespeare compressed events that occurred in 45 B.C. to 42 B.C. into six days of this play. After Caesar defeats armies led by the sons of Pompey, he returns to Rome in triumph. Three times Mark Antony offers him a kingly crown and each time he refuses it. Some are afraid that Caesar is becoming too powerful, so Cassius and Brutus head a band of conspirators. Despite warnings, Caesar goes to the Capitol and is killed by the conspirators. At his funeral Brutus attempts to explain the killing and then allows Mark Antony to speak. He skillfully turns the crowd against the conspirators who are forced to flee the city. Brutus and Cassius head an army that is opposed by Mark Antony, Caesar's nephew Octavius Caesar and Lepidus. The armies meet at Philippi where the troops of Cassius are routed and he orders his servant to kill him. Brutus commits suicide and the triumvirate is victorious.

Difficulties:

- A large number of men is needed; only two women are in the cast.
- Outstanding actors are required for Brutus, Antony, Cassius and Caesar.
- In Act IV, Scene 3 a stage direction says that Lucius provides "Music, and a song," but there are no words in the script.

King Lear

Genre: Tragedy

Date of First Performance: 1605

Places Depicted: King Lear's palace; Earl of Gloucester's castle; Duke of Albany's palace; before Gloucester's castle; a wood; a heath; before a hovel; chamber in a farmhouse; before the Duke of Albany's palace; French camp near Dover; fields near Dover; British camp near Dover

Characters:

Lear, King of Britain	Goneril, daughter to Lear
King of France	Regan, daughter to Lear
Duke of Burgundy	Cordelia, daughter to Lear
Duke of Cornwall	
Duke of Albany	Oswald, steward to Goneril
Earl of Kent	A captain
Earl of Gloucester	Gentleman attendant on Cordelia
Edgar, son to Gloucester	A herald
Edmund, bastard son to Gloucester	Servants to Cornwall
Curan, a courtier	Knights of Lear's train
Old man, tenant to Gloucester	Captains
Doctor	Messengers
Fool	Soldiers, other attendants

Plot: Elderly British King Lear wants to retire and decides to divide his kingdom among his three daughters: Goneril, Regan and Cordelia. The first two tell their father what he wants to hear and he rewards each of them with one-third of his kingdom. But Cordelia's simple statement of love and duty infuriates him and he takes her share and divides it between Goneril and Regan. The King of France, however, takes Cordelia as his wife. Lear is supposed to spend a month alternately with Goneril and Regan; however, they reduce his retinue and heap other indignities upon him so he leaves with his fool. Some friends help him get to Dover where Cordelia has landed with a French invasion. There Cordelia finds him and cares for him. The French are defeated in battle, Goneril poisons Regan and then stabs herself, Cordelia is hanged and Lear dies.

Difficulties:

- Charles Lamb, writing *On the Tragedies of Shakespeare* in the early nineteenth century, declared, "The Lear of Shakespeare cannot be acted." Of course, it has been acted by such famous performers as Edwin Booth, Laurence Olivier and James Earl Jones. Most people will agree, however, that it is one of the most difficult roles to act that has ever been created.

- Act III, Scene 7 portrays the blinding of Gloucester which is a challenge to the director to stage well.

- The Fool sings twice, soft music plays once, and at various times the script calls for horns, drums, sennet and alarum.

Macbeth

Genre: Tragedy

Date of First Performance: 1606

Places Depicted: A desert place; a camp near Forres; a heath; the King's palace; Macbeth's castle at Inverness; before Macbeth's castle; a park; a cavern; Macduff's castle at Fife; before the King's palace in England; room in castle at Dunsinane; country near Dunsinane; country near Birnam Wood

Characters:

Duncan, King of Scotland	Lady Macbeth
Malcolm, son to Duncan	Lady Macduff
Donalbain, son to Duncan	Gentlewoman attending Lady Macbeth
Macbeth, general of Scottish army	Hecate
Banquo, general of Scottish army	Three Witches
Macduff, nobleman of Scotland	
Lennox, nobleman	Boy, son to Macduff
Ross, nobleman	An English doctor
Menteith, nobleman	A Scottish doctor
Angus, nobleman	A soldier
Caithness, nobleman	A porter
Fleance, son to Banquo	An old man
Siward, general of English forces	Murderers, messengers, lords, officers
Young Siward, his son	Soldiers, other attendants
Seyton, officer attending Macbeth	Apparitions

Plot: After Macbeth and Banquo, two generals under King Duncan in eleventh-century Scotland, are victorious in battle, three witches hail Macbeth as Thane of Glamis, Thane of Cawdor and future King of Scotland. They also tell Banquo his children will be kings. This prediction is the inciting incident that motivates the plot. The result is that King Duncan is killed by Macbeth with the help of his wife and Macbeth is crowned

King of Scotland. He next kills Banquo but his son, Fleance, escapes. Macbeth kills Lady Macduff and her children but Macduff escapes. Lady Macbeth become mentally ill and commits suicide. Finally, Macbeth is killed by Macduff, allowing Duncan's son, Malcolm, to become king.

Difficulties:

- The scenes with the three witches can be hard to stage, especially the one with the apparitions (Act IV, Scene 1).
- The banquet scene (Act III, Scene 4) where Banquo's ghost appears can also present problems.
- Swordfighting is always difficult such as the scenes in which Macbeth kills Young Siward and Macduff fights with Macbeth (Act V, Scenes 7 and 8).

Measure for Measure

Genre: Dark comedy

Date of First Performance: 1604

Places Depicted: An apartment in the Duke's palace in Vienna; a street; a monastery; a nunnery; hall and room in Angelo's house; room in prison; street before the prison; moated grange at St. Luke's; fields; street near the city-gate; the city-gate

Characters:

Vincentio, the Duke of Vienna

Angelo, the deputy

Escalus, an ancient lord

Claudio, a young gentleman

Lucio, a fantastic

Provost

Friar Thomas

Friar Peter

A justice

Varrius

Elbow, a simple constable

Froth, a foolish gentleman

Pompey, clown, servant to Mistress Overdone

Isabella, sister to Claudio

Mariana, betrothed to Angelo

Juliet, beloved of Claudio

Francesca, a nun

Mistress Overdone, a bawd

Abhorson, an executioner

Barnardine, a prisoner

Two gentlemen

Boy

Lords, officers

Citizens

Attendants

Plot: Duke Vincentio decides to travel and leave the city of Vienna in the hands of Angelo and Escalus so moral reforms may be introduced. Instead of leaving, the Duke disguises himself as Friar Lodowick and stays to watch what happens. Juliet has illegally conceived Claudio's child and Angelo decides to make an example of Claudio by sentencing him to death. His sister Isabella, who is about to become a nun, pleads for mercy and Angelo suggests she buy her brother's life with her chastity. Isabella refuses but Claudio begs her to reconsider. The disguised Duke suggests she make a date with Angelo and then substitute Mariana, who had a past relationship with Angelo. They carry out their plan, but afterward Angelo orders the head of Claudio be sent to him immediately. At the prison, they substitute the head of another prisoner. After more complications in the plot, the Duke reveals himself and orders Angelo to wed Mariana immediately. Then the Duke announces the law requires "measure for measure" and orders Angelo's execution. After Mariana and Isabella beg for his life, the Duke pardons Claudio, proposes marriage to Isabella, orders Claudio to marry Juliet and pardons Angelo.

Difficulties:

- Excellent actors are needed to play the Duke, Angelo and Isabella. Disguising the Duke as Friar Lodowick so people do not recognize him may present a problem.
- One song by the Boy in Act IV, Scene 1 needs music.

The Merchant of Venice

Genre: Comedy

Date of First Performance: 1596

Places Depicted: A street in Venice; a room in Portia's house in Belmont; a room in Shylock's house in Venice; before Shylock's house; a garden at Portia's house; a court of justice in Venice; on an avenue to Portia's house

Characters:

Duke of Venice	Portia, a rich heiress
Prince of Morocco	Nerissa, her waiting-maid
Prince of Arragon	Jessica, daughter to Shylock
Antonio, a merchant	
Bassanio, his friend	Old Gobbo, father to Launcelot
Salanio, friend to Antono and Bassanio	Leonardo, servant to Bassanio
Salarino, friend to Antonio and Bassanio	Balthasar, servant to Portia
Gratiano, friend to Antonio and Bassanio	Stephano, servant to Portia
Salerio	Magnificoes of Venice
Lorenzo, in love with Jessica	Officers of the Court
Shylock, a rich Jew	Jailer
Tubal, a Jew, his friend	Servants to Portia
Launcelot Gobbo, a clown, servant to Shylock	Other attendants

Plot: In Venice; Bassanio wants to borrow three thousand ducats from Antonio so he may ask Portia to marry him. Antonio borrows the money from Shylock who demands a pound of flesh if the money is not repaid in three months. Shylock's daughter Jessica elopes with Lorenzo; Portia and Bassanio marry, as do Portia's maid Nerissa and his friend Gratiano. Meanwhile, Antonio has bad luck with his financial affairs and cannot repay Shylock who demands that Antonio be arrested. In a court of justice in Venice, Portia is disguised as a lawyer and Nerissa as her clerk. Portia says Shylock may have his pound of flesh but if he sheds a drop of blood he dies. Portia reminds all that anyone who covets the life of another owes one-half of his goods to that person and one-half to the state. Shylock must also become a Christian.

In the end Antonio learns three of his argosies are safe and Jessica receives a deed giving her Shylock's possessions after his death.

Difficulties:

- This play needs excellent actors to portray Shylock and Portia. In Act III, Scene 1 Shylock has a famous speech which begins "Hath not a Jew eyes?" In Act IV, Scene 1 Portia has an equally well-known speech starting "The quality of mercy is not strained, . . ."

- There is one song in Act III, Scene 2 and musicians play in Act V, Scene 1. Music must be found for these occasions.

The Merry Wives of Windsor

Genre: Comedy

Date of First Performance: 1600

Places Depicted: Before Page's house in Windsor; a room in the Garter Inn; a room in Doctor Caius's house; a field near Windsor; a field near Frogmore; a street in Windsor; a room in Ford's house; a room in Page's house; Windsor Park; a street leading to the park

Characters:

Sir John Falstaff

Fenton, a gentleman

Shallow, a country justice

Slender, cousin to Shallow

Ford, gentleman dwelling at Windsor

Page, gentleman dwelling at Windsor

William Page, a boy, son to Page

Sir Hugh Evans, a Welsh parson

Doctor Caius, a French physician

Host of the Garter Inn

Robin, page to Falstaff

Mistress Ford

Mistress Page

Anne Page, her daughter

Mistress Quickly, servant to Doctor Caius

Bardolph, swindler attending on Falstaff

Pistol, swindler attending on Falstaff

Nym, swindler attending on Falstaff

Simple, servant to Slender

John Rugby, servant to Doctor Caius

Other servants

Plot: Supposedly, Queen Elizabeth asked Shakespeare to write a play about Falstaff in love. (The character of Falstaff had appeared in *Henry IV*, Parts 1 and 2 and had died in *Henry V*.) To please the queen, this was the play Shakespeare wrote. In Windsor two women, Mistress Ford and Mistress Page, attract the attention of Sir John Falstaff, an old lecher who thinks of himself as a lady-killer. Although both of the ladies are married, they get love letters from Falstaff that are almost identical. The two ladies plot unmercifully against Falstaff with the result that he gets carried in a laundry basket of dirty clothes and thrown into the Thames. To avoid an irate husband, he has to disguise himself as an old fat woman and is beaten by Ford. In his third humiliation, he is disguised as Herne the Hunter wearing a buck's head while others dressed as fairies pinch him and burn him with tapers. A happy ending finds that the Pages and the Fords forgive him.

Difficulties:

- Falstaff must appear to be fat. He says, "I am in the waist two yards about."

- Because this play has more prose lines than any other Shakespearean play, directors may think it will be easy to direct. That is not so. As directors know, comedies are usually more difficult to produce than serious plays.
- There are three songs in the play needing music.

A Midsummer Night's Dream

Genre: Comedy

Date of First Performance: About 1595

Places Depicted: The palace of Theseus in Athens; Quince's house in Athens; a wood near Athens

Characters:

Theseus, Duke of Athens	Hippolyta, Queen of Amazons
Egeus, father to Hermia	Hermia, in love with Lysander
Lysander, in love with Hermia	Helena, in love with Demetrius
Demetrius, in love with Hermia	Titania, Queen of fairies
Philostrate, Master of Revels	
Quince, a carpenter	Oberon, King of the fairies
Snug, a joiner	Puck or Robin Goodfellow
Bottom, a weaver	Peaseblossom, a fairy
Flute, a bellows-mender	Cobweb, a fairy
Snout, a tinker	Moth, a fairy
Starveling, a tailor	Mustardseed, a fairy
Other attendants on Theseus and Hippolyta	Other fairies and elves

Plot: Generally considered to be the most joyful poetic comedy ever written, the plot concerns the vagaries of love among Theseus and Hippolyta; Hermia, Helena, Lysander and Demetrius; and Oberon and Titania. The latter two are attended by a court jester, Puck, and dancing-singing fairies and elves. Add to this mix rustic comedians, led by Bottom, who put on the play of *Pyramus and Thisbe*. Of course, there is a happy ending.

Difficulties:

- The lyrical poetry needs study and astute interpretation.
- The director, if not a dancer, may need a choreographer's help with the dancing. There can be dances of fairies and elves in several scenes, and the rustics do a Bergomask dance at the end of *Pyramus and Thisbe*.
- In Act II, Scene 1, First Fairy may sing "Over hill, over dale," rather than speak it. In the next scene, the fairies sing Titania to sleep. If Puck and Oberon are singers, they may also sing rather than speak several passages.
- One suggestion for the music is to consider Mendelssohn's incidental music for this play.

Much Ado About Nothing
Genre: Comedy
Date of First Performance: 1599
Places Depicted: Before Leonato's house in Messina; a room and a hall in his house; Leonato's orchard and garden; a street; Hero's apartment; church; prison
Characters:

Don Pedro, Prince of Arragon
Don John, his villainous brother
Claudio, young lord of Florence
Benedick, young lord of Padua
Leonato, Governor of Messina
Antonio, his brother
Balthasar, attendant on Don Pedro
Conrade, follower of Don John
Borachio, follower of Don John
Friar Francis

Hero, daughter to Leonato
Beatrice, niece to Leonato
Margaret, gentlewoman attending on Hero
Ursula, gentlewoman attending on Hero

Dogberry, a constable
Verges, a headborough
A sexton
A boy
Messengers, watch, other attendants

Plot: Noted for the witty dialogue between Beatrice and Benedick, this play tells the story of their growing love and also the relationship of Claudio and Hero. Learning of Claudio's love, Don Pedro offers to woo Hero for him, which he does; however, Don Pedro's evil brother, Don John, tells Claudio that Don Pedro is wooing Hero for himself. On the night before Hero and Claudio's wedding day, Don John conspires to make Claudio think Hero is unfaithful to him. At the altar, Claudio rejects her. She faints and it is reported that she is dead. In the last act, it is revealed that Hero is innocent and she and Claudio are married. Then Beatrice and Benedick decide to get together.

Difficulties:
* Exceptional actors are needed for Beatrice and Benedick and outstanding comedians for Dogberry and Verges.
* There are two songs and two dances for which appropriate music must be found.

Othello
Genre: Tragedy
Date of First Performance: 1604
Places Depicted: Streets in Venice; council-chamber; seaport in Cyprus; street in Cyprus; hall in castle; before the castle; beyond the castle; within the castle; bedchamber
Characters:

Duke of Venice
Brabantio, a senator
Gratiano, brother to Brabantio
Lodovico, kinsman to Brabantio
Othello, a noble Moor in service of Venice
Cassio, his lieutenant
Iago, his ancient or ensign
Roderigo, a Venetian gentleman
Montano, former governor of Cyprus
Clown, servant to Othello

Desdemona, daughter to Brabantio and wife to Othello
Emilia, wife to Iago
Bianca, mistress to Cassio

Other senators
Sailor
Messenger
Herald
Officers, gentlemen
Musicians, attendants

Plot: Othello, a Moorish general, marries Desdemona, daughter of Brabantio, who is incensed by the marriage. Othello also offends Iago by choosing Cassio to be his lieutenant and Iago then decides to seek revenge. Othello is sent to the island of Cyprus to protect it from the Turks and Desdemona accompanies him. Iago preys upon Othello's jealousy and convinces him Desdemona is unfaithful. The result is that Othello kills Desdemona and stabs himself. Iago, who killed Roderigo and Emilia, his wife, is condemned to torture.

Difficulties:

- The roles of Othello and Iago demand great actors like Laurence Olivier who in his long career had the opportunity to play first Iago and then later Othello. Other famous performers who played the title role were Paul Robeson and Orson Welles.
- There are two songs sung by Iago and Desdemona that will need music.
- Trumpets also are used in two scenes and musicians play in one.

Richard II

Genre: History

Date of First Performance: 1595

Places Depicted: King Richard's palace in London; Duke of Lancaster's palace; the lists at Coventry; the court; Ely House; Windsor castle; wilds in Gloucestershire; a camp in Wales; before the castle at Bristol; the coast of Wales with a castle in view; before Flint castle in Wales; the Duke of York's garden at Langley; Westminister Hall; a street leading to the Tower in London; Duke of York's palace; a royal palace; Pomfret castle

Characters:

King Richard II

John of Gaunt, Duke of Lancaster, uncle to the king

Edmund of Langley, Duke of York, uncle to the king

Henry Bolingbroke, Duke of Hereford, son to John of Gaunt

Duke of Aumerle, son to Duke of York

Thomas Mowbray, Duke of Norfolk

Duke of Surrey

Earl of Salisbury

Lord Berkeley

Earl of Northumberland

Henry Percy, surnamed Hotspur, his son

Bushy, servant to King Richard

Bagot, servant to King Richard

Green, servant to King Richard

Queen to King Richard

Duchess of York

Duchess of Gloucester

Lady attending on queen

Lord Ross

Lord Willoughby

Lord Fitzwater

Bishop of Carlisle

Abbot of Westminster

Lord Marshal

Sir Stephen Scroop

Sir Pierce of Exton

Captain of band of Welshmen

Two gardeners, keeper

Lords, heralds, officers

Soldiers, messenger, groom

Other attendants

Plot: The historic period of this play is April 29, 1398, to the beginning of March, 1400. Henry Bolingbroke charges Thomas Mowbray, the Duke of Norfolk, with misappropriation of funds and high treason. To settle this dispute, King Richard banishes Norfolk for life and Henry for six years. Shortly thereafter, Henry's father, John of Gaunt, dies and Richard unjustly confiscates his estates to raise funds for the Irish wars. This gives Henry an excuse to return from exile to assert his rights. Many nobles join Henry who asks that his inheritance be returned. Richard agrees. Later, Richard is forced to abdicate: his crown is removed and he is taken to the Tower as Henry is hailed as King Henry IV. Richard, who kills two servants, is murdered by Exton, who thought he was doing what Henry wanted, but instead Henry banishes Exton and vows to go to the Holy Land to wash the blood off his guilty hand.

Difficulties:

- King Richard II is a weak king who requires a subtle characterization.
- The scene near the end in which Richard kills two servants with an ax and then is murdered by Exton is difficult to stage.
- In several places, flourishes (fanfares) are called for.

Richard III

Genre: History

Date of First Performance: About 1593

Places Depicted: A street in London; the palace; the Tower of London; before Lord Hastings' house; Pomfret Castle; the Tower walls; Baynard's Castle; before the Tower; before the palace; Lord Derby's house; an open place in Salisbury; the camp near Tamworth; Bosworth Field; another part of the field

Characters:

King Edward IV
Edward, Prince of Wales, later King Edward V, son to the King
Richard, Duke of York, son to the King
George, Duke of Clarence, brother to the King
Richard, Duke of Gloucester, later King Richard III, brother to the King
A young son of Clarence
Henry, Earl of Richmond, later King Henry VII
Cardinal Bourchier, Archbishop of Canterbury
Thomas Rotherham, Archbishop of York
John Morton, Bishop of Ely
Duke of Buckingham
Duke of Norfolk
Earl of Surrey, his son
Earl Rivers, brother to Elizabeth
Marquis of Dorset, son to Elizabeth
Lord Grey, son to Elizabeth
Earl of Oxford
Lord Hastings
Lord Stanley, also called Earl of Derby
Lord Lovel
Sir Thomas Vaughan

Elizabeth, Queen to King Edward IV
Margaret, widow of King Henry VI
Duchess of York, mother to King Edward IV
Lady Anne, widow of Edward, Prince of Wales, son to King Henry VI; later married to Richard III
A young daughter of Clarence

Sir Richard Ratcliff
Sir William Catesby
Sir James Tyrrel
Sir James Blount
Sir Walter Herbert
Sir Robert Brakenbury, Lieutenant of Tower
Sir William Brandon
Christopher Urswick, a priest
Another priest
Tressel and Berkeley, gentlemen attending on Lady Anne
Lord Mayor of London
Sheriff of Wiltshire
Ghosts of those murdered by Richard III
Lords and other attendants
A pursuivant, a scrivener, a page, a priest
Citizens, murderers, messengers, soldiers

Plot: Historically, this play covers the final part of the Wars of the Roses which ended in 1485. Richard, Duke of Gloucester, is a deformed hunchback who ruthlessly aspires to be king by killing all who stand in his way. Among others, he has his brother, Clarence, murdered. He kills the husband and father-in-law of Lady Anne but tells her he did it because he loves her. She marries him. King Edward IV dies and Richard manages to get himself crowned king while holding Edward's two sons in the Tower and seeking their deaths. As King Richard III, he has Queen Anne killed so he might marry his niece, Elizabeth. She is betrothed to the Earl of Richmond who leads an army against Richard and kills him in combat. Richmond, who becomes King Henry VII, proposes to marry Elizabeth, thus ending the Wars of the Roses.

Difficulties:

- Richard is one of the most villainous characters ever created for the stage. To make him believable is the problem.
- Richard's deformity (he is a hunchback) may be difficult for the actor to play. Just a suggestion of the ailment is probably better than overplaying it.
- Needed are trumpets, drums, sennets, alarums and excursion.

The Taming of The Shrew

Genre: Farce comedy

Date of First Performance: About 1594

Places Depicted: Cutting the two scenes of the Induction and six lines at the end of the next scene (the first scene of the play) can be done without harming the farce. If you take these cuts you will need the following: a public place in Padua before Baptista's house; before Hortensio's house; inside Baptista's house; Baptista's garden; inside Petruchio's country house; near Baptista's house; on the road to Padua; before Lucentio's lodging; and inside Lucentio's house.

Characters:

Baptista, a gentleman of Padua	Katharina, daughter of Baptista
Vincentio, a merchant of Padua	Bianca, daughter of Baptista
Lucentio, son to Vincentio	A widow
Petruchio, a gentleman of Verona	
Gremio, old dandy, suitor to Bianca	A pedant
Hortensio, suitor to Bianca	A tailor
Tranio, clever servant to Lucentio	A haberdasher
Biondello, young servant to Lucentio	An officer
Grumio, small servant to Petruchio	Other servants

Plot: Baptista, a rich merchant in Padua, has two daughters. Bianca, a gentle, charming young lady, has many suitors but she cannot marry until her older sister, Katharina (also called Kate), is wed. Unfortunately, Kate does not have any suitors because she has a shrewish disposition. Petruchio arrives on the scene from Verona and is interested in wooing Kate when he hears of her large dowry. The rest of the play is concerned with Petruchio's taming Katharina. In the last scene Kate demonstrates what an obedient, gentle wife she has become—more so than Bianca.

Difficulties:

- Two excellent actors are needed for Petruchio and Katharina.
- Farce comedies are always difficult to act and direct.

The Tempest

Genre: Pastoral romance

Date of First Performance: 1611

Places Depicted: On a ship at sea; before Prospero's cell on an island; another part of the island

Characters:

Alonso, king of Naples	Miranda, daughter to Prospero
Sebastian, his brother	
Prospero, the rightful Duke of Milan	Ariel, an airy spirit
Antonio, his brother, the usurping Duke of Milan	Iris, role assumed by spirits in Prospero's pageant
	Ceres, role assumed by spirits in Prospero's pageant
Ferdinand, son to Alonso	
Gonzalo, honest old Counsellor	Juno, role assumed by spirits in Prospero's pageant
Adrian, lord	Nymphs, role assumed by spirits in Prospero's pageant
Francisco, lord	
Caliban, a savage, deformed slave	Reapers, role assumed by spirits in Prospero's pageant
Trinculo, a jester	
Stephano, a drunken butler	Other spirits
	Master of the ship
	Boatswain
	Mariners

Plot: The play opens with a shipwreck amidst thunder and lightning, which was caused by Prospero, a former Duke of Milan. Twelve years earlier he had been banished from Milan by his brother Antonio, who became the Duke with the help of Alonso, the King of Naples. Since that time Prospero and his daughter Miranda have been living on a tropical enchanted island with two servants: Caliban, an evil monster, and Ariel, an airy diminutive spirit, who is invisible to all except Prospero. The major dramatic question is: Will Prospero get his dukedom back? On board the wrecked ship are Antonio, Sebastian, Gonzalo, King Alonso and his son Ferdinand. In the three to four hours that elapse from the beginning to the end of the play, Ferdinand and Miranda fall in love, Prospero gets his dukedom back, Ariel is set free, and they are all sailing the next day on calm seas back to Naples and Milan.

Difficulties:

- The opening scene, the shipwreck, is the most difficult one to stage, but it can be a very effective and exciting beginning to the play if handled well.
- It is imperative that you have an excellent actor to play Prospero, magician and

ruler of the island, as he carries the show.

- The casting of Ariel must also be well done. He is described as a small, airy, quick spirit who moves like a dancer. In addition he sings four solos and accompanies himself. In Act II, Scene 1 he plays solemn music.
- Juno and Ceres sing, as do Stephano and Caliban. At the masque in Act IV, Scene 1, Iris, Ceres, Juno, reapers and nymphs sing and dance. "Shapes" are dancers in Act III, Scene 3. Appropriate music must be found for the above songs and dances.

Twelfth Night

Genre: Comedy

Date of First Performance: 1600 or 1601

Places Depicted: Duke's palace in Illyria; seacoast; Olivia's house; a street; Olivia's garden; and a cellar in her house.

Characters:

Orsino, duke of Illyria	Countess Olivia
Sebastian, twin brother to Viola	Viola, twin sister to Sebastian
Sir Toby Belch, uncle to Olivia	Maria, Olivia's woman
Sir Andrew Aguecheek, foolish knight	
Malvolio, steward to Olivia	Valentine, gentleman attending the Duke
Fabian, servant to Olivia	Curio, gentleman attending the Duke
Feste, Olivia's clown and singer	A priest
Antonio, a sea captain, friend to Sebastian	Lords, sailors, officers, musicians
A sea captain, friend to Viola	Other attendants

Plot: This joyous comedy starts with twins, Viola and Sebastian, being separated by a shipwreck. Viola lands on the coast of Illyria and fears her brother is dead. She disguises herself as a boy, Cesario, and obtains work as a page to Duke Orsino. The Duke sends Cesario to talk to the Countess Olivia, with whom he is enamored; but unfortunately for him Olivia is attracted to Cesario. Meanwhile, Cesario/Viola finds she is in love with the Duke. This is the complicated situation which becomes more complicated before the happy ending.

Difficulties:

- Viola and Sebastian must look enough alike that they can be mistaken for each other when she is dressed as a man.
- Another casting problem may be finding an actor-singer to play Feste, who should be funny and have a good singing voice as he sings four solos and accompanies himself on the lute. (If he cannot play the lute, a page may accompany him.)
- A third difficulty may be obtaining one or two pages to play the lute and pipe.
- Also, this play will require research to locate appropriate music to put with the lyrics of the songs that are in the script.

✧ Suggested Reading ✧

Shakespeare

Aagesen, Colleen, and Margie Blumberg. *Shakespeare for Kids*. Chicago: Chicago Review Press, 1999.

Bishop, T.G. *Shakespeare and the Theatre of Wonder*. Cambridge: Cambridge University Press, 1996.

Bloom, Harold. *Shakespeare: The Invention of the Human*. New York: Riverhead Books, 1998.

Crowl, Samuel. *Shakespeare Observed: Studies in Performance on Stage and Screen*. Athens, Ohio: Ohio University Press, 1992.

Fraser, Russell. *Young Shakespeare*. New York: Columbia University Press, 1988.

Kennedy, Dennis. *Looking at Shakespeare*. Cambridge: Cambridge University Press, 1993.

Miola, Robert S. *Shakespeare and Classical Tragedy*. Oxford: Clarendon Press, 1992.

Reese, M.M. *Shakespeare: His World and His Work*. New York: St. Martin's Press, 1980.

Rowse, A.L. *Shakespeare the Man*. New York: Harper and Row, Publishers, 1973.

Sams, Eric. *The Real Shakespeare*. New Haven: Yale University Press, 1995.

Schoenbaum, S. *Shakespeare: The Globe and the World*. New York: Oxford University Press, 1979.

———. *William Shakespeare: A Documentary Life*. New York: Oxford University Press, 1975.

———. *William Shakespeare: Records and Images*. New York: Oxford University Press, 1981.

Thomson, Peter. *Shakespeare's Professional Career*. Cambridge: Cambridge University Press, 1992.

Wagenknecht, Edward. *The Personality of Shakespeare*. Norman: University of Oklahoma Press, 1972.

Shakespeare's Plays in Single Editions

The Arden Shakespeare
The New Folger Library Edition of Shakespeare's Plays
The New Penguin Shakespeare
The New Variorum Shakespeare

The Newly Revised Signet Classic Shakespeare Series
Samuel French's Acting Editions

Music in Shakespeare's Plays

Long, John H. *Shakespeare's Use of Music*. Gainesville: University of Florida Press, 1971.

Naylor, Edward Woodall, ed. *Shakespeare Music: Music of the Period*. New York: Da Capo Press, 1973.

Noble, Richmond. *Shakespeare's Use of Song*. Oxford: Clarendon Press, 1966.

Seng, Peter J. *The Vocal Songs in the Plays of Shakespeare*. Cambridge: Harvard University Press, 1967.

Sternfeld, F.W. *Music in Shakespearean Tragedy*. London: Routledge and Kegan Paul Limited, 1963.

Vincent, Charles, ed. *Fifty Shakspere Songs*. Boston: Oliver Ditson Company, 1906.

Directing

Benedetti, Robert L. *The Director at Work*. Englewood Cliffs, N.J.: Prentice-Hall, Inc., 1985.

Berry, Ralph. *On Directing Shakespeare: Interviews with Contemporary Directors*. London: Hamish Hamilton Ltd., 1989.

Brook, Peter. *The Empty Space*. New York: Avon Books, 1968.

———. *The Shifting Point*. New York: Harper & Row, Publishers, 1987.

Dean, Alexander, and Lawrence Carra. *Fundamentals of Play Directing*. 4th ed. New York: Holt, Rinehart and Winston, 1980.

Jones, David Richard. *Great Directors at Work*. Berkeley: University of California Press, 1986.

Hodge, Francis. *Play Directing*. 3rd ed. Englewood Cliffs, N.J.: Prentice-Hall, Inc., 1988.

Leiter, Samuel L. *The Great Stage Directors*. New York: Facts on File, Inc., 1994.

Loney, Glenn, ed. *Staging Shakespeare: Seminars on Production Problems*. New York: Garland Publishing, Inc., 1990.

Morrow, Lee Alan, and Frank Pike. *Creating Theatre.* New York: Vintage Books, 1986.

O'Neill, R.H., and N.M. Boretz. *The Director as Artist.* New York: Holt, Rinehart and Winston, 1987.

Rodgers, James W., and Wanda C. Rodgers. *Play Director's Survival Kit.* West Nyack, N.Y.: The Center for Applied Research in Education, 1995.

Acting

Adler, Stella. *The Technique of Acting.* New York: Bantam Books, 1988.

Albright, Hardie, and Arnita Albright. *Acting: The Creative Process.* 3rd ed. Belmont, Calif.: Wadsworth Publishing Company, 1980.

Barton, John. *Playing Shakespeare.* London: Methuen London Ltd., 1984.

Barton, Robert. *Acting: Onstage and Off.* 2d ed. New York: Harcourt Brace Jovanovich College Publishers, 1993.

Benedetti, Robert L. *The Actor at Work.* 5th ed. Englewood Cliffs, N.J.: Prentice-Hall, Inc., 1990.

Cohen, Robert. *Acting in Shakespeare.* Mountain View, Calif.: Mayfield Publishing Company, 1991.

———. *Acting One.* 2nd ed. Mountain View, Calif.: Mayfield Publishing Company, 1992.

Crawford, Jerry L. *Acting in Person and in Style.* 4th ed. Dubuque, Iowa: Wm. C. Brown Publishing, 1991.

Gielgud, John, with John Miller. *Acting Shakespeare.* New York: Charles Scribner's Sons, 1991.

Gronbeck-Tedesco, John L. *Acting Through Exercises.* Mountain View, Calif.: Mayfield Publishing Company, 1992.

Hagen, Uta. *Respect for Acting.* New York: Macmillan Publishing Co., Inc., 1973.

Harrop, John, and Sabin R. Epstein. *Acting with Style.* 2nd ed. Englewood Cliffs, N.J.: Prentice-Hall, Inc., 1990.

Kahan, Stanley. *Introduction to Acting.* 3rd ed. Newton, Mass.: Allyn and Bacon, Inc., 1991.

McGaw, Charles, and Larry D. Clark. *Acting Is Believing.* 5th ed. New York: Holt, Rinehart and Winston, 1987.

McTigue, Mary. *Acting Like a Pro.* Cincinnati: Betterway Books, 1992.

Miller, Allan. *A Passion for Acting.* New York: Back Stage Books, 1992.

Moore, Sonia. *The Stanislavski System.* 2nd rev. ed. New York: Penguin Books, 1984.

Novak, Elaine Adams. *Styles of Acting.* Englewood Cliffs, N.J.: Prentice-Hall, Inc., 1985.

Olivier, Laurence. *On Acting.* New York: Simon and Schuster, 1986.

Richardson, Don. *Acting Without Agony.* Boston: Allyn and Bacon, Inc., 1988.

Skura, Meredith Anne. *Shakespeare: The Actor and the Purposes of Playing.* Chicago: University of Chicago Press, 1993.

Stanislavski, Constantin. *An Actor Prepares.* Translated by Elizabeth Reynolds Hapgood. New York: Theatre Arts Books, 1936.

———. *Building a Character.* Translated by Elizabeth Reynolds Hapgood. New York: Routledge/Theatre Arts Books, 1977.

———. *Creating a Role.* Translated by Elizabeth Reynolds Hapgood. New York: Routledge, 1989.

———. *My Life in Art.* Translated by J.J. Robbins. Boston: Little, Brown and Company, 1924.

Stanislavsky, Konstantin. *Stanislavsky on the Art of the Stage.* Translated by David Magarshack. London: Faber and Faber, 1988.

Woods, Leigh. *On Playing Shakespeare.* New York: Greenwood Press, 1991.

Yakim, Moni, with Muriel Broadman. *Creating a Character.* New York: Back Stage Books, 1990.

Voice and Dialects

Anderson, Virgil A. *Training the Speaking Voice.* 3rd ed. New York: Oxford University Press, 1977.

Blunt, Jerry. *Stage Dialects.* New York: Harper & Row, Publishers, Inc., 1967. (With tapes.)

———. *More Stage Dialects.* New York: Harper & Row, Publishers, Inc., 1980. (With tapes.)

Hill, Harry, with Robert Barton. *A Voice for the Theatre.* New York: Holt, Rinehart and Winston, 1985.

Machlin, Evangeline. *Speech for the Stage.* Rev. ed. New York: Theatre Arts Books, 1980.

Mayer, Lyle V. *Fundamentals of Voice & Diction.* 8th ed. Dubuque, Iowa: Wm. C. Brown Publishers, 1988.

Manners and Customs

Oxenford, Lyn. *Playing Period Plays.* London: J. Garnet Miller Ltd., 1958.

Russell, Douglas A. *Period Style for the Theatre.* Boston: Allyn and Bacon, Inc., 1980.

Stage Fighting

Gordon, Gilbert. *Stage Fights.* New York: Theatre Arts Books, 1973.

Hobbs, William. *Stage Combat.* New York: St. Martin's Press, 1981.

Keezer, Claude D. *Principles of Stage Combat.* Schulenburg, Tex.: I.E. Clark, Inc., 1983.

Stage Makeup

Corson, Richard. *Stage Makeup.* 7th ed. Englewood Cliffs, N.J.: Prentice-Hall, Inc., 1986.

Swinfield, Rosemarie. *Stage Makeup Step-by-Step.* Cincinnati: Betterway Books, 1995.

Technical Theatre

Collison, David. *Stage Sound.* 2nd ed. New York: Drama Book Service, 1982.

Cunningham, Glen. *Stage Lighting Revealed.* Cincinnati: Betterway Books, 1993.

Ionazzi, Daniel A. *Stagecraft Handbook.* Cincinnati: Betterway Books, 1996.

———. *The Stage Management Handbook.* Cincinnati: Betterway Books, 1992.

Kelly, F. M., revised by Alan Mansfield. *Shakespearian Costume for Stage and Screen.* London: Adam & Charles Black, 1970.

Kidd, Mary T. *Stage Costume Step by Step.* Cincinnati: Betterway Books, 1996.

Rose, Rich. *Drawing Scenery for Theater, Film and Television.* Cincinnati: Betterway Books, 1994.

Thurston, James. *The Theatre Props Handbook.* Cincinnati: Betterway Books, 1987.

✧ Index ✧